Healing, aromatic and edible plants of Crete

Author: **Antonis Alibertis**, naturalist
Atalantis 12, 71 409 Ayios Ioannis, Heraklion, Crete.
Tel/Fax: 2810 323398

Photographs: Antonis Alibertis
Cover: Yiannis Galanis
Translation: Jill Pittinger
Layout: Dimitra Yenetzaki

© Copyright **"Mystis"**

Central distribution**: Mystis**
Kalisperidon 15, 71 307 Heraklion, Crete.
Tel: 2810 226518, 346451 Fax: 2810 221908
E-mail: mystis@her.forthnet.gr

Printed by: **TYPOKRETA**
Heraklion Industrial Park, Crete,
Tel. 2810 380882-6
E-mail: typokreta@her.forthnet.gr
www.kazanakis.gr

ISBN: 978-960-6655-20-3

ANTONIS ALIBERTIS

Healing, aromatic and edible

Plants
of
Crete

I N T R O D U C T I O N

ear Reader –
Crete has been renowned since very ancient times- in fact since the Minoan period - for its herbs and its plants in general. We learn from a papyrus of the 18th Dynasty that the Egyptians imported Cretan herbs and used them both to treat their sick and for the embalming of the dead. Ancient Greek doctors and herbalists sang their praises, as did the Romans. We know today that 10% of the around 2,000 plants of Crete are endemic, that is to say they grow exclusively on the island. I decided, therefore, to write a book about the plants of Crete, and especially the herbs. You may want to ask a question, however. Who is this person who knows so much about the herbs of Crete?

About myself:
I am a lover of Nature; for the past 25 years I have dedicated my free time – and still continue to do so – to reading books about the plants and herbs, to the search for - and discovery of - rare plants in the mountains and ravines, and to the photography and listing of the plants not only of Crete but of the whole of Greece. I am a friend who would like to share his knowledge, his wealth of observations and his inexhaustive photograph material with the reader of this book, and impart a little of his love for this beautiful, many-facetted and celebrated world of Cretan plants and herbs. The book you now have in your hand saw the light of day because words are blown away on the wind, and knowledge fades if it is not recorded.

The book should not be considered either as a collection of medicinal cures or food recipes, or as a complete catalogue of the healing and aromatic plants of Crete. It is, rather, the product of an attempt to get to know most of the plants which grow on the island and are useful to Man, an aid to help us understand them better and distinguish between them more easily, and a catalogue of their peculiarities and their uses, compiled with a lot of effort from scientific works and also from folklore, hearsay, and both personal and older knowledge and experience. My book would have achieved success if it is considered to constitute an opportunity to learn to love this wonderful world around us - this world which we have neglected and, unfortunately, are destroying for a number of different reasons.

A short history of botany

Some assert that God, others that Nature, fashioned Man and placed him in the 'earthly paradise', surrounding him with thousands of plants full of healing virtues and nutritional substances, so that he would lack for nothing. It seems that with relative alacrity, Man discovered their properties and used them as best he could; this is evidenced by finds which have been preserved from the oldest civilisations.

The therapeutic use of herbs was known to the Chinese from the period of Emperor Huang-gi-Ti, 2000 BC, who wrote a handbook about them. Ayurvedic medicine, practised in India since time immemorial, was based on herbs. An ancient Egyptian papyrus dating from 2800 BC refers to the therapeutic application of certain common herbs such as garlic, mint, and marjoram. We learn from archaeological discoveries that the Egyptians used herbs for nutrition, aromatisation, the preparation of cosmetics and also of salves essential for the embalming of their dead - the mummies so familiar to us. The Greeks, our ancient forefathers, developed the therapeutic remedies of the Egyptians further and proceeded to the production of new salves and medicines. They still, of course, continued to use the herbs in cookery, aromatisation and as dyes, and they also introduced them into their religious rites. Hippocrates and Dioscurides contributed much to this work. In turn, Greek theories were adopted by the Romans; particularly worthy of note here are Galen and Pliny.

All of this knowledge passed from the Romans to the Arabs, who enthusiastically embraced the theories concerning the therapeutic properties of the herbs, incorporated them into their own traditions and – luckily - preserved and disseminated them. Of their writings, the most important is the **Medical Canon** of the Persian naturalist Avicenna, who was born in 980 AD. The knowledge held by the Arabs was passed to Europe both by them and by the crusaders, and preserved until the Renaissance, particularly in monastic establishments. Subsequently, due to the famous (perhaps somewhat infamous) lectures of the Swiss alchemist and naturalist Paracelsus (1530), the systematic studies carried out by the great European botanists and the discovery of the New World, botanical knowledge increased to an unexpected degree. A huge variety of plants were brought to Europe from every country in the world. However, with the beginning of modern scientific research in the 18th century, botany and medicine diverged.

During the last two centuries, in the face of the impressive progress made in medicine and chemistry, this millennia-old heritage of Mankind unfortunately suffered a second fate – it was almost forgotten. In fact, the first synthetic drugs began to appear in the 19th century and herbs remained only as old, superseded medical remedies, or retained their application in cookery or perfumery. In spite of all this, in recent years people have begun to rediscover their nature, and at the same time their inestimable therapeutic, aromatic and nutritional value.

Herbs have returned to the stage once more.

Wherever he may be, in whatever corner of the world, Man is surrounded by plants which are sympathetic to him and suited to his requirements; certainly, they may not always be the same ones, but they can fulfil the same needs. It is unfortunate that, while he has such great need of these plants, Man is at the same time the greatest threat to them. The arrogance which accords him the title 'Lord of Nature' blinds him, and does not permit him to see that he himself is a destroyer, laying waste to the 'earthly paradise' around him which he clearly does not respect. This state of affairs seems even more ill-omened if we realise that he has sufficient means not only to protect that earthly paradise it but also to enhance it and make it even more of one.

Happily, many scientists today are persuaded of the value of herbs and are carrying out systematic research in that direction. Man is feeling more and more the need to return to his roots, to rediscover Nature and be reunited with it. Indeed, the ranks of people who, like us, are making this return, are now multiplying; for some, certainly, it will become a love and a passion.

The object of this book

We are going to try, together, to get to know the majority of the herbs and aromatic plants of the island. While the book will tell us about their usage, we must not in any way consider it a medical authority. We will surely be struck by the enormous potentiality of certain plants, **but must always have in mind that these are general properties, which are not especially suited to every individual and the peculiarities of his/her health. We will pay particular attention to those plants which are poisonous and regard them with care and caution. <u>In all instances, the prior advice of a doctor is essential before any plant is used, in any way.</u> We should never play with drugs, just as we should never play with our own life.** The book will also help us to recognise the plants which can be eaten and constitute a pleasant and healthy variation to our diet.

This certainly does not mean that we should go forth with the book under our arm to cut, uproot and trample everything underfoot. Let us only collect the plants we need, and in the quantity that we require.

It would be a blessing from God if some of our fellow human beings could cultivate some of these plants, before it is too late. It would be a great misfortune if some species disappeared, and this is something which can happen very easily under current conditions. Thankfully, cultivation has already begun, with satisfying results, of some plants such as dictamos (**Origanum dictamnus**) in Ebaros, Crete, and lavender (**Lavandula angustifolia**) near Levidi in the Peloponnese. Why, therefore, should this cultivation not be extended to a larger number of plants? Crete undoubtedly offers itself for similar experiments. Not only certain Cretan plants could be cultivated, but also others originating from neighbouring regions such as the Peloponnese or the Aegean islands.

A visit to the Mediterranean Agronomic Institute in Souda (MAICh) astonished us with the work that has been done there relating to the protection, conservation and multiplication of many endemic species of Cretan flora. Warm thanks are due to all who work there! More could certainly be done by the State, for instance a number of important biotopes where these particular plants grow could be placed under protection.

What the book contains

For greater clarity, the plants are presented in alphabetical order and according to their families, genus, species, sub-species and varieties. One or more photographs of every plant, accompanied by a simple description, constitute the basis of each presentation. Thereafter, the biotope and the distribution of the plant on the island are defined. The plant references end with their properties and their uses, and often with a few suggestions regarding their application.

At the end of the book there is an alphabetical index of the scientific Latin names of all the plants mentioned, as well as one of their popular names in English, where they are known. The list of references is comprehensive and indicates the volume of the study that has been undertaken.

The name of each plant consists of two Latin words. The first indicates the genus, and the second, the species. For example: in the case of ***Tulipa cretica***, the word ***Tulipa*** refers to the genus, and ***cretica*** to the species. If the latter is followed by **ssp.** or **var.** this refers to the sub-species or variety. The name of the individual who discovered, described and 'christened' the plant follows immediately afterwards.

An asterisk * next to the name of the plant indicates that it is endemic, i.e. it grows only in a particular country or region, e.g. Greece, Crete or Sitia. We therefore describe it as endemic to Greece, Crete etc.

The months during which the plant is in flower are given with Latin numerals, whereby I = January, II = February etc (e.g. VI – VIII = from June to August).

A helpful glossary, illustrated with sketches, will allow everyone to achieve a better understanding of the text and the special terminology whose use is obligatory.

Since the book refers constantly to the properties and usages of the plants, some completely decorative species have been included, such as tulips (***Tulipa***), irises (***Iris***), gladioli (***Gladiolus)*** hermodactyli (***Hermodactylus***) and some wild ranunculi (***Ranunculus)***.

Acknowledgements

Thanks are due to all those who contributed to the publication of this book:

To Manolis Avramakis for the addition of a number of popular local names in Greek, the loan of some slides and the location of relative information via the Internet; to Mihalis Damanakis for material and spiritual support; to Kostas Kokolakis for his readiness to participate in excursions into the mountains and valleys of Crete; to Vasilis Orfanos, always available to help with his inexhaustible knowledge of linguistics and his vast experience where books are concerned; and of course to Antonis Tsintaris and Georgios Manouras the publishers...............

The usage of plants

Plants can be used in two ways: internally and externally. In accordance with how they are used, we can speak of an infusion, maceration, decoction, tisane/tea, juice, extract, tincture, syrup and powder, or poultice, embrocation, compress, plaster, collyrium, gargle, rinse, wash and bath.

INTERNAL USE

Infusion, maceration: This necessitates steeping a plant or a part of one (flowers, roots, bark, stems/twigs or leaves) in hot or cold water for a certain period of time.

Tisane/tea/decoction: This necessitates boiling a plant or a part of one (flowers, roots, bark, stems/twigs or leaves) in a liquid (water, alcohol, tsikoudia, raki, wine, mead, brandy or beer). If we boil a plant or a part of one in alcohol we can speak of a **tincture** and if we boil it with sugar, of a **syrup**.

Juice: The process is the same as that used to produce fruit juice, with the help of a mixer. The juice is taken by the teaspoon, either as it is or mixed with honey – or even in milk.

Extract: A very concentrated essential oil, which is produced by distillation.

Solution: The liquid obtained from infusion, decoction or maceration.

Powder: The dried plant matter is pounded in a mortar. The powder is normally taken mixed with milk.

EXTERNAL USE

Plaster: This is a kind of compress which has been soaked in a very dilute solution. Since it is very slow-acting, it has to be changed every two hours.

Embrocation: Liquid from the tisane or decoction is poured onto the affected area, and then rubbed in for a long time.

Poultice: According to the circumstances, the plant is either placed directly on the skin or wrapped in a light, thin gauze. The method of application depends upon its particular properties.

Collyrium: As this is an eye-wash, a very weak solution has to be used.

Compress: A large piece of cotton wool or flannel is soaked in an infusion or decoction and placed on the affected area.

Foot or hand baths: The chemical constituents are absorbed by osmosis, and the treatment is more rapid.

Rinse/Wash: For the stomach or uterus a very thin solution has to be used, at body temperature (37° C); the results are immediate.

ADVICE ON THE GATHERING OF HERBS

- We should not invade the natural environment with the intention of gathering whatever we find in front of us for our own satisfaction. Cut or gather some of the plants and leave the rest to multiply.
- If the roots of the plant are not needed, avoid pulling them up and harvest only the parts needed.
- Since all of the parts of a plant – roots, stems, leaves, flowers, bark, fruits, seeds, juice and essential oils – may be of use, there is one more reason for gathering only the part we need and not destroying the whole plant.
- The leaves can be harvested from the stems without cutting them.
- If the plant is deciduous, the leaves are gathered before flowering; if it is an ever-green, they can be gathered all the year round.
- Gather the flower-heads of the plants when they are in full flower and not when they have dried up.
- Tie the plants in little bunches and hang them out of the sun, in a well-ventilated place.
- Store the herbs, if possible, in glass jars which are hermetically sealed.
- Avoid gathering wild greens and herbs which are not healthy-looking, e.g. those which have yellowing or diseased leaves.
- Do not collect herbs when the weather is damp; they will mildew rapidly.
- Spread out the leaves or flowers very thinly on a tray and stir them lightly at regular intervals.
- In the case of wild greens from the mountains, wash them very well before cooking. Take even greater care if they are to be eaten raw, adding a little vinegar to the water in which they are washed.

Into the world of plants and herbs

Let us now travel together into the world of plants and herbs without being intimidated by their Latin names. Their use is necessary, otherwise we cannot be sure that we are talking about the same plant. There are not only many common names for the same plant, but the same name is often also used for different plants.

PTERIDOPHYTA

ADIANTACEAE family

Adiantum capillus veneris L. VI-X
Maidenhair fern

DESCRIPTION: Composite leaves on stems up to 60 cm in length, winter-hardy, with brownish-black leaf-stems, very scaly at the base. Leaflets with surfaces of a vibrant green colour, rounded, cuneate at the base, slightly torn at the margins, and resembling little fans. The microscopic-sized seeds ripen in July-August.

HABITAT: Limestone cliffs, mouths of caves, walls of springs, springs and watercourses.

PROPERTIES, USES: Known to us from the time of Dioscurides under the name of 'Aphrodite's tresses'. In the past, the plant was used to treat respiratory infections and hair loss. We know that its antitussant and soothing properties are mostly contained in the leaves (tisane, decoction). We can drink up to three spoonfuls per day and give it without fear to children suffering from colds. A spoonful of leaves in a glass of water makes a pleasant drink. If it is used for decorative purposes, the pot containing the plant should be placed on a plate which should always be filled with water.

ASPLENIACEAE
(Spleenwort family)

Asplenium ceterach L. (= Ceterach officinarum) Willd.   V-VI

DESCRIPTION: Leaves up to 25 cm, winter-hardy, with an elongated blade, pinnate, divided into 9-12 semicircular parts, ciliate and dark green in the upper section, brownish gold in the lower. The microscopic seeds ripen in May-June. In the summer, the leaves roll up.

HABITAT: Hollows and clefts in the rocks, sun-drenched locations.

PROPERTIES, USES: The 'asplenion' referred to by Dioscurides has diuretic and expectorant properties. It is used as a vermifuge (for intestinal worms). If we are suffering from renal colics and infections of the urinary tract, we can use it as a tisane and drink one glass a day. Folk healers used it as a plaster, in general for skin pimples and in particular for acne in young people.

EQUISITACEAE
(Horsetail family)

60 million years ago, the horsetails were regular trees, but now their height does not exceed two metres. Three species grow on Crete.

Equisetum telmateia Ehrh.   III-V

DESCRIPTION: A plant with a perennial rhizome and single, hollow stems with sections bearing toothed wrappings. In the spring short-lived, fertile spikes appear with fruit-bearing heads of ochre or ochre-brown colour, resembling ancient columns or spindles, and also infertile spindles, much-branching with leaf-like whorled branches, of a height exceeding 1 metre and resembling little Christmas trees.
HABITAT: This plant spreads easily! Found on the banks of streams and in sandy soil that is damp to marshy.
PROPERTIES, USES: As it is rich in silica and potassium, it is designated diuretic, styptic, haemostatic, healing and cleansing. Actually, because of their silica content, the sterile stems are an excellent means of enriching our organism with mineral salts, a good medicine for fractures and - what is more - a means of preventing arteriosclerosis. The Egyptians used the plant to treat wounds. In fact it staunches any kind of bleeding, from that of the nose to that of the menstrual flow. It is even capable of easing nocturnal incontinence. It is also used in severe respiratory conditions as well as stomach and mouth infections. According to each individual case, it is used in a tisane, poultice or as a juice. The high silica content in the cells is also used for polishing metals, furniture and ivory.

The fertile stems of the plant which appear in spring and look like spindles can be cooked like asparagus. Pliny asserted that in the raw state they constituted a good tonic. Nevertheless, they are better consumed after being cooked.

13

Warning! An alkaloid substance in the plant – ekuisetine - can halt development and cause intestinal problems.

NOTE: **Equisetum arvense L.** (common horsetail) is characterized by short-lived spore-bearing shafts with notable sheathing on its nodal joints.

Equisetum ramosissimum Desf. The above characteristics do not apply. The plant grows in wet places, and the sheathing on the joints is almost absent.

Equisetum ramosissimum

Equisetum telmateia

HYPOLEPIDACEAE family

Pteridium aquilinum (L.) Kuhn   V-VII

DESCRIPTION: The leaves approach 2 metres in length and spring from a deep and creeping rhizome; thus huge populations are generated. The leaf blade is two or three times pinnately-lobed with a triangular outline. If we look at the top of the leaf we can see the shape of an eagle. In the younger foliage, the leaflets are rolled and recall the pastoral staff of a Catholic bishop.

HABITAT: In forests and on the edges of forests, in shady soil, damp or dry.

PROPERTIES, USES: The foliage makes a pleasant bed-litter which does not rot in the winter. The ancient Greeks considered this eagle-wing shaped plant a heavenly one, sent by the god Helios. The volutes which were the main embellishment of the Ionic capitals were very probably inspired by the 'pastoral staffs' of this plant. The young leaves are cooked like asparagus; the Japanese consume large quantities of them. The Indians of North America eat them raw. This practice should be avoided, however, because it may be responsible for lowering the body's reserves of vitamin B. The roots are also eaten either ground or roasted. The leaves and the roots are used as a dye substance; the leaves yield a light yellowish-green colour; the roots a deep orange. Both of these dyes are fixed by the use of alum.

SPERMATOPHYTA GYMNOSPERMAE

CUPRESSACEAE family

Cupressus sempervirens (L.) *var. horizontalis* III-V

Funeral cypress

DESCRIPTION: A resinous tree, typical of the Mediterranean shores, which can reach a height of 15-30 metres. It has spreading branches and a pyramid-like top. The leaves are needle-like (acerose), dark green. The male flowers are small, elongated, and yellow. The female flowers (cones) are rounded, green, and have a period of development of two years.

HABITAT: The White Mountains and on Psiloritis (Idi). The tallest and finest trees are to be found in the Samaria Gorge. The tortuous, twisted root plunges deep underground and allows the tree to grow in dry soil without suffering distress in the unbearable summer heat. Its longevity can be as much as 500-700 years.

PROPERTIES, USES: Ovid tells us that the cypress (*Cupressus*) originated from the transformation into a tree of Cyparissos, a beautiful youth loved by Apollo, who unwittingly killed a sacred stag. Others affirm that it was worshipped on Cyprus, hence its name (Cuprus > Cupressus). To Plato, it symbolized the immortality of the soul.

The durability of its wood led to the great exploitation of the tree from the earliest times onwards. The capitals at Knossos and Phaestos were made of cypress wood, as were the beams set into the walls to make them more resistant to earthquakes. It was also used for ship-building and was exported to mainland Greece and Egypt for the purpose. It must have been for such a reason that in 1414, Venice prohibited the export of Cretan cypress wood.

The essential oils of the cypress are used in inhalations and embrocations for the decongestion of the respiratory system. The cones are diuretic, sudorific (sweat-inducing), astringent, haemostatic and impart a black colour to hair.

The Assyrians and Babylonians used the essential oil of the cypress to treat irritation of the anal passage and haemorrhoids. Dioscurides suggested its use in dysentery, erysipelas, to repair broken nails and remove parasites. Hippocrates advised its use for urinary infections. In general, it was taken in antiquity as a tisane, in order to stop diarrhoea and remittent fevers (malaria).

It is still used in the villages today against hair loss and glandular fever. 6-8 cypress cones are boiled in red wine, then strained and a little sugar added, and the decoction given to the patient to the equivalent of two glasses per day. The same beverage, without sugar, can stimulate the menstrual flow.

NOTE: There is the variety *Cupressus sempervirens* var. *pyramidalis* (Italian cypress) which is upright and pillar-like, and shaped rather like a paintbrush. This variety was imported into Crete and is more frequently used as a decorative tree and a windbreak.

Juniperus oxycedrus L. *ssp. macrocarpa* (Sm.) Ball IV-V
Prickly juniper (cedar)

DESCRIPTION: A tree 1–10 metres in height. Leaves (needles) up to 25 mm, with a spiky tip. Very unobtrusive, almost inconspicuous flowers. The fruits (berries) are 12-15 mm in diameter, dark brown or black, and covered in a waxy coat. The fruits of certain types of these trees are edible, with the flavour of dates.

HABITAT: In stony and sandy soils near the sea, particularly in the south and west of the island (Matala, Elafonisos, Gavdos, Chrysi etc).

PROPERTIES, USES: In antiquity, it was believed that the use of this plant in a beverage induced vigour and longevity. It was used in ritual cleansing and for this reason was burned in sacred places. Later on, the oil from the fruits was considered to be a panacea, especially for typhus, cholera, dysentery and worms.

The berries are still used today for infections of the urinary tract and for detoxification of the body in cases of arthritis or gout.

They are also used to treat colics and flatulence, as an aid to digestion, to soothe contractions of the uterus during childbirth, and to assist in the decongestion of the respiratory tract.

The wood is so greatly resistant to rot that it was once used in the construction of houses, in furniture-making, and in sculpture.

NOTE: The **sub-species oxycedrus** L. is found at high altitudes and forms clumps of thick bushes. Its fruit are considerably smaller. Its oil, mixed with wax and fat to form an ointment, is used to treat eczema and other skin conditions - even cancerous ones (!) - and for pains in the ears and nose.

Juniperus oxycedrus ssp. oxycedrus

EPHEDRACEAE
(Joint pine family)

Ephedra cambylopoda C.A. Meyer
(=Ephedra fragilis ssp. cambylopoda (C.A. Meyer) K. Richter)   IV-V
Joint pine

DESCRIPTION: A perennial shrub, climbing and much-branched. Hard but easily snapped, jointed stems, up to 4 metres in length, greenish-blue in colour and whip-like. The leaves are opposite, microscopically small, and scale-like. The flowers are small, yellow-greenish. The fruit is small, red, and fleshy.

HABITAT: Rocks and maquis, from the sea up to the mountain region.

PROPERTIES, USES: The Chinese realized the efficacy of ephedrine in cases of asthma almost 5,000 years ago. It is an alkaloid related to adrenaline but slower-working and longer-lasting. It acts as a tonic for the nervous system, as an antihistamine against congestion and is angiosystolic (it causes the blood vessels to dilate).

As a beverage, therefore, it is used to treat asthma, catarrh, coughs, allergy-generated fever, renal insufficiency and to calm the nervous system. It brings about a gentle but stable stimulation which is lasting and can be a help in moments of depression.

Dioscurides used it as an expectorant.

Because of its biochemical constituents, it is also used in the preparation of antiaphrodisiac drugs, especially for the treatment of gonorrhea and syphilis.

It is a suitable plant for decoration.

PINACEAE (Pine family)

Pinus brutia Ten.　　　　　II-IV
Calabrian pine

DESCRIPTION: An evergreen tree with a slender trunk which exceeds 20 metres in height. The leaves (needles) are thin, 80-120 mm, arranged in pairs. The cones are ovoid, almost stalkless, and perpendicular to the branch which bears them.

HABITAT: In the mountains and on hills near the sea, especially in the south of the island.

PROPERTIES, USES: The pines were dedicated to Poseidon, god of the sea, because they gave the best wood for the construction of curved parts of a ship. The resin has always been used in the production of Greek retsina wine. It is also used to make colophonium (a yellow resin used for rubbing the strings of a violin bow). Its pharmaceutical use is as an antitussant, and also for the treatment of boils, ulcers and suppurating growths. It is also used to treat festering wounds in animals. In general the pine, if only for the fact that it cleans the air around it – something badly needed, especially in the big cities – is of great use to Man. The hospitals for tuberculosis sufferers are often built amidst pine trees.

Alas, however! Despite their usefulness, the pines have one great enemy – us! We set fire to them and burn them down to the ground, either through carelessness or on purpose. Only rarely are forest fires the result of an accident.

NOTE: *Pinus pinea* (Stone pine, Umbrella pine) and *Pinus halepensis* (Aleppo pine) are found on Crete but they have been introduced there from elsewhere. The seeds of the stone pine (pine nuts) are edible and find many uses, such as in a stuffing for turkey.

Pinus pinea

ANGIOSPERMS: DICOTYLEDONS

Acanthus spinosus L.   **IV-VII**
Spiny acanthus

DESCRIPTION: A perennial, 40–90 cm in height, resembling the donkey acanthus, with single upright stems. The leaves are 9 cm, dark green, stalked, winged, and have spiny teeth. The inflorescence is a dense spike. The flowers are large and stalkless. The bracts are thorny. The corolla is pinkish-white to pinkish-green +/- darkening; the

upper lip is entire and domed, the lower lip three-lobed.

HABITAT: On the edges of roads, in olive groves, in dry places.

PROPERTIES, USES: As a sedative. According to Dioscurides, the roots have beneficial properties for tuberculosis sufferers and for those who suffer from convulsions or hernia.

In architecture, the leaf of the acanthus was immortalized by Callimachos (3rd century BC) in the Corinthian capital, and became a symbol of Greek culture.

Left: ***Acanthus mollis*** which is cultivated for decoration.

AIZOACEAE (Aizoon family)

Mesembryanthemum crystallinum L.
Ice plant   **V-VIII**

DESCRIPTION: An annual, up to 80 cm, creeping, much-branched, covered with cells full of water that glitter like crystals. Leaves 6-12 cm, alternate, ovate, flat, fleshy, succulent and slightly sinuate. Flowers 2–3cm in diameter, with very narrow petals of a whitish-pearl colour, longer than the sepals.
HABITAT: On sandy and rocky beaches, near the sea.
PROPERTIES, USES: The tender leaves are eaten in salads. Soda was once produced from the plant.

ANACARDIACEAE (Cashew family)

Pistachia lentiscus L.   **III-VI**
Mastic tree, Lentisc

DESCRIPTION: An evergreen shrub, rarely a small tree, up to 3 metres in height; dark green in colour, even in the midst of summer. The leaves are pinnate with unpaired terminal leaflet, with 8-12 lanceolate leaflets up to 5 cm and a winged petiole. Short, dense axillary inflorescences. The anthers of the male flowers are dark red, those of the female flowers greenish. The fruits (drupes) have a diameter of about 4 mm and are red at first, then later black.
HABITAT: In phrygana (garrigue), maquis and forests.
PROPERTIES, USES: On Chios, a variety of this tree is cultivated from which **mastic** is extracted; this is a type of aromatic gum

22

which was once in demand in the harems of the Ottoman sultans for perfuming the breath. A sweet drink is also produced, of the same name and for the same purpose. Mastic is widely used in confectionery and mainly exported to Turkey.

The therapeutic virtues of the plant are due to the astringent substances which are present in the roots and tender leaves. A wine made by steeping branches of the lentisc in grape must relieves the stomach and stops diarrhoea.

The resin was once used for toothache, rheumatism and gout. It is still used in the production of varnishes. Dioscurides mentions that it removes facial freckles and helps in the healing of fractures.

The wood of the tree, with its beautiful veining, is used in furniture manufacture and veneering. It was also once used for the manufacture of toothpicks.

The Chios lentisc ⇨
⇩

Nerium oleander L.
Oleander

V-VIII

DESCRIPTION: An evergreen shrub up to 5 metres in height. Leaves 12x2 cm, in pairs or threes, linear to lanceolate, apiculate, delicate dark green. Glossy on the upper surface, fuzzy and light-coloured on the underside, with a very membranous epidermis to protect it against sun and drought. Reddish-pink flowers with a funnel-like corolla, roundish petals and glandular sepals. Penetrating scent, and bitter tasting.

HABITAT: Originates from Colchis, in the eastern region of the Black Sea. Self-sowing on the beds and banks of torrents, streams and rivers, and generally in damp biotopes.

The oleander is used as a decorative plant and for this reason is found along the sides of main roads, in gardens and at the entrances to houses. Its flowers, with a single or double corolla, are exquisite. Their colour varies from pinkish-carmine to yellow with intermediate shades of pink and white.

PROPERTIES, USES: The milky juice is used for infections of the scalp and for cardiac conditions. Folk medicine used its leaves for infections of the skin, scabies, syphilis and herpes.

WARNING! This plant is poisonous! The parts of it which are the most useful, and at the same time the most dangerous - if not to say deadly - are the leaves, containing an alkaloid substance and certain crystals whose properties resemble those of dactylidine. Chewing of the leaves or other parts of this plant is strictly prohibited!

People once used to clog ratholes with the leaves; the rats, in order to get out, had to eat the leaves and thus expired. Goats which eat them (a rare occurrence) produce milk that is bitter and cannot be drunk (!).

Vinca major L.
Greater periwinkle

III-VI

DESCRIPTION: A perennial, evergreen, vine-like, with infertile creeping stems and flowering shoots which climb upwards initially and then fall to the ground to take root. The leaves are green, shiny, opposite, ovate-lanceolate and delicately ciliate. The flower is 3-5 cm in diameter, +/- light blue-violet. The corolla is funnel-like with 5 roundish petals.

HABITAT: Banks of streams, forest clearings, damp biotopes.

PROPERTIES, USES: In Italy the plant is considered a symbol of purity and used to decorate the coffins of those who have died young.

In France, it is called 'the witches' violet', because it was used in witches' philtres.

In Greece it is considered a harbinger of spring and planted in public gardens. The flowers, which resemble little blue eyes, open during the first days of spring.

The leaves are gathered during the flowering time and used fresh or dried. The plant is almost scentless, but has a bitter taste which becomes insipid when it is dried.

In medicine, it is used as a menstrual stimulant and to stop diarrhoea. Its tannin and lactic acid content give it antiseptic, cleansing and sedative properties, and it can be used for haemoptysis, fever, leucorrhoea, infections of the throat and wounds. It has great application in cases of intestinal ulcers (rinses) and mastitis (poultices). It rejuvenates and cleans the blood.

In bygone days it was used to stop the secretion of milk in nursing mothers (1-2 spoonfuls of a tisane in a glass of water, morning and evening), for conditions of the lungs and for a cough.

It is widely used in leather manufacture.

Hedera helix L.   **IX-XI**
Ivy

DESCRIPTION: A perennial plant, evergreen, woody, climbing, with glossy foliage. Can reach 20 metres in length. The laterally growing roots are shaped like grappling-hooks, enabling it to attach itself to any kind of surface: soil, walls, trees. The leaves are alternate, tough, smooth, triangular and dark green. The sterile branches have three to five lobed leaves, and the fertile branches smaller, ovate leaves, acute or elliptic. Insignificant flowers with yellow anthers, forming green umbels. The fruit (berries) are roundish, blue-black, and have a bitter taste.

HABITAT: A parasitic plant which attaches itself to trees, sucks out their juices and often chokes them with its embrace, on soil where no other plant whatsoever has any chance of survival. 'Eats' into walls, causing cracks in them.

The plant has a longevity of as much as 100 years, and it has existed in nature for more than 60 million years.

PROPERTIES, USES: A magic plant, and a symbol of immortality from the very earliest times, ivy was dedicated to Dionysos (Roman Bacchus). Garlands for festivals were made from its leaves and stems. It also, along with the vine, symbolized drunkenness. In antiquity its tight embrace was likened to the passionate intertwining of lovers.

The leaves contain resin, acid, gum and essential oils, and have a bitter flavour that is insipid to nauseating. In times past, the leaves and fruits were used in yellow fever, and also as a contraceptive and anticoagulant. An infusion (one pinch in one litre of water) has very positive results in respiratory conditions.

It also has properties as a stimulant, menstrual stimulant and dilutant. Folk healers regarded it as effective against tuberculosis of the bowels, dysentery (ivy flowers in wine two times daily), burns (an ointment made from flowers, leaves and wax all pounded together), ozaena, chronic rhinitis, small ulcers, scurf, erysipelas and skin diseases. In remote villages its leaves were used as a dressing for wounds.

Great caution is advised in any kind of internal use of this plant, which should always be under medical supervision. In large doses it is poisonous and emetic, and can cause disturbances of the nervous system and even meningitis.

By contrast, for external use (in a poultice) ivy constitutes one of the best medicines. It is a tonic, febrifuge, sudorific, regulates menstruation and can return tissues which have been attacked by ulcer, oedema and even tumours (!) to their original condition. It is also an excellent analgesic for rheumatism and other pain. The fresh leaves in a poultice are antineuralgic, decongestant and can treat cellulite. They can dissolve superfluous fat and to some degree return the body to its former beauty. The also help in the extraction of pus from wounds. Dioscurides considered them a panacea. Ivy is also used in homeopathy.

Hedera helix

*Aristolochia cretica** Lam.   III-IV
Cretan birthwort

DESCRIPTION: A perennial plant with a rhizome, almost creeping and with stems measuring 30-60 cm. Leaves up to 6.5 cm, triangular-ovate, and cordate at the base. Flowers 5-12 cm, unconventional in shape, with a tubular corolla flattened out in the upper part and bent and constricted at the base, in ochre-brown +/- greyish tones, the centre completely covered with long hairs. The exterior is downy.

HABITAT: A plant of Asiatic origin which was introduced into Crete from Karpathos; found mainly on stony soil.

PROPERTIES, USES: Generally, it is believed that the aristolochias are able to help women at the time of childbirth and prevent any kind of complication that might occur. Their name is characteristic of this belief: (from the Greek words for 'excellent' and 'to give birth'.

Their flavour is aromatic, piquant and very bitter, like that of quinine. They all have more or less the same properties. The useful parts of the plant are the flowering stems, the roots and the seeds, which have to be dried and then preserved in glass containers.

The aristolochias, with their antibiotic properties, can clean and treat wounds, stop haemorrhages, bring to the surface thorns and splinters which have gone deep, soothe pain, remove the poison of snakes and insects, treat jaundice, anaemia and chloro-

27

sis, strengthen contractions of the uterus at the time of childbirth, heal skin cancers, stop the development of malignant tumours, stimulate the lymphatic glands and give greater liveliness to various cells.

As an extract, three spoonfuls per day for one month are recommended. For the tisane, we can boil 25 g of stems, fresh leaves and roots in a litre of water, wine or vinegar and drink up to 3 cups per day. To prepare an ointment, the roots are pounded in a mortar and mixed up with animal fat.

WARNING! This is a poisonous plant because of the alkaloid substances it contains. The extract from the roots, in a large dose, can cause nausea, terrible headaches, apoplexy, mental disturbances, nightmares and increased sexual potency. For children and babies, a stronger dose can have fatal consequences. From the medical point of view, this can be considered among the best of medicines, if it is used with great care.

NOTE: Two other types of aristolochia are also found on the island:

- *Aristolochia parviflora* Sm. which flowers in March-April in the Elounda region.
- *Aristolochia sempervirens* L. (Evergreen birthwort) which flowers from March to August up to an altitude of 200 metres.

Aristolochia cretica

Aristolochia sempervirens

Cionura erecta (L.) Griseb.
(= Marsdenia erecta (L.) R.)   V-VI

Milkweed

DESCRIPTION: An evergreen plant with a rhizome, 50-100 cm in height. Stalked, cordate leaves at the base. White flowers with a diameter of 1 cm, in a raceme.

HABITAT: Amongst rocks and pebbles, on the banks of streams and near the sea.

PROPERTIES, USES: **Warning! This is a poisonous plant! Its toxic properties were known in antiquity (Dioscurides). The leaves used to be added to little balls of bread and fed to rabid dogs, foxes and wolves, causing paralysis of the extremities.**

Cynanchum acutum L. (= Cynanchum
monspeliacum L.)   VI-IX

Stranglewort

DESCRIPTION: A perennial plant, 1-3 metres in height, climbing, woody,with milky juice. Leaves 2-8 cm, opposite, delicate, cordate to ovate, often curved, with a stalk 1-5 cm long, green-greyish. Flowers with a diameter of 8-12 mm, fragrant. White corolla, rarely pink, with 5 thin lobes, containing a secondary, very small corolla with 10 white lobes and 5 stamens. The fruits (capsules) are up to 8 cm long, smooth, and open along their length when ripe, to scatter seeds which have long, white, silky hairs.

HABITAT: Found on the banks of rivers, near the sea, in wet locations and salt meadows.

PROPERTIES, USES: **Warning! This is a poisonous plant! The milky juice constitutes a fierce purgative.**

Berberis cretica

BERBERIDACEAE (Barberry family)

Berberis cretica L.　　　　　V-VII
Cretan barberry

DESCRIPTION: A deciduous shrub up to 1.5 metres in height, which has yellowish wood, narrow, entire leaves and thorns consisting of three segments. The flowers are in a raceme with 3 small sepals, 6 large yellow and 6 small nectar-bearing petals. The fruits (berries) are fleshy and blue-black.

HABITAT: Found in the mountain and sub-alpine zone, on stony ground.

PROPERTIES, USES: The plant has toning, purgative, and energizing properties and is a bile (gall) stimulant. The roots and the bark are used in a tisane for infections of the lungs, kidneys, liver (jaundice) and also to expel gallstones via the gastrointestinal tract. One spoonful of the juice from the berries in cold water constitutes an excellent, refreshing drink.

Leontice leontopetalum L.　　　II-IV
Leontice

DESCRIPTION: A perennial plant, 30-50 cm, with a rhizome, erect, much-branching, green-blue. Leaves up to 20 cm, 2-3 pinnate with ovate, entire leaflets. Raceme with 15-40 flowers, in the axil of the upper leaves. The flower has six large yellow sepals and 6 small sepals of the same colour.

HABITAT: Sunny locations, on plains and in mountains of low altitude.

PROPERTIES, USES: According to tradition, the thread which Ariadne gave to Theseus to enable him to escape from the Labyrinth was spun from the fibres of the leontice. The roots of the plant were once used to make soap to clean fabrics, and also as a medicine to treat epilepsy.

31

BORAGINACEAE (Borage family)

Alkanna tinctoria (L.) Tausch.   I-V
Dyer's alkanet

DESCRIPTION: A perennial plant, 10-30 cm, hairy, prickly, greyish-white. The leaves are obovate, the lower ones stalked, the upper ones stalkless and periblastic. Terminal inflorescences, at first short and dense and then becoming elongated. Flowers 6-8 mm, blue or mauve with a few hairs on the inside of the corolla. Calyx with five lobes, covered by coarse hairs. The bracts are slightly larger than the calyx.

HABITAT: At low altitudes, near the sea, on sandy beaches and uncultivated soils.

PROPERTIES, USES: The root, mixed up with oil, gives a red colour which is used in confectionery, pharmaceuticals, the production of fragrances, and in distillation. It is also used for the colouration of alcohol in thermometers. The subterranean parts of the plant are astringent and used in gastrointestinal conditions.

NOTE: *Alkanna sieberi* A. DC. has larger flowers which are white with a blue-lilac center, and is found up to an altitude of 1000 metres.

Alkanna sieberi
⇩

Anchusa azurea **Miller** (- *A. italica* **Retz**)   **III-VI**

Large blue alkanet

DESCRIPTION: A perennial, 20-150 cm, erect. Lanceolate leaves covered with dense white prickly hairs, the lower leaves 10-30 cm long and stalked, the upper leaves smaller and stalkless. Inflorescence with large, alternate flowers. The corolla is funnel-shaped, dark-blue to brilliant violet in colour with a white centre surrounded by light violet (violet buds), with 5 outspread, rounded petals and linear sepals.

HABITAT: Found on all soils at moderate or low altitudes.

PROPERTIES, USES: The tender leaves are eaten like spinach. The roots and the bark contain a red substance that has been used since early times as a dye and a softener. The flowers, in an infusion, are sudorific, while the roots and seeds are an expectorant and purgative. 'With schnapps and sugar, the little flowers strengthen the heart and give joy to the melancholy', wrote Tragus, a German botanist of the 16th century.

The skin of the root is excellent for jam-making. It is said that those who eat it will never be consumptive or dropsical, but will remain cheerful, be rejuvenated, and enjoy good health (!). All of this however, is subject to the precondition that we collect the skin very early, before the appearance of the leaves, otherwise the virtues of the plant will pass into the stems and leaves.

Borago officinalis L.   III-V
Borage

The name of this plant originates from the Latin 'burra' ('thick cloth'), and is probably due to its texture.

DESCRIPTION: An annual plant, 20-70 cm in height, robust, covered in coarse hairs, with a strong aroma of cucumber. Huge leaves, up to 20 cm, ovate-lanceolate, stalked and wrinkled. Nodding flowers on long flower-stalks. Corolla 2-3 cm in diameter, with outspreading, lanceolate petals, a brilliant blue-violet in colour. Very short calyx. Together, all the anthers form a cone projecting out of the centre of the flower.

HABITAT: Found at a low altitude, amongst rubbish and rubble.

PROPERTIES, USES: It originates from Syria, has the flavour of hay, the aroma of wine and contains various nitreous substances which dissolve in alcohol. It also contains acid, vegetable, calcium and potassium salts dissolved in water. It is aromatic, a constituent of honey, and edible. It is used to treat inflammation, conditions of the liver and the respiratory system, scarlet fever, measles, chicken pox, acute rheumatism and rheumatic and arthritic pain.

It is drunk as a tisane or tea, made from 10 g of flowers to one litre of boiling water, and in an infusion made with 25 g of flowers. We can add sugar, honey or 'petimezi' (raisin syrup), especially if it is intended for small children. As a beverage, the leaves and flowers have diuretic, sudorific, emollient and febrifuge properties, and it is used as an expectorant and antitussant.

Folk healers recommended the juice of the fruit of borage as a heart tonic and to treat hysteria, and for nursing mothers as a beverage, mixed with fennel, to increase the secretions from the mammary glands.

The leaves and flowers are eaten in salads or can be cooked like spinach. The wilted leaves, as a poultice, ripen abcesses and boils, and soothe burns.

Pliny believed that a distillation of the flowers in wine 'gives joy to men'. Modern research has indicated that the plant irritates the suprarenal glands which produce adrenalin, and for this reason gives the individual courage in difficult conditions.

Cerinthe major L.   II-IV
Honeywort

DESCRIPTION: A plant 15-60 cm in height. Large leaves, the lower ones spatulate, tough, and covered with white 'warts' which have a few hairs. The upper leaves are stalkless, cordate at the base. The flowers are in dense, short, terminal racemes. The corolla is 10-30 mm, funnel-shaped, yellow, sometimes brownish-mauve at its base.

HABITAT: At moderate and low altitudes, on all soils.

PROPERTIES, USES: According to Dioscurides, a poultice made from the leaves of this plant removes blemishes from the fingernails and face.

The name of the plant comes from the Latin meaning 'a plant of wax', probably so-called because this is a plant which attracts bees and thus contributes to honey-making. It was once used to treat eye conditions.

NOTE: *Cerinthe retorta* **Sm**. has smaller, two-coloured flowers, surrounded by purple bracts. It is met in a limited number of biotopes (Kavousi).

Cerinthe retorta

Cynoglossum columnae Ten.   III-V
Houndstongue

DESCRIPTION: An annual, 25-60 cm in height. Downy leaves, lanceolate, stalkless or periblastic. Corolla 5-6 mm with 5 reddish-purple petals, sometimes darkening or purplish-blue. Flat fruits, rounded, with raised edges, covered with hooked prickles.

HABITAT: Stony locations.

Cynoglossum creticum Miller   IV-V
Cretan houndstongue

DESCRIPTION: A plant up to 60 cm in height, biennial, branching in its top section, hairy. Leaves 5-15 cm, oblanceolate, covered on both surfaces by thick hair, the lower leaves being stalked, the upper ones stalkless, alternate, and slightly periblastic. Flowers on a short stalk. Corolla 5-9 mm, five-lobed, pink, later turning blue with darker veining. Flat fruits with dense prickles.
HABITAT: Up to the mountain zone.

Cynoglossum lithospermifolium Lam. *ssp. cariense* (Boiss.) Greuter & Burdet (= *Mattiastrum lithospermifolium*) IV-VI

DESCRIPTION: An annual plant, grassy. Stems 7-35 cm (- 50), with dense, coarse hairs. Basal leaves lanceolate-spatulate, stalked; the other leaves are stalkless and smaller. Corolla 3-5 mm, tubular, blue-violet or mauve. The fruits are flat, round or ovoid, with a membraneous, brown, winged edge.
HABITAT: The plant originates from Asia Minor and is met only in the alpine and sub-alpine zone of the White Mountains of Crete - nowhere else in Europe.

Cynoglossum sphacioticum * Boiss. & Heldr.   IV-VII

DESCRIPTION: A perennial plant, 10-18 cm, hairy, with lanceolate leaves that are stalkless, and dense inflorescences. Corolla 4 mm, of a delicate blue to violet colour. Tubular calyx. Round fruits, full of microscopically-sized prickles.
HABITAT: Found in the White Mountains, in the alpine and sub-alpine zone, amidst

heaps of stones, along with **Cynoglossum lithospermifolium**.

PROPERTIES, USES: All four species have roughly the same properties. Their odour resembles that of the dog or the goat, and their taste is unpleasant and nauseating. **Apart from inulin, amongst the other elements the plants contain is an alkaloid –cynoglossin -which classifies them as poisonous.** This is the reason why, in bygone days, they were used as a narcotic and tranquilliser to treat psychological disturbances. Some people used them for renal colic and colic of the gall bladder, and for severe gastrointestinal conditions accompanied by diarrhoea. The flowers contain a rich nectar which attracts bees.

Heliotropium supinum L.   V-VII
Heliotrope sp.

DESCRIPTION: An annual plant, branching from the base. Leaves up to 3.5 cm, stalked, roundish, downy on the underside. Flowers 1-2 mm which are the smallest of those of the four species of **Heliotropium** (**H. dolosum, H. europaeum, H. hirsutissimum**) found on Crete. After flowering, the calyx enlarges and takes on the shape of a little flask which surrounds the fruit.

HABITAT: Sandy soils, the banks of dried-up streams, near to the seashore.

PROPERTIES, USES: The seeds and leaves were once used in embrocations to make pimples disappear. The plants are dehydrating, solvent, and cleansing. **The seeds and the roots contain cynoglossin, a toxic alkaloid. According to Dioscurides, they can cause sterility and miscarriage.** It was believed in bygone days that the raceme-shaped inflorescences resembled the

Cynoglossum sphacioticum

37

H. hirsutissimum

tails of scorpions and had the power to heal the bites of those arthropods (ancient homeopathy!)

writers, it was believed that the hard seeds, which Pliny called little pearls, were able to shatter stones in the kidneys and the gall bladder (again, homeopathy!).

Lithodora hispidula (Sibth. & Sm.) Grieseb.   III-V
Gromwell

DESCRIPTION: A phrygano plant, 1- 35 cm, much-branching. Stalkless leaves, dark green, ovate-linear, covered with hairs as long as 15 mm, especially on the underside. Terminal inflorescences with 1-4 flowers. Funnel-shaped corolla with a diameter of up to 10 mm, five-lobed, blue-violet in colour. The fruits have an ant-like appearance.
HABITAT: In phrygana (garrigue), at low altitude.
PROPERTIES, USES: According to ancient

Symphytum creticum (Willd) **Run. Ex Greuter & Rech.fil.** (= *Procopiana cretica* (Willd) **Gusuleac)** IV-V

Cretan comfrey

DESCRIPTION: A perennial plant 10-50 cm, much-branching, hairy. Ovate leaves, often cordate at the base. Dense inflorescence. Corolla whitish-pink and five-lobed, with outspread lobes, turned backwards at the edge.

HABITAT: Ravines and shady, rocky locations.

PROPERTIES, USES: John Gerard (1597) speaking of **Symphytum officinale**, believed that its application was in cases of back pain which are due to violent movements, such as those associated with women's wrestling (!).

Symphytum officinale contains a chemical substance, allantoin, which helps in the development of bones, cartilage and muscle cells. If the plant is pounded and then placed in a poultice on the affected place, the allantoin is absorbed by the skin and healing is accelerated. In bygone days, a bath in water to which a part of the plant had been added, was considered to be the popular, folk way of restoring the maidenhead of a betrothed young woman who had wanted to regain her lost virginity (an old way of 'patching up' lost virtue!). In the form of a poultice, the plant is used in dislocations, sprains, and wounds in general. As a tisane, it also has a healing effect on peptic ulcers.

As an ointment, it is used for split skin, including that of the breasts, for haemorrhoids , and for arthritis.

Note: **Symphytum officinale** does not exist on Crete. **Symphytum creticum**, known until recently by the name of **Procopiana** *cretica*, probably exhibits similar and also other properties.

S. officinale

39

CACTACEAE (Cactus family)

Opuntia ficus-barbarica A. Berger
(= *Opuntia ficus-indica*)   III-VII
Prickly pear

DESCRIPTION: A cactus which can reach a height of 5 metres. Large branches, thick and flattened, resembling tennis racquets in shape, and covered with thousands of small, sharp thorns. In spring, vase-like receptacles crowned with large golden yellow flowers appear on the edges of the branches, and as time passes, these turn into juicy, reddish or yellowish fruits, shaped like little barrels and covered with clumps of sharp spines.

HABITAT: Found at low altitudes.

PROPERTIES, USES: The plant originates from North America; it was brought to Europe by Christopher Columbus, and to Crete by the Venetians.

The fruits are eaten raw, preferably chilled. They are pleasant-tasting, in spite of the many seeds they contain. The flowers can be used in a tisane to treat diarrhoea. The fresh 'tennis racquets', when heated, constitute an excellent softening poultice for boils and other skin eruptions.

Avoid consumption of the fruits at midday because, due to the heat, the little thorns are detached by the slightest movement and become dangerous.

CAMPANULACEAE (Bellflower family)

Petromarula pinnata * (L.) A. DC.
Rock lettuce   **IV-V**

DESCRIPTION: A biennial plant which reaches up to 80 cm in height, with basal rosettes and smooth stems. The leaves are divided, pinnately-lobed, up to 30 cm. The spike is dense with blue flowers. The corolla is divided to its base with 5 linear lobes that are turned backwards.

HABITAT: On walls of abandoned houses and rocks up to an altitude of 1200 metres.

PROPERTIES, USES: The rock lettuce is eaten in the same way as all the lettuces.

PARACEAE (Caper family)

Capparis spinosa L. ssp. *sicula*
(Veillard) Holmboe (= *Capparis ovata*)
Caper   **IV-IX**

DESCRIPTION: A shrub, 30-100 cm, with prostrate branches on the ground or hanging from rocks and walls. The leaves are alternate, ovate, slightly fleshy, sometimes downy, with two hook-like stipules, spiny at the base. Solitary flowers, with 4 sepals and 4 white petals and numerous long, ray-like stamens which are violet in colour. The fruits are well-known as 'caper buds'.
HABITAT: On walls and rocks in the coastal zone.
PROPERTIES, USES: All – or nearly all – of the caper is edible. The tender shoots are cooked like asparagus. The little branches can be cooked like spinach, before the axillary thorns of the leaves have developed. The root can be cooked like salsify. It is the buds that are eaten most of all, and have been known since antiquity as **capers**. They are either preserved in vinegar and salt (even very small buds can be used). They have a piquant, slightly bitter flavour, and stimulate the appetite as well as the liver functions.
The largest buds, when they are ready to open, are covered in salt and left to dry in the sun, then stored away from dampness. The leaves can be boiled; to remove the bitterness, it is a good idea to change the water several times. Add olive oil and vinegar to make a pleasant-tasting salad.
The root and the buds have diuretic properties; they are menstrual stimulants and may even be aphrodisiac. In addition, they cleanse the liver and treat arteriosclerosis.

CAPRIFOLIACEAE
(Honeysuckle family)

***Lonicera etrusca* G. Santi *(=Lonicera glabra* (Lowe) Pau)**   **V-VII**
Honeysuckle

DESCRIPTION: A small shrub with oblong, opposite, smooth leaves, up to 8 cm. The upper leaves of the flower-bearing stems are opposite, joined at the base. Umbels with 8-12 flowers on long peduncles grow from the leaf axils. The corolla is yellowish or whitish-yellow inside, and reddish on the outside.

HABITAT: Found in the mountain zone.

PROPERTIES, USES: As all the woodbines, this was a great inspiration to the ancient Greeks in their art. It is a nectar-producing plant with ophthalmic, diuretic and anti-catarrhal properties.

Folk medicine uses honeysuckle to whiten the teeth and relieve inflamed gums. For this purpose we can burn branches of wild honeysuckle, quench them with water, pound them and rub the teeth and gums with the powder.

If we stir together at boiling point 6 g of this powder with an equal quantity of frankincense and 15 g of wax, we will have an excellent ointment for eczema, burns and haemorrhoids.

43

Sambucus ebulus L.   **VI-VII**
Dwarf elder, Danewort

DESCRIPTION: An annual plant with a woody rhizome which produces stems 60-200 cm long. It has an unpleasant, bitter smell and taste. Large leaves with 5-13 leaflets that are oblanceolate, acute, and toothed. The flowers are whitish and aromatic, in umbels 5-16 cm in diameter. The berries are black, and pea-sized. The plant spreads very easily.

HABITAT: Along roadsides, on fences and on the banks of streams.

PROPERTIES, USES: The tubers contain acid, fatty substances, sugar, gum, large quantities of plant albumen and a bitter substance.

The leaves, mixed with the leaves of wormwood in a poultice and placed on the stomach of a child, will remove intestinal worms by means of bowel movements. In antiquity the plant was used as a purgative. The flowers, in an infusion, are expectorant, antitussant, and sudorific, and above all a disinfectant for the bowels. In external use, the leaves are antirheumatic.

The violet-coloured fluid from the fruits was used for many years to colour wine and in the dying of wool and leather.

WARNING! This is a poisonous plant, if it is consumed in large quantities. Prolonged mastication can cause the secretion of large amounts of saliva, and even nausea and vomiting.

Sambucus nigra L.   **V-VI**
Elderberry

DESCRIPTION: A deciduous shrub, decorative, up to 10 metres in height, which has become acclimatised. Hollow shoots which have a soft pith and, like the leaves, a strong odour. The leaves have 5-7 leaflets. The flowers are small, white, fragrant, in corymbs bending towards the ground. The fruits are black berries. This is probably the 'aktea' of Theophrastus and Dioscurides.

HABITAT: In the immediate neighbourhood of human activity (villages, houses, groves), in damp localities.

PROPERTIES, USES: The flower-bearing nodes and fruits are edible and used in the production of delicious marmalades, jellies, wine and liqueur. The nodes ('eyes') are also used to prepare a type of **caper,** involving maceration in vinegar; this is an effective treatment for influenza, pneumonia, asthma, bronchitis, colds and sore throats. The very ripe fruits are eaten raw or with cheese in a salad. The juice of the berries prevents the development of influenza. The leaves are a dilutant. In a light tisane, they are useful in cases of oedema and kidney complaints, such as urine insufficiency and uric lithiasis. A gargle is used to treat mouth ulcers, inflamed throats and tonsilitis.

The flowers, in a very hot infusion together with milk, are anti-catarrhal and sudorific. The internal part of the pith of the stem is purgative, and used against dropsy. The pith and the root are emetic. Sleeping beneath this bush is not recommended; it is said to be the cause of erotic and sensual dreams, followed by a bad awakening which is accompanied by unbearable tension and vomiting. Once upon a time, the pith was removed from the hollow stems and they were used as flutes and blowpipes. Ancient folk used them in hunting, to blow out little poisonous darts.

The crushed leaves are thought to be insect-repellent.

Agrostemma githago L.   V-VII
Corn cockle

DESCRIPTION: A plant up to 1 metre in height, hairy, erect. Narrow, lanceolate leaves, acute. Flowers of a light reddish-mauve colour, with emarginate petals. The very hairy calyx column ends in 5 long, narrow teeth, considerably longer than the petals.

HABITAT: Rare, in cornfields, on the Askifou plateau.

PROPERTIES, USES: The corn cockle has such a beautiful flower that it would be worth using as a decoration. Unfortunately it is tending to disappear on Crete, mainly because the cultivation of grain is being reduced.

WARNING! This is a dangerous, toxic weed which even animals avoid! The grain which contains its seeds is almost unusable, not to say dangerous. The round black seeds have narcotic properties. In antiquity they were used in a tisane to treat scurf and scabies.

Dianthus aciphyllus * **Sieber ex. Ser.**
Pink sp.   V-VII

DESCRIPTION: A perennial plant, woody, very dense at its base. The leaves are opposite, linear, and acute. The flower-bearing stems are strong, with more than 3 flowers which are unperfumed. The petals are 10 mm, dentate, pinkish-carmine with reddish-carmine veining.

HABITAT: Found on rocks and precipices in the centre of the island (Juktas). Worth cultivating.

Dianthus fruticosus L. (=*Dianthus arboreus*)   V-VII
Pink tree

DESCRIPTION: A small shrub up to 50 cm, woody. Leaves up to 40 mm, linear, fleshy, and with rounded tips. Numerous, fragrant flowers. Calyx 18-22 mm, narrowing at the tip. 10-12 obovate, acute hypocalyx scales. Petals 10 mm, dentate, pink, and hairy at the base. 10 stamens.
HABITAT: Rocks and crevasses at low altitudes (Almyros).

Dianthus pulviniformis * Greuter IV-VII

DESCRIPTION: A perennial plant, woody at the base. The flower-bearing stems are 3-5 cm, with 2-3 very small flowers. Petals 3-4 mm, dentate, light pinkish-violet in colour.
HABITAT: Found on rocks and precipices on the slopes of Kedros, at an altitude above 1000 metres.

Dianthus sphacioticus *
Boiss. & Heldr.   VI-VIII

DESCRIPTION: A perennial plant with a thick trunk, woody at the base, and many non-flowering stems. Ovate-lanceolate leaves. Flowering stems 2-10 (-15) cm, with 2-5 pairs of leaves and solitary terminal flowers. Petals 3-4 mm, entire, light pink in colour; calyx 13-16 mm, surrounded by 6 hypocalyx scales at the base.

HABITAT: White Mountains, in the alpine and sub-alpine zone (Pachnes, Ammoudara).

PROPERTIES, USES: The flowers of **Dianthus cariophylus**, the decorative plant that adorns balconies and verandas, are used to make confectionery and perfumes as well as to aromatise beverages.

All the species of **Dianthus** (the flower of Zeus) have more or less the same pharmaceutical properties. They are used as an infusion or tisane mixed with chamomile against anaemia, debility, stomach pain, bad functioning of the gastrointestinal tract, and especially against flatulence and hiccups.

NOTE: 13 species and sub-species of **Dianthus** have been recorded on Crete.

Dianthus juniperinus ⇨

Paronychia macrosepala Boiss.   IV-VI
Paronychia sp.

DESCRIPTION: A plant of 5-30 cm, low-growing, much-branched. Leaves grey-green, and downy. Flowers have large, membranous bracts, 6-10 mm, which cover the green sepals.
HABITAT: From the sea up to the sub-alpine zone.
PROPERTIES, USES: The plant contains substances useful to medicine. It is recommended for inflammation of the lungs, bronchitis, and asthma.

Silene behen L.   III-V
Catchfly sp.

DESCRIPTION: An annual plant, 15-20 cm, hairless. Single or branching stems. The leaves are greenish-blue. Slightly branched inflorescence. Calyx 11-17 mm, compressed at the lips, whitish with red veining and resembling a little amphora in shape. Mauve, two-lobed petals.
HABITAT: Found at low altitudes.

Silene colorata Poiret   II-IV
DESCRIPTION: An annual plant, 30-60 cm, with erect stems, branching, downy at the base. Branched inflorescence. The lower leaves are obovate, the rest linear. Calyx 9-16 mm. The petals are purple, two-lobed.
HABITAT: Soils at low altitudes, usually near the sea, where whole populations may be observed.

Silene gallica L.   V-VI
Small-flowered catchfly

DESCRIPTION: An annual plant with stems 14-45 cm, erect, single or branching, hairy, glandular. The lower leaves are oblong-ovate, the upper leaves linear. Flowers in a unilateral raceme. Calyx 7-10 mm, with veins. Pink petals, slightly two-lobed.
HABITAT: Found on soils at low and medium altitude.

Silene succulenta Forsskal   IV-VI

DESCRIPTION: A perennial. Fleshy, woody at the base with numerous stems, prostrate or decumbent, hairy, glandular. Leaves obovate or oblanceolate. Flowers quite large, 15-20 mm, in the axils of the upper leaves. Narrow, club-like calyx. 'Trimmed' petals, divided, white, sometimes pink or whitish-pink, which open after sunset or under a cloudy sky.
HABITAT: On little-frequented sands of the southern beaches of the island.

*Silene variegata** (Desf.)
Boiss. & Heldr.   V-VII

DESCRIPTION: A perennial, low-growing, with short stems up to 10 cm. Juicy leaves, greyish-blue, the lower ones ovate-spatulate, the upper ones smaller, obovate. Greyish-violet calyx with 10 veins. Reddish-brown petals, deeply divided.
HABITAT: Alpine and sub-alpine zone, on shingle slopes.

Silene vulgaris (Moench) *ssp. macrocarpa* Turrill   IV-V
Bladder campion

DESCRIPTION: A large perennial, up to 1 metre, hairless. Leaves 7-10 cm, lanceolate. Branched inflorescence of white, pink or greenish flowers, the petals deeply divided. Calyx very swollen, flask-like, ochre-coloured with 20 veins.

HABITAT: Common up to the mountain zone in cultivated fields, dry meadows and

Silene bellidifolia

on banks.

PROPERTIES, USES: As children, we took great delight in breaking open the swollen calyxes to cause a kind of 'detonation'. The tender stems are roasted and eaten with butter and lemon.

NOTES: The name was given to these plants in memory of the Silenes of Dionysiac mythology, who anointed their bodies with 'saliva of the silene' to protect them from snakes.

Another 19 species are found on Crete.

Stellaria media (L.) Vill.   I-V
Common chickweed

DESCRIPTION: This is an annual, up to 40 cm. The lower leaves are smooth, ovate and acutel, on long petioles; the upper leaves are stalkless. The spike is non-glandular. The flowers are stalked. Corolla 8-10 mm, with sepals the same length as the five white petals which are torn down to the base and give the impression that there are actually 10 in number, arranged in pairs.

HABITAT: A common weed in cultivated fields at low and medium altitudes.

PROPERTIES, USES: The plant has countless medicinal properties, especially as a treatment for sore throats (coughs, inflamed vocal chords, colds). The leaves are cooked like those of spinach, and are delicious. Eaten raw, they help to limit 'middle-age spread'. Birds covet the seeds and it is said that when they eat them, they sing more sweetly. The plant was once used as a poultice for the healing of wounds, to make boils disappear, and to alleviate rheumatic pains of the joints. It is believed that the fresh plants, in a beverage, are a powerful means of detoxification and sufficient to banish fatigue and weakness. The plant is also recommended for conditions of the urinary tract and inflammation of the bladder.

NOTES: - *Stellaria cupaniana* **Jord & Fourr**. (= *Stellaria media ssp. cupaniana* = *ssp. neglecta* = *ssp. postii*): This has sepals and petals of equal length, and stems covered with glandular hairs.

- *Stellaria pallida* (Dumort.) **Piré** (= *Stellaria media ssp. apetala*): This has very small, almost non-existent petals.

CHENOPODIACEAE
(Goosefoot family)

Atriplex halimus L.   IV-X
Shrubby orache

DESCRIPTION: A perennial, evergreen shrub up to 3 metres, branching, and greenish silvery-white in colour. Leaves up to 6 cm on long stalks, ovate-rhomboidal or ovate. Insignificant flowers, unisexual, without a corolla, at first forming spikes and then becoming yellowish or greenish panicles.

HABITAT: Near the sea, on salty, infertile and dry soils, on stony ground, old walls and ruins.

PROPERTIES, USES: Since the foliage is dense and does not fall in the winter, it seems to constitute an ideal windbreak for the protection of gardens near the sea. The leaves are eaten raw, boiled as a salad or pickled, and are emollient.

NOTE: As a protection against the sun, the leaves are whitish and thus reflect the abundant light.

among which are nitrogen, carbohydrates, and cellulose, but no fat. Normally, the fleshy rhizomes and the leaves are used for their cooling, sedative and cleansing (purgative) properties. They are a treatment for infections of the scalp, pediculosis (skin infection of the extremities) and scurf. The scalp should be washed with the juice and the painful area rubbed with a paste mixed with wax.

Beta sp. L.
Beet

DESCRIPTION: This is a plant suited to cultivation with long stalks and numerous leaves. It is grown as a vegetable, for decoration, as animal feed and even for the sugar it contains (sugar beet). In the wild form, 3 species have been recorded on Crete: ***Beta adanensis* Aellen**, ***B. macrocarpa* Guss**. and ***B. vulgaris ssp. maritima* (L.) Arcang**. ***Beta vulgaris ssp. vulgaris*** is the common beetroot familiar to us all.

PROPERTIES, USES: The beets contain a large number of biochemical substances,

Chenopodium album L.   **V-VIII**
White goosefoot, Fat hen

DESCRIPTION: An annual with reddish stems, sometimes large, and fluted. Leaves lanceolate or rhomboid, petiolate and with a powdery appearance. Insignificant greenish flowers, in terminal spikes. Fruit wrapped in 5 sepals.

HABITAT: A common weed on the edges of roads, near to inhabited localities and in cultivated fields.

PROPERTIES, USES: This plant was cultivated on a large scale as a vegetable, until in the 16th century it was usurped by the arrival from Asia of the spinach (***Spinacia oleracea***) that is so well-known to us all. Nevertheless, experts say that it is much more digestible than spinach, with a clearly better flavour, and contains more iron and proteins.

We eat the leaves and the tender stems as a salad, or cooked like spinach. They contain proteins which are cleansing, sedative and cooling. The tender stems must be gathered before the plant flowers; afterwards, they have a tart flavour. Naturally, it is essential to wash the leaves very well to get rid of the powdery substance on them.

NOTE: ***Chenopodium*** is a Greek word and means 'goosefoot'; it probably refers to the shape of the leaves.

Salicornia europaea **L.**
Glasswort, Marsh samphire

DESCRIPTION: An annual, fleshy, green, turning yellow or red after maturity. Opposite, semi-transparent leaves, resembling juicy scales.
HABITAT: Found on salt flats near the sea.
PROPERTIES, USES: The plant has the ability to store up to 17% of salt in its cells. It is very rich in calories, iodine, sodium and potassium and is considered to have very strong antiscorbutic properties. It is cooked like fresh beans. "If we add it as a salad garnish around a plate of cold roast meat or fish, it has the worth of any iodine therapy", says Clotilde Boisvert, one of the best specialists in the cooking of wild plants.

Salsola kali **L.**　　　　**VI-VIII**
Prickly saltwort

DESCRIPTION: A plant 10-100 cm in height, fleshy and much-branching, yellowish or greyish-green. The lower leaves are opposite, linear, and thorn-tipped. 1-3 very small flowers in the leaf axils, free petals of a light yellow colour and 2 sepals smaller than the petals, completely thorny.
HABITAT: Low altitudes, near the beaches.
PROPERTIES, USES: In olden times, the plant was used to produce soda. The consumption of the tender shoots lowers arterial pressure. The plant is also diuretic, an appetite stimulant, a vermifuge and an ulcer combatant. The seeds are much liked by sheep.

CISTACEAE (Rockrose family)

Cistus creticus L.   III-V

Cretan cistus, cretan rockrose

DESCRIPTION: A perennial shrub up to 1 metre, aromatic and dense. Leaves 12-25 mm, ovate-lanceolate, opposite, green with undulate margins and glandular hairs which secrete a gum - ladanum. Flowers 4-6 cm, large, with a corolla of a vibrant pinkish-lilac colour, white in the centre. 5 ovate sepals and 5 petals which are slightly two-lobed and wrinkled. The styles are the same length as the golden-yellow stamens.

HABITAT: Found in areas of phrygana (garrigue) and maquis.

PROPERTIES, USES: Herodotus tells us that people used to gather the gum – ladanum – from the beards and feet of goats, to which it had adhered. Today, as in the Middle Ages, it is gathered with the help of rakes fitted with rubber or hairy straps. This is done around midday, when the gum has softened and can adhere more easily.

The gum was used to make incense and ointments. Today, it is mostly used in perfumery. It is considered, sedative, styptic, warming, anti-catarrhal, antispasmodic and expectorant. It has also been used with good results in cases of sleeplessness, toothache and tetanus. The seeds of the plant are used to make a boiled decoction which stops diarrhoea, and the leaves are used to produce an aromatic tea.

Folk tradition believes that the wood of the plant protects against the evil eye and spells. For those who make 'paximadi' (twice-baked rusk) in a traditional oven, there is no better wood to use for fuel than that of cistus.

WARNING! For whatever internal use, the prior approval of a doctor is needed.
NOTE: Laudanum is a tincture of opium; <u>ladanum</u> is the oily gum of cistus.

Cistus salvifolius L.   IV-VI
Sage-leaved cistus

DESCRIPTION: Resembles **Cistus creti-cus**, but the leaves are 1-4 cm and stalked, ovate-elliptic, rough on the underside, covered on both surfaces with hairs which lie flat. Stalked flowers 3-5 cm in diameter, white, solitary or up to 4 together with 3 sepals at the base.

HABITAT: On stony slopes and generally on poor soils.

PROPERTIES, USES: Villagers used the plant as a fuel for ovens. The leaves and the flowers were used to make a tisane to treat bowel colic, haemorrhoids, dysentery, renal colic, bladder and liver conditions, and skin infections (30 g are boiled in 600 g of water until only half the liquid is left). As a poultice, it is used for rheumatism and arthritis.

NOTE: Two other varieties are found on Crete – **Cistus parviflorus Lam.** and **Cistus mospeliensis L.**

C. parviflorus

C. monspeliensis

COMPOSITAE (Asteraceae) (Daisy family)

Achillea cretica L.   IV-V
Cretan sneezewort

DESCRIPTION: The plant has a perennial rhizome and stems up to 40 cm. The young leaves are cylindrical and downy, the regular leaves 2-6 cm, narrow, and pinnately-lobed. The inflorescences consist of white flowers up to 10 mm in diameter, forming umbels.

HABITAT: Rocky soils at low altitudes (Kolymbari, Matala etc.)

PROPERTIES, USES: Is this the flower of Achilles which healed the wounds of Telephos? It is said that if achillea is rubbed on a wound, it staunches the bleeding. In the form of a drink, the plant has stomachic, styptic and solvent properties, cleans oily skin, prevents baldness, improves the function of the glands, helps maintain body weight, and helps fight the cold - and unrequited love (!).

As an infusion, a little spoonful in a glass of water three times per day restores the appetite of those who have lost the desire to eat. It is also recommended for the treatment of pains in the stomach, bowels, gall bladder and kidneys, and for haemoptysis and inflammation of the respiratory tract.

Anthemis chia L.   II-IV

Daisy sp.

DESCRIPTION: Stems up to 40 cm, with a few hairs. Leaves 2-pinnate, with sections spread out at an angle of up to 90°, and triangular or ovate lobes. The inflorescences are up to 45 mm in diameter, on long peduncles. The flowers have labiate florets larger than the disc. External bracts, triangular-lanceolate, acutely pointed at the tip, with membranous brown edges.

HABITAT: Soils at low altitudes.

PROPERTIES, USES: 25-30 g of dried flowers may be boiled in 150 g water. Bran is added and the mixture used as a poultice for external inflammation – e.g. skin infections and conditions, ulcers, split skin and haemorrhoids.

NOTE: The classification of the species of the **Anthemis** genus causes many headaches, since it is complicated to the naked eye. Another 12 species grow on Crete, among which 5 are endemic: **A. abrotanifolia*, A. ammanthus*, A, filicaulis*, A. glaberrima*, A. tomentella***.

A. abrotanifolia

A. filicaulis

59

Artemisia arborescens L.   **IV-VI**

Wormwood

DESCRIPTION: A perennial shrub, aromatic, bitter, covered in silvery-white down. Stems 50-100 cm. Leaves pinnately-lobed or two times pinnately-lobed, the lobes narrow and rounding at the tip. Roundish flower-heads, 6-7 mm, which form large panicles of many flowers.

HABITAT: Found at low altitudes, on roadsides and in abandoned fields.

PROPERTIES, USES: Distillation of the leaves and flowers produces an oil which is a vermifuge, tonic, sudorific, antiseptic and a febrifuge. **In the past, a strong drink produced by distillation – absinthe – caused particular harm to the nervous system.** Many submitted to its charm and sang its praises, foremost among them Edouard Manet, Charles Baudelaire, Arthur Rimbaud, Oscar Wild, Paul Gauguin, Toulouse Lautrec and Van Gogh. The latter was said to have been the first famous victim of absinthism; he went insane.

The dried flowers, in a tisane, three cups per day, exhibit diuretic properties for the treatment of kidney colic, amenorrhoea, stomach upsets and fever. For dropsy, 18-30 g of the powder from dried artemisia in one litre of water, one glass per day.

A handful of leaves placed in one litre of white wine for two weeks produces a drink which stimulates the appetite (one liqueur glass per day, before a meal, for a maximum of three days). The same beverage taken after the meal is beneficial to the stomach, while in the morning, before breakfast, it is effective in cases of intestinal worms (tapeworms, threadworms).

The plant is also used in the preparation of dyes and to aromatise various drinks.

WARNING! The consumption and use of this plant is completely prohibited for nursing mothers, pregnant women (it is a uternine stimulant), and nervous and irritable individuals, as well as those who suffer from buccal and gastrointestinal conditions. Its rich essential oil, when used, can cause nervous disturbances.

Aster tripolium L.   IX-XI
Sea aster

DESCRIPTION: An annual or perennial. Stems 20-60 mm (-100), branching, erect and hairless. The leaves are opposite, lanceolate, the lower ones stalked, the upper ones stalkless. Corymb-like inflorescence with many beautiful heads. Labiate florets 10-30 mm, a vibrant blue-violet in colour.
HABITAT: Found in brackish water and on salt flats (Georgioupolis).
PROPERTIES, USES: The whole plant, and particularly the root, is used to treat ophthalmic conditions and sore throats. It should have been cultivated for decoration.

Atractylis gummifera L.   VII-IX
Pine thistle

DESCRIPTION: An annual, prostrate, with large thorny leaves forming a dense rosette around a large, single flower-head 3-7 cm in diameter. The florets are pinkish-lilac, turning white during the ripening period, and surrounded by thorny bracts.
HABITAT: Found on the edges of fields and roads, and in fallow locations.
PROPERTIES, USES: According to Theophrastus, the roots are edible but fatal to dogs and pigs. If one wants to learn what chance a sick person has to get well, all that it is necessary to do is to wash the person for three days in a mixture of wine and one part of this plant. If he/she survives, recovery is certain!

Bellis perennis L.   **II-VI**
Daisy

DESCRIPTION: A perennial with a basal rosette. Leaves up to 4 cm, spatulate or obovate, erect, hairy, with a single vein, and stalked. Flower-bearing stems 4-15 cm, leafless. Flower-heads 15-30 mm with many labiate white florets which have reddish shading on their undersurface.

HABITAT: Up to the sub-alpine zone, in meadows, lawns and forests.

PROPERTIES, USES: The plants make a sedative and emollient beverage, a good antiseptic for wounds and grazes, and an excellent rinse for the genitals. The plant certainly has solvent and cleansing properties.

NOTE: Another 3 species are found on Crete: **B. annua**, **B. longifolia***, and **B. sylvestris**.

B. annua

Calendula arvensis L.   XII-V
Field marigold

DESCRIPTION: An annual, up to 30 cm. Branching, hairy stems. Leaves up to 8 cm, alternate, longish, stalkless; their margins +/- entire. Terminal flower-heads 1.5-2 cm in diameter, on short pedicels, with 2 series of linear bracts which have membranous edges. Labiate yellow, and tubular yellowish-orange florets. The fruits (achenes) take three different forms.

HABITAT: Common in fields, clearings, and vineyards etc.

PROPERTIES, USES: The flowers are a menstrual stimulant, sudorific, sedative and antiseptic. The leaves are bitter and tasteless, and their odour is repellent enough to cause vomiting; after scalding, they are used as a poultice for acne. As a powder or ointment, they are a treatment for pimples, calluses, fistulae, irritating rashes and any other kind of skin condition. In the case of pimples, erysipelas and eczema, a piece of cotton wool can be moistened in a maceration/decoction of the flowers and placed on the affected area. This same decoction, for internal use, is recommended as a menstrual stimulant and to regulate the periods. Again as a decoction, 15 g of leaves in 400 g of water constitute a beverage which can stimulate the liver.

Cattle and sheep eat these plants, but pigs avoid them.

NOTE: The flowers open in the morning with the first rays of the sun, and close at sunset in the evening.

Carthamus lanatus (L.) ssp. baeticus (Boiss. & Heldr.) Nyman   V-VIII
Carthamus

DESCRIPTION: An annual, 15-75 cm, glandular, branching in its upper part, and covered in woolly hairs which are shed with the course of time. Lanceolate, pinnately-lobed leaves with thorny teeth. Flower-heads 2-3 cm, solitary, with tubular golden florets, wrapped in thorny leaf-bracts. The plant is said to smell of rancid butter; the juice it produces is reddish.
HABITAT: Infertile places at low and medium altitude.
PROPERTIES, USES: The dried flowers are sometimes sold -, fraudulently - as saffron, since the latter is very expensive. The plant is antiseptic and used to treat gangrene.

Centaurea aegialophila Wagenitz IV-VI
Centaury sp.
DESCRIPTION: A plant with very short stems. The leaves are stalked, entire, cordate or cordate to deeply toothed, or ovate, light green, and covered with a light white down. The flowers are solitary or in pairs. The florets are pink, with purple shading at the tip, the external florets being longer than the internal ones. The bracts have membranous, dentate margins and with a short terminal thorn, 1-3 mm.
HABITAT: Sandy beaches in the north-east of the island, and on Karpathos.
PROPERTIES, USES: As a poultice to treat inflammation of the tips of the fingers, below and around the nails.

Centaurea calcitrapa L.   IV-VI
Red star thistle

DESCRIPTION: A biennial or perennial plant, up to 100 cm. The young leaves are downy and greyish, the rest are green and glandular. The basal leaves are lanceolate, pinnately-lobed, the upper ones sagittate. The flower-heads have pinkish-mauve florets and a white centre. The hypanth measures 6-8 mm, and is ovate with greenish bracts ending in a sharp thorn 10-18 mm long.
HABITAT: Acid soils, at low altitudes.
PROPERTIES, USES: The petals have toning, healing, febrifuge, diuretic and purgative properties.

Centaurea raphanina* Sibth. & Sm.
Centaury sp.   IV-VI

DESCRIPTION: A perennial, almost stemless. Basal rosette of entire leaves, sometimes deeply-toothed or lobed. Flower-heads 2-4 cm with tubular florets that are light pink or white. The bracts are entire or slightly dentate, with a terminal thorn.
HABITAT: Found up to the mountain zone.
PROPERTIES, USES: The plant is eaten boiled, as a salad, and stimulates the appetite. It is said to have tonic and diuretic properties and is thus used in conditions of the kidneys and bladder. In a decoction, it is used as a collyrium and soothes pain in the eyes. Boiled leaves are used in a poultice for eye complaints.

Centaurea solstitialis L.   VI-VIII
St. Barnaby's thistle

DESCRIPTION: A biennial, with stems of 30-100 cm, much-branching and sinuately-winged. The leaves are ash-grey, covered with spidery hairs, the lower ones deeply-toothed, and have dried by the time of flowering. The upper leaves are lanceolate with entire margins and short, terminal thorns. Solitary flower-heads with gold-yellow florets. The bracts have a large yellow, terminal thorn.

HABITAT: Found up to the alpine zone.

PROPERTIES, USES: During the time that the rosettes have tender leaves they are eaten cooked, in a salad. The flowers are a febrifuge, and the roots have stomachic properties.

NOTE: *Centaurea idea** **Boiss. & Heldr**. differs in that it has a short and unbranched middle stem, which carries only one flower-head at the centre of the plant, and in its glandular florets. As a tisane, it tones up the appetite and aids digestion.

Chrysanthemum coronarium L.
(= *Glebionis coronaria*)   III-V
Crown daisy

DESCRIPTION: An annual, up to 80 cm, much-branching, with numerous 2-pinnately-lobed leaves. Smooth stems. Large flower-heads 5-6 cm in diameter, with tubular yellow and labiate dark yellow florets (***var. bicolor*** has florets that are labiate and whitish-yellow at the tips but darker in the centre).

HABITAT: Common in fallow fields. Often covers large areas of ground.

PROPERTIES, USES: The young stems are boiled along with other wild greens and eaten as a salad. The flowers were once used in cases of jaundice. It is said that the plant, uprooted before sunrise and hung from the shoulder, protects against charms and spells.

C. coronarium

Chrysanthemum segetum L. (*Glebionis segetum*)   IV-VI
Corn marigold

DESCRIPTION: An annual, up to 60 cm, hairless, slightly fleshy. The stem is very leafy, very slightly branched. The leaves are oblong or obovate, torn or coarsely toothed, the upper leaves +/- periblastic and less divided. Flower-heads 2-5 cm in diameter, solitary. Yellow florets, tubular and labiate. Ovate bracts with membranous edges. Winged fruits.

HABITAT: Cultivated and abandoned fields.

PROPERTIES, USES: The roots are cooked like salsify. The plant is considered to be healing. A yellow colouring is extracted from the flowers.

Cichorium intybus L.   V-VI
Chicory

DESCRIPTION: A perennial, slightly hairy or hairless, 40-100 cm, with a carrot-like root. The basal leaves are large, lobed or toothed, and form a round rosette from the centre of which the flower-bearing stem develops. The flower-heads are 4 cm in diameter and open in the morning. Labiate blue florets with dark-blue stamens.

HABITAT: Abandoned and cultivated fields at low and moderate altitudes.

PROPERTIES, USES: One of the best edible plants. It has tonic, diuretic, purgative, stomachic, febrifuge and appetite-stimulating properties, and the Romans even believed it was an aphrodisiac. The Egyptians knew about chicory as early as the 4th millennium, and it was certainly one of the 'bitter greens' that the Hebrews ate with their Passover lamb. Salads of raw or boiled chicory are much in demand. The rosettes of leaves are gathered before the flowering stem develops. The tender flower-bearing stems are just as tasty as the leaves.

The roots contain a bitter, milky substance which gives the plant special properties. If we add the powdered dry root to café au lait, the beverage becomes more digestible. The leaves contain a bitter substance, chlorophyll, a sugary substance, albumen and many salts such as potassium nitrate, sulphur, phosphorus and magnesium.

A tisane of the leaves, with the addition of salt and lemon juice, strengthens the digestive system, is a treatment for jaundice, liver pains, swellings of the gall bladder, remittent fevers and kidney complaints.

WARNING! The gathering of chicory

should be avoided near polluted areas (busy roads, rubbish dumps) because the plant has the characteristic of absorbing whatever chemical substances are to be found in its immediate vicinity.

Cichorium spinosum L.   IV-V and VII-X

Spiny chicory, Stamnagathi

DESCRIPTION: A perennial, small phrygano plant, spiny, with short stems (4-18 cm), branching from the base. The leaves are pinnately-lobed or dentate. The flower-heads are similar to those of chicory, but smaller and with fewer labiate florets.

HABITAT: Found near beaches and (strangely!) in the mountains and on plains at an altitude of above 1000 metres. It is also cultivated.

PROPERTIES, USES: The tender stems are eaten raw or boiled with olive oil and lemon dressing. Fricassé of lamb with 'stamnagathi' is a very special dish.

NOTES: The tender stems, if they are not gathered at the right time, become woody and inedible. The plant has all the properties of *Cichorium intybus*.

Cichorium pumillum Jacq. (= *C. endivia ssp. divaricatum*) which flowers in **VII**, resembles *C. intybus* but is an annual or

biennial; its lower leaves are hairy and the flowering stem is thick and robust. Some varieties are cultivated.

C. spinosum

Cynara cornigera Lindley   IV-VI
Wild artichoke

DESCRIPTION: A perennial plant, robust. Stems around 40 cm, erect. Leaves arranged in a rosette, up to 40 cm, deeply lobed, with light-coloured veins on the upper surface. Flower-heads up to 50 mm with tubular, yellowish florets. Thorny bracts.

HABITAT: In phrygana (garrigue) and on rocks at low altitudes.

PROPERTIES, USES: All of the artichokes, whether cultivated (*Cynara scolymus* L.) or wild (*C. cardunculus* L. and *C. cornigera*) have more or less the same properties. They contain calcium, phosphorus, vitamins, organic acids, bitter substances, cynarin and inulin.

Like the tender base of the bracts, the lower part of the flower-head – the hypanth – is highly edible. Often these parts are all that is eaten. What a pity! The rest of the plant is very bitter in flavour but it has the unique ability to stimulate bile secretion, restrict urine secretion, and reduce the level of cholesterol in the blood, arterial pressure, and hypertrophy of the prostate.

The flowers and leaves, in an infusion, are used to treat fever, with one or two glasses per day. The fresh leaves, pounded and used in a poultice, are used to treat haemorrhoids. For tonsillitis and sore throats, we can apply a poultice of boiled leaves, leaving it in place the whole night.

WARNING! Cynarin, in combination with milk, can cause stomach disturbances. As both the beverage and the extract are extremely bitter to the taste, there should be no hesitation in adding honey.

Cynara scolymus

NOTES: In the past, **C. cardunculus** (Cardoon) was cultivated as a decorative and edible plant. It has stiff, pinnately-lobed or twice pinnately-lobed leaves with yellow spines on the lobes that are 15-35 mm long, flower-heads smaller than those of the cultivated artichoke, bracts with spines 1-5 cm long, and tubular deep blue-violet flowers.

The stems and leaf rosette of **C. cornigera**, after its spines and fibres have been carefully removed with a knife, can be used to make a sublime-tasting dish of lamb in egg and lemon sauce ('avgolemono').

C. cardunculus

Dittrichia viscosa (L.) Greuter VIII-XI
Stink aster?

DESCRIPTION: A perennial plant up to 1 metre, glandular, sticky, strong-smelling. Erect stems, much-branched, thickly haired, thinning towards the tip. Leaves 3-7 cm, alternate, +/- lanceolate, the upper leaves semi-periblastic. Numerous flower-heads 1-1.5 cm, forming +/- longish inflorescences. Hypanth with scale-like linear bracts. The female flowers are labiate and yellow, the male flowers are tubular and yellowish-orange.

HABITAT: Abandoned fields, the edges of roads, rubbish tips, damp locations. Often in large populations.

PURPOSES, USES: The strong, rancid smell emitted by the plant was once considered sufficient to repel insects, and in particular fleas. It was used in conditions of the bladder. The parts of the plant above ground were used as a dye, yielding the colour of oil.

Echinops spinosissimus Turra VII-VIII
Spiny globe thistle

DESCRIPTION: A spiny plant, very erect. Stems 50-100 cm, branching, covered with glandular hairs. Large leaves, woolly, whitish, 2-pinnately-lobed, with spiny lobes. Clusters of round, thorny flower-heads, greyish-green to light silver in colour. Florets 3.5-7 mm, tubular, light-blue to violet.

HABITAT: Abandoned fields and stony soils up to the mountain zone.

PROPERTIES, USES: To combat neurasthenia, 200 g of spiny globe thistle, 500 g of elm and 200 g of "Bermuda Grass". can be boiled in 2 litres of water, and a cup of the liquid drunk in the morning and evening.

Helminthoteca echioides (L.) Holub. (= *Picris echioides* L.)   IV-VII
Bristly ox-tongue

DESCRIPTION: An annual or biennial plant, 30-60 cm, much-branched, covered in tough hairs (pigs' bristles). Leaves covered with whitish vesicles (pustules), the lower leaves obovate, toothed and with a winged stalk, the upper leaves stalkless. Numerous heads with labiate yellow florets. The external bracts are triangular, broad, and very characteristic.

HABITAT: Common on soils where there are grazing plants. A weed, harmful to cultivated crops.

PROPERTIES, USES: The plant, dried and powdered, is used as an embrocation for myrmiciasis (a type of swelling on the skin). It is also used as a poultice for inflammation.

It is eaten boiled with olive oil and lemon juice, together with artichokes and courgettes. Widows, it is said, have a special predilection for it – hence one of its popular Greek names, 'hirovotano'.

Inula candida (L.) Cass. V-VII
Inula sp.

DESCRIPTION: A plant with thin stems up to 30 cm and basal leaves 3-9 cm, ovate or lanceolate. The heads are moderately sized with many small, labiate yellowish florets.

HABITAT: Found in rocky locations at low altitude, usually near the sea. Endemic to western Crete (Kastelli Kissamou).

PROPERTIES, USES: Dioscurides recommended the use of an ointment made from pounded seeds to banish wrinkles and to maintain a fresh-looking complexion (smooth skin).

Lactuca serriola L. VI-VIII
Prickly lettuce

DESCRIPTION: An annual or biennial plant up to 180 cm, producing a rich milky juice (latex), slightly bitter and sticky, which thickens when in contact with air to take on a colloidal appearance. Basal rosettes of broad leaves, lobed and covered in the lower part, above and around the central vein, with tough, thorny hairs (bristles). The flowerheads are small with labiate florets in a light yellow colour, which open in the evening and close again in the morning with the rising of the sun. The popular Greek name, which means 'compass', was given because of the characteristic of the plant to turn as far as possible to face the sun.

HABITAT: Of Mediterranean origin, found in cultivated fields and on roadsides.

PROPERTIES, USES: The plant is used to treat arthritic-rheumatic pains, gonorrhoea, eye conditions and chronic wounds. It is diuretic and purgative. Given that the plant has emollient, sedative, tranquillising and slightly narcotic properties, it also dampens sexual arousement.

Pliny mentions that one doctor used it to cure the Emperor Augustus of a liver condition. In the Middle Ages, it was recommended to assist sleep.It works 'wonders' in cases of illness characterised by spasms, such as asthma, whooping cough, chronic stress, tachycardia and hysteria.

WARNING! Generally, lettuces can grow out of dirty water, industrial waste-water and dung, and thus be carriers of microbes which cause tuberculosis, cholera, hepatitis, dysentery etc. For this reason, they must be scrupulously washed and if necessary, left for an hour in a light solution of water and vinegar or lemon juice.

NOTES: - *Lactuca sativa* L., our well-known lettuce with its watery leaves and the round, domed heads which resemble a cabbage, originated either from Egypt or from Siberia.
- *Lactuca saligna* L. is a small, hairless plant without thorns. Its leaves are narrow, the upper ones sagittate, with their two lobes embracing the stem.

Matricaria recutita L. (= *Matricaria chamomilla*)   III-IV
Scented mayweed, Chamomile

DESCRIPTION: An annual, aromatic plant, branching, up to 60 cm. The leaves are 2-3 times pinnately-lobed, the sections linear to thread-like. Numerous flower-heads up to 25 mm in diameter. The florets are labiate, turning back on themselves at the tips. The bracts have whitish-green tips. The flowers are fragrant and slightly bitter.
HABITAT: Found near villages, houses, generally in inhabited locations.
PROPERTIES, USES: The medicinal properties are endless. Today, in an infusion, it is used as a digestive aid, as an antispasmodic, for aerophagia, for unsettled stomach, stomach cramps, anorexia, as a light purgative, as an emetic, gall-stimulant, appetite-stimulant, to soothe stomach pain, for neuralgia, for hysteria, for hypochondria (spleen), for trigeminal pain, rheumatic pain, myalgia, period pain and as a tonic for the blood circulation.

As a compress and a simple infusion, it is used externally for inflammation of the skin and eyes (moisten a piece of cotton wool in a tepid infusion and place on the painful area). As a gargle, it is used for any kind of stress and for purulent tonsillitis, and as a poultice

M. recutita

for abscesses, boils and other infections of the skin.

The ancient Greeks knew it as a febrifuge and dedicated it to Apollo.

Young Cretan women used to wash their hair in an infusion of chamomile to give it blonde highlights.

WARNING! It can be destructive if taken in large quantities. Its alkaloid content can cause damage to the digestive system. It can cause a predisposition in adults towards rheumatic pains if taken in a large dose and continuously (overuse), and in children to develop cerebral hyperaemia. It is also harmful to corpulent and sensitive women, in whom it causes persistent headaches, sleeplessness and trembling of the hands.

NOTE: Greek chamomile contains 9.36% of essential oil and is considered to be among the best.

Onopordum bracteatum Boiss. & Heldr. ssp. *creticum* Franco   VI-VIII
Donkey thistle

DESCRIPTION: A biennial, up to 100 cm. Yellowish, greenish or whitish stems, hairy, winged, and with palm-like spines. Leaves 30 x 8 cm, white, woolly in the lower section. Recognised by its robust bracts which are spiny, hairless, completely lanceolate, and flower-heads 30-70 mm in diameter. The florets are tubular and mauve, rarely white.
HABITAT: Found in mountain areas.
NOTE: ***Onopordum*** = onos (donkey) + pordi (from the verb meaning to be confused or lost).

O. bracteatum ⇨

Onopordum illyricum ssp. cardunculus (Boiss.) Franco VII-VIII
Illyrian Scotch thistle

DESCRIPTION: A biennial plant up to 200 cm in height. Winged stems, spiny, with thick yellowish hairs. Leaves up to 35x15 cm, stalkless, green to whitish, with triangular side lobes, +/- entire. Heads 40-50 mm in diameter. The bracts of the hypanth have a 'brick roof' appearance, with barbs that are often coloured, and revolute. Tubular purple florets.
HABITAT: At moderate altitude, on road-sides and in stony locations.

Onopordum majorii (Beauverd.)V-VII

DESCRIPTION: Plants up to 1.5 m, with white hairs and narrow wings. Leaves up to 45 cm, pinnate, greyish-green, covered in sparse hairs in the top part and dense in the lower. The whole plant resembles a huge candelabra. Flower heads enormous, with a diameter of 70-100 cm.
HABITAT: Found in the east of the island and on Karpathos, at relatively low altitude.

Onopordum tauricum Willd. IV-VII

DESCRIPTION: A biennial plant which can reach 2 metres, green, with no white wool. Winged stems, frequently branching, and spiny. Leaves up to 25 cm, pinnately-lobed. Large heads, round with a diameter of up to 70 mm. Tubular florets, pinkish-purple and spiny bracts, the upper ones growing upwards, the lower ones drooping.
HABITAT: On uncultivated soils, at moderate and low altitudes.
PROPERTIES, USES: Some people eat the hypanths like artichokes, before they flower.

Onopordon majorii

The plants are diuretic and stomachic, and are used against pleurisy. They are eaten by goats, as well as by donkeys.

NOTES: According to experts, it is very difficult to differentiate between the species of **Onopordum** without the help of a microscope. However, it appears that the identification of the four types which grow on Crete is relatively easy. Whatever the case may be, these plants with their large, beautiful flowers (heads) can never go unnoticed.

Onopordon tauricum

Picnomon acarna (L.) Cass.　　IV-VI
Picnomon

DESCRIPTION: An annual, 10-50 cm, branching, with spidery hairs. Winged, spiny stems. Leaves lanceolate with strong yellow thorns, 4-15 mm. Heads with tubular florets, pinkish-carmine, surrounded by longer, spiny leaves.

HABITAT: Found on roadsides, in uncultivated and stony places up to the mountain zone.

PROPERTIES, USES: Its roots were once used to treat sore throats, toothache and stomach disturbances, while the fruits were used to treat convulsions in children.

Pulicaria dysenterica (L.) Bernh.VII-X
Common fleabane

DESCRIPTION: A plant with a perennial rhizome and annual stems, hairy, branching, up to 100 cm. Oblong-lanceolate leaves, glandular, stemless, the upper ones periblastic. Flower-heads on long pedicels, the side ones longer than those in the middle. Labiate florets with 3 teeth. Unpleasant smell and taste.
HABITAT: Damp soils, marshes and generally wet locations.
PROPERTIES, USES: According to Linnaios, it was used successfully during epidemics of dysentery.

The rhizome, in an infusion, has disinfectant properties. The plant was also used to remove lice (its seeds resemble lice in form and gave the impression that they would be effective against the insects.) Ancient homeopathy!

Reichardia picroides (L.) Roth   III-V
Reichardia sp.

DESCRIPTION: A perennial, 5-45 cm, hairless, with a milky juice. Fragile stems. The basal leaves are dense, entire or pinnately-lobed. Heads up to 30 mm in diameter, with yellow, labiate florets.
PROPERTIES, USES: The plant is eaten raw and leaves a pleasant flavour of fresh milk in the mouth. It is also eaten boiled, on its own or with other mountain greens. It is appetite-stimulating and slightly diuretic.

Scariola venimea (L.) J & C. Presl. VI-VIII
Pliant lettuce

DESCRIPTION: A perennial plant with stems 30-80 cm, branching in the upper part. The leaves are smooth, green-blue, the lower ones lobed, the upper ones entire, with 2 linear sections at the base. The inflorescence consists of numerous heads made up of 4-5 labiate, lemon yellow florets, toothed at the tips.

HABITAT: Rocky locations up to the mountain zone.

PROPERTIES, USES: The milky juice, after desiccation, was once used for respiratory conditions.

Scolymus hispanicus L.   V-VIII
Spanish oyster plant

DESCRIPTION: A biennial or perennial, branching and +/- haired, with a thick, stake-like root. The stems are winged and spiny. The leaves are pinnately-lobed with dentate sections, and spiny. The heads are 1-2 cm in diameter, growing from the leaf axils. The florets are labiate, golden-yellow in colour. The plant resembles ***Carthamus lanatus***.

HABITAT: Sterile and uncultivated soils at low altitudes.

PROPERTIES, USES: The roots consist of a woody, central section and a white, fleshy external sheath. The latter is held in great esteem by Cretan cooks who use it together with the fleshy ridges of the leaves to prepare delicious soups and lamb fricassee or lamb in egg and lemon sauce - a sheer culinary delight. The inedible part of the margin and the spines of the leaves are removed by grasping the midrib with two fingers and running it through them from the base to the tip.

Pliny mentions that the sculptor Xenocrates used to wash with an extract of scolymus mixed with wine, to neutralise the bad odour of sweat; this probably constituted the first deodorant!

Scorzonera cretica Willd.   IV-V

Cretan viper's grass

DESCRIPTION: A perennial with a cylindrical rhizome. Stems up to 50 cm, hairy. Leaves about 30 cm, linear. The flower-heads are large, up to 50 mm, with labiate yellow florets.

HABITAT: Found on rocks and in sterile areas at low and medium altitudes.

PROPERTIES, USES: The roots were eaten in antiquity. Today, the plant is known as a type of salsify.

NOTE: *Scorzonera idaea* * **(Gand.) Lipsch.** is endemic to Psiloritis (Idi) in the alpine and sub-alpine zone. This is a dwarf plant up to 4 cm, with a cylindrical rhizome and similar rosettes with leaves 3-6 cm, linear and sinuate.

S. idaea

Senecio vulgaris L.   I-XII

Groundsel

DESCRIPTION: An annual with a branching stem, up to 30 cm, and lobed leaves. The heads have tubular florets, lemon-yellow in colour. they rarely produce a few labiate florets.

HABITAT: A common weed in cultivated and fallow areas.

PROPERTIES, USES: The plant is almost devoid of scent and has a grassy, insipid flavour. It is considered a good sedative and emollient, and a dilutant of a number of salts. For this reason its use is suggested in cases of renal, bladder or liver colic, emphractic jaundice and leucorrhoea. It has also been used for haemoptysis, period pains and as a haemostatic, because it assists sustolic contraction of the blood vessels. It is given as a tisane, 2-3 cups per day.

Boiled in milk, mixed up with mallow leaves and bran, it is used hot as a poultice for exanthema and skin infections, and mastitis, haemorrhoids, bruising as a result of wounds, abscesses, anthrax and also for stomach pains.

A delight for birds, especially for canaries and goldfinches, it is also a good food for sheep, deer, pigs, cattle and rabbits.

S. vulgaris

Silybum marianum (L.) Gaertner IV-VI
Holy thistle, Milk thistle

DESCRIPTION: A biennial, branching plant with a basal rosette. Alternate leaves, very characteristic, hairless, and a brilliant green in colour, with white veining or spots, pinnately-lobed, spiny, the lower leaves stalked, the upper leaves with a cordate base wrapping the wingless stem. Solitary flowerheads, on long stalks, with a diameter of around 4 cm, reddish-violet tubular florets and bracts terminating in terrible spines which are 2-5 cm long.

HABITAT: Often found in large populations on the edges of roads and in meadows, usually in company with stinging nettles and other plants greedy for nitrogen.

PROPERTIES, USES: All parts of this plant are edible – the leaves, hypanth, stems and roots. The hypanths are superior in flavour to artichokes. The shoots of the first year are eaten raw as a salad or cooked like spinach. The fruits contain silymarin, a substance used in the treatment of conditions of the gall bladder and the liver. As it is also haemostatic,

it is used to treat nosebleeds, wounds and menstrual bleeding. It has a beneficial influence on the circulation (in cases of headache, dizziness, hypotension, general indisposition) and on allergies (nausea, allergic catarrh, itching and asthma).

Tradition tells us that the white spots on the leaves are drops of the milk of the Virgin which fell on the plant while she was feeding the Holy Child.

Sonchus oleraceus L.   IV-VI
Smooth sow-thistle

DESCRIPTION: An annual plant, 20-70 cm, greyish with a milky juice. The basal leaves are entire, the upper ones pinnately-lobed, pinnate or deeply toothed, all with soft spines. The heads are 20-25 mm, with labiate yellow florets, surrounded by white.

HABITAT: Common in cultivated fields and in ditches along the sides of roads. It can flower all the year round if the soil is damp enough.

PROPERTIES, USES: The plant is eaten boiled, as a salad, often together with other wild greens; the leaves and stems can be cooked like spinach. The roots are eaten raw or in a soup.

It is said that Theseus, before he confronted the Minotaur, that monster of Greek legend, asked to eat a plate of sonchus.

There is a belief that the plant heals stomach ulcers when eaten raw. Compresses of the pounded stems have therapeutic value in the treatment of eye inflammations and scorpion bites.

NOTE: **Sonchus asper ssp. asper** and **ssp. glaucescens** are also found on Crete. They resemble **Sonchus oleraceus** and have the same properties and uses.

S. oleraceus

S. oleraceus

Taraxacum sp. (*Taraxacum alepicum, T. bithynicum, T. hellenicum, T. minimum*)
Dandelion   **VIII-V**

T. alepicum

DESCRIPTION: This is an herbaceous, prostrate plant with a thick root. The rosette has stalked, deeply divided leaves, parts of which are often triangular and always apiculate, becoming more oblong towards the top of the plant. The heads of the flowering stems have numerous labiate yellow florets which open from the centre towards the outer edge. The plant flowers from autumn until the spring, according to the species. The seed is an achene with a winged, stalked pappus which disintegrates with the slightest breath of wind.

HABITAT: Found on dry and damp soils which are often pebbly or stony, from the sea right up to the sub-alpine zone, according to the species.

PROPERTIES, USES: All of the species are edible. They should be washed well, if necessary in water to which salt has been added, strained, and dressed with olive oil, lemon salt and pepper, to make a delicious salad.

The plants are rich in potassium, and can be used in cases of urine deficiency (anouria) and all conditions of the urinary tract. In their raw state, they are also described as appetite-stimulating, tonic, and an aphrodisiac.In an infusion or tisane, they provide for the good function of the glands, and are good for the digestion and a menstrual stimulant. Also as an infusion, they seem to be useful in cases of chronic dermatitis, arthritis, liver and spleen distention, scurvy, mental stress, dropsy and chronic eczema.

Mixed with nettles and **Achillea cretica** in a tisane, the plant strengthens a constitution exhausted after a long illness or stress.

For rheumatism sufferers, an infusion made with the roots (10 g to 200 g of water) is recommended; one glass per day.

The milky juice of the plants is used once daily for pimples, boils, rashes and skin irritations caused by insects.

T. minimum

83

Tragopogon lassithicus * Rech. fil.
Lasithian goat's beard   **V-VII**

DESCRIPTION: A perennial, small, up to
20 cm, with linear leaves on simple stems.
The flower-heads have labiate florets in a soft
yellow shade, washed with reddish-brown at
the centre and the tips. Hypanth with 5
bracts larger than the florets.
HABITAT: Found only on Dikti and Psiloritis; should definitely be protected.

Tragopogon sinuatum **Ani-Lall**
(= *Tragopogon porrifolius*)   **IV-V**
Salsify, Goat's beard, Oyster plant

DESCRIPTION: A biennial, felty, up to
120 cm. Linear leaves, widening at the base.
Large heads with labiate pinkish-lilac florets,
the same length as the bracts of the hypanth,
which have darker, rarely white, veining.
HABITAT: Found in meadows and set-aside
fields, at low and medium altitude.
PROPERTIES, USES: Theophrastus gave it
the name which it still bears today – trago-
pogon – because of the resemblance of its
tuft with the beard of a goat.
The plants are eaten raw as a salad, or boiled.
The root, when it is boiled, has the flavour of
oyster, whence it acquires its common English name of 'oyster plant'. It can also be
roasted and used like coffee.
All of the species, but especially those which
have leaves like those of the leek, have a large
number of biochemical properties. They can
be used as a diuretic and purgative - 20-25 g
in one litre of water - for arthritis, rheumatism and skin conditions. All of the parts of
the plant, on the analogy of 1 part to 5 parts

of water, can be used to treat renal colic (one
glass every morning, before a meal).

T. sinuatum

Tussilago farfara L.
Colt's foot

II-VI

DESCRIPTION: A perennial plant with a thick tuber which, in spring, throws out hairy, scaly flower-stems, with only one head bearing yellow labiate florets, male at the centre and female at the periphery. The leaves appear after flowering, which explains the Latin name 'filius ante patrem' (meaning 'the son before the father'), and are felty on the underside. The fruit takes the form of a white tuft and vaguely resembles the hoofprint of a donkey.

HABITAT: Found on cool, damp calcareous clay soils.

PROPERTIES, USES: The plant was known to Dioscurides. He and Pliny recommended the inhalation of smoke from the burning leaves and roots of the plant for asthma and coughs. Syrup made from the leaves also constitutes a very good medicine for coughs. The flowers, which have a sweet flavour and a pleasing scent, are also antitussant, anti-inflammatory and sedative. Hippocrates cleaned festering wounds with an infusion of the plant.

As a powder, it is used for skin ulcers and as a tincture for toothache and rheumatic and arthritic pains. The tender leaves are eaten raw as a salad with other wild greens, or they can be boiled. The leaves and flowers, when boiled, are used as a poultice for skin inflammations, pimples and abcesses. The high zinc content of the leaves explains their healing ability.

Xanthium brasilicum Well. et *saccharatum* Wallr. (= *Xanthium stumarium* L.)
Rough cocklebur   **VII-IX**

DESCRIPTION: An annual, up to 1 metre, very branching. Hairy, entire or 3-5 lobed leaves, toothed and on a long stalk. Unisexual flowers, in terminal or axillary clumps, the male above the female, the latter with 2 florets and a spiny base.

HABITAT: Found on sandy beaches, the banks of streams and sides of roads, at low altitude. Of uncertain origin.

PROPERTIES, USES: Sheep, goats and cattle graze readily on this plant. It was once used for scrofula, leprosy and catarrh.

Xanthium spinosum L.   **VII-X**
Spiny cocklebur

DESCRIPTION: An annual, 30-70 cm. Alternate, three-lobed leaves, the middle lobe larger, dark green on the surface with veins covered in white down and whitish and woolly on the underside. The base of the flower-stalk has three-part spines which are yellowish-straw coloured. The male florets are in little terminal inflorescences and there are two female florets in the leaf axils.

HABITAT: Found at low altitude, in clearings, on rubbish tips, and on stream banks. It originates from South America and was brought to Europe by the Portuguese.

PROPERTIES, USES: Goats and cattle like to eat this plant, especially the fruits. It was used in dyeing, for the yellow colour it produces.

Calystegia sepium (L.) R. Br.   VI-IX
Larger bindweed, Bellvine

DESCRIPTION: An annual, climbing, with a milky juice. Can reach up to 5 metres. Leaves cordate to sagittate. Flowers 30-70 mm, large, bell-like, white, and surrounded by 2 bracts which cover the calyx and thus help us to distinguish it from plants of the ***Convolvulus*** species. The flowers open with the light of day and close again when the sky becomes cloudy. Remarkably, they remain open in moonlight.

HABITAT: Cool, damp soils, marshes and the banks of rivers and streams.

PROPERTIES, USES: Animals like the leaves. The plant is healing and slightly purgative.

Convolvulus arvensis L.   IV-VIII
Field bindweed

DESCRIPTION: A perennial plant with stems 10-100 cm. Sagittate leaves. Flowers 2 cm in diameter, fragrant, pink, white or intermediate shades of the two, solitary or in pairs. Small bracts, at some distance from the flowers.

HABITAT: Common in fields, gardens and on roadsides.

PROPERTIES, USES: A weed which is only destroyed with great difficulty. Animals like the plant, which is used to treat dropsy.

Cuscuta palaestina Boiss.   IV-VI
Dodder

DESCRIPTION: An annual parasite, climbing. Flowers in dense inflorescences. The corolla is very small, in the shape of a little bell, white to straw-pink in colour, and consists of 4 petals.

HABITAT: Found up to the sub-alpine zone.

PROPERTIES, USES: This parasite embraces its host plant, in order to drain off the nutritious substances through strong suckers which resemble cupping-glasses. The people of antiquity compared it with the hair of nymphs (nereids) and of devils, from which its common Greek names derive.

It has therapeutic properties in cases of constipation and melancholy (!),

NOTE: Three further species are recorded from Crete: ***Cuscuta atrans, Cuscuta planifolia*** and ***Cuscuta epithymum***.

Cuscuta epithymum?

C. palaestina
⇩

Sedum acre L. *ssp. neglectum* (Ten.) Murb.   V-VII
Wallpepper

DESCRIPTION: A perennial, low-growing, hairless. Flowering stems 5-12 cm, relatively few in number. Leaves (scales) 3-6 mm, elliptic, lamina-like. Flowers with outspread petals, a vibrant yellow colour, with reddish-orange tips.

HABITAT: Stony locations, on roadsides, up to the sub-alpine zone.

PROPERTIES, USES: The plant has smoothing properties (it removes callouses and bunions), and is antitussant (in a syrup made with one part of the plant and sugar). It was once used for its abortive properties - with doubtful efficacy, however.

WARNING! Poisonous when taken in a large dose.

NOTES: Plants of the **Sedum** family live exclusively among the rocks, on stony and sandy soil. For this reason, its stems and leaves are fleshy, and thus retain the atmospheric moisture and early morning dew by means of a very evolved subterranean system of thin, superficial rootlets. 18 species have been recorded on Crete.

Sedum hispanicum

Umbilicus rupestris (Salisb.) Dandy
Navelwort   IV-V

DESCRIPTION: A perennial, 10-50 cm. Basal leaves orbicular and fleshy, like little plates, with a little depression like that of an umbilicus (belly button) at the centre. The plant has a single stem, erect, sometimes branched, and covered over more than half of its length with little flowers 7-20 mm, which are pendent, bell-shaped, whitish-green, yellow or pink.
HABITAT: Found in clefts in the rocks and on walls at low and medium altitude.
PROPERTIES, USES: A cooling and diuretic plant.
NOTE: *Umbilicus horizontalis* (Guss.) – Pennywort – has horizontal flowers.

U. horizontalis

CRUCIFERAE (Mustard family)

Brassica cretica (L.) Lam.   IV-V
Cretan cabbage

DESCRIPTION: A perennial, up to 1 metre, with fleshy, greyish-green leaves. Basal leaves 10-15 cm, deeply toothed, those on the stem stalkless and with auricles. The flowers are white in the sub-species **ssp. nivea** and ochre-yellow in **ssp. cretica.**
HABITAT: The progenitor of our cabbage grows on the rocks of the gorges and cliffs, up to the mountain zone.
PROPERTIES, USES: Generally, the cabbages exhibit a multitude of biochemical properties and work positively against a large spectrum of conditions: nervous insomnia, rheumatic and arthritic conditions, ischialgia, wounds of all kinds, inflammations, abcesses, boils, burns, skin complaints, scurf, leprosy, gout (podagra), jaundice and dysentery.

90

In an infusion, the plants are used as an anti-dote to mushroom poisoning.

As a poultice, they help singers to regain their voices; they also combat inflammation of the reproductive organs (e.g. the testicles and paramitrion).

The leaves, when they are pressed with a hot iron, constitute a good poultice for ulcers and skin wounds. Women can even use them, softened by ironing, on the breast in cases of mastitis, or for any other kind of swelling.

Due to their anti-inflammatory properties, villagers used their leaves and the pounded seeds to treat dog and rat bites, as well as for swelling and pain in the joints.

Cabbage soup is diuretic, detoxifying, soothes a cough and helps to treat eye conditions (as a wash, after it has been filtered).

Sauerkraut, French choucroute, is made by fermenting cabbage in a closed container, with the addition of various other ingredients such as pepper, vinegar etc.

The cabbages supply our bodies with the necessary sulphur and are an excellent purgative. They are a wonderful medicine against insomnia and nerves. "Those suffering from stress, participants in competitions, and all who suffer from melancholy or neurasthenia or chronic fatigue, should eat lots of cabbage", M. Messegué tells us.

Brassica nigra (L.) Koch   III-IV
Black cabbage

DESCRIPTION: An annual, large, hairless and branching, and a vibrant green in colour. The basal leaves are rough, deeply-toothed to pinnate, the upper ones stalked, lanceolate, and tangential to the stem. The flowers are arranged in a terminal raceme. Petals 7-9 mm, of a light yellow colour. Erect siliqua, elongated and rectangular, with round seeds, brownish-black in colour and with a meshed surface.

HABITAT: Cultivated and self-sowing in zones of low and medium altitude.

PROPERTIES, USES: The seeds contain a large quantity of oil which is, however, of limited use. The plant is used in the manufacture of a table mustard stronger than that produced from **Sinapis alba.** From its seeds, medicine and pharmacology produce the mustard dust which is used in mustard-plasters. Some chemists sell sinapi in various preparations (poultices, adhesive plasters, ointments).

Cattle like the tender green parts of the plant. The tender shoots are gathered and eaten boiled, as a salad. They can, however, cause flatulence.

Capsela bursa-pastoris (L.) **Medicus**
Shepherd's purse   **II-IV**

DESCRIPTION: An annual or biennial with a number of forms. Basal rosette with dentate leaves. Insignificant white flowers. Siliqua in the form of an upturned and top-heavy triangle which recalls the handwoven bags or purses of shepherds (bursa pastoris).

HABITAT: Very common on plains and up to the mountain zone.

PROPERTIES, USES: The plant contains a bitter substance and a resinous element which dissolves in water and alcohol. It can be used to produce a good oil for lamps.

As it is antiseptic, styptic, colloidal and a tonic it combats diarrhoea, dysentery, hypertension, nosebleeds and bleeding from the womb, haemoptysis and haematuria (infusion of 20-30 g in 600-900 g of water, one cup every two hours). Fresh plants in a poultice stop haemorrhage, and can be used in first aid.

A mixture of 150-200 g of tincture to 300 g of alcohol, left for 8-10 days, can be given

(120-150 drops per day) to those who suffer from lithiasis and stones in the urinary tract. Expulsion of the indissoluble residue from the kidneys and bladder will follow.

Mixed with an egg yolk and camphor, it is used as a poultice for haemorrhoids, infected wounds, joint pains and rheumatic and arthritic muscle pains.

Some sips of a hot tisane, before and during the process of childbirth, helps the contractions of the womb and also to minimalise the bleeding which follows. As a menstrual regulator, it is very useful at the time of the menopause.

Capsela bursa-pastoris

Cardamine hirsuta L.   III-IV
Lady's-smock sp.

DESCRIPTION: An annual, 10-30 cm. Basal rosette with leaves +/- hairy, dense, winged (3-7 leaflets each). Very small white flowers. Siliqua longish, erect, and considerably larger than the flowers.

HABITAT: Damp and shady locations up to the mountain zone.

PROPERTIES, USES: Nectar-producing, tonic, antiscorbutic and diuretic. Eaten as a salad, like spinach, and in a soup.

Eruca sativa Miller (= *Eruca vesicaria ssp. sativa*)   II-IV

Rognette, Roka, Rucola

DESCRIPTION: An annual, 20-90 cm, branching, hairy, with a strong, unpleasant smell and sharp flavour. Deeply-toothed or pinnate leaves. Sepals fall early, petals 15-20 mm, yellowish or whitish, with violet veining. Siliqua 12-25 mm, erect, with a lanceolate beak.

HABITAT: Fields, uncultivated soils, rubbish dumps, on roadsides, at low altitudes.

PROPERTIES, USES: The leaves are eaten raw as a flavouring in salads. They are said to be aphrodisiac (!). The seeds were once used as a diuretic, digestant, and antiscorbutic.

Hirschfeldia incana (L.) Lagrèse-Fossat (= *Brassica geniculata*)   III-V

DESCRIPTION: An annual plant up to 1 metre with erect stems, often branched, almost leafless. Basal leaves stalked, pinnately-lobed and consisting of 5 lobes, the terminal one larger and dentate, with a kind of membrane at the tip of the teeth. The flowering-head develops gradually, one or two flowers at first and then considerably more. Flowers up to 5 mm, yellow. Siliqua 8-12 mm, short, cylindrical, and linear.

HABITAT: Found in areas at low and medium altitude, and on roadsides.

PROPERTIES, USES: The tender shoots, a little before flowering, are much in demand. They are eaten boiled, as a salad. Cooked in the frying pan with eggs, they make a delicious omelette.

H. incana

H. incana

Nasturtium officinale R. BR.   IV-VIII
Nasturtium, water-cress

DESCRIPTION: A perennial, 10-60 cm, creeping, stoloniferous, juicy, and hairless. Stems angular in cross-section. Stalked, opposite pinnate leaves, with ovate leaflets. Small, white flowers. Linear siliqua, 13-18 mm.

HABITAT: Found in streams, wells, on the edges of marshes, small lakes and rivers.

PROPERTIES, USES: This plant is eaten raw as a salad during the period of flowering, It is, however, better when boiled, since the larvae of a parasitic worm of the liver (hypatic Fasiola) live on the plant. At altitude, the flavour changes and becomes bitter. The plant contains oils, iodine, iron, potassium, sulphur, phosphorus, salt, manganese, and ascorbic acid. It is used for rachitis (rickets) and constitutes the ideal plant for those who suffer from diabetes. It also has purgative, diuretic, tonic, anti-inflammatory, antiscorbutic and even aphrodisiac properties. For this reason we say in Greek that someone who has regained his strength 'has cardamised' (cardamom is the popular Greek name for the plant).

The crushed plant is used as a poultice to treat skin complaints (ulcers, pain, swelling, abscesses) and to speed up the healing of wounds.

The application of the crushed plant mixed with honey is said to remove freckles.

are 20-30 mm, ochre-yellow or white with violet veining. The fruits are long, up to 80 mm, and form 'strings of worry beads' which easily crumble.

HABITAT: Found in cultivated and abandoned fields, on rubbish dumps, and on roadsides.

PROPERTIES, USES: The plant is an irritant, and a tough weed. It is only destroyed by uprooting before the seeds have ripened. The seeds, which have the flavour of garlic, were once used in cases of rheumatism. Biochemically, the plant resembles mustard

Raphanus raphanistrum L.   II-V
Wild radish

DESCRIPTION: An annual, 30-60 cm, with coarse hairs. The leaves are deeply-toothed or pinnate, with ovate, dentate lateral lobes and a larger middle lobe. The flowers

(*Sinapis*) and has the same heating, tonic and appetite-stimulating properties.

Folk medicine uses it against stomach pains. A purée-type soup is made with its turnip-like roots, mixed with olive oil, and when it is hot, placed on the abdomen in the stomach area as a poultice. For pain in the mouth, boil 3-4 roots, add 2 soup-spoons of vinegar and a little salt to the infusion, and gargle with it. We can give the juice from the roots mixed with sugar to children suffering from whooping cough, one spoonful per hour.

The hot tisane is also good in cases of acute respiratory conditions, sore throat, influenza, coughs and even kidney conditions.

NOTE: ***Raphanus sativus L.*** produces edible turnip-like roots, the well-known radishes. It has bile-stimulant properties and tones up the appetite as well as the digestive functions.

Avoid consumption of these plants if you have a bad tooth - they destroy the tooth enamel.

Sinapis alba L.   II-V
White mustard

DESCRIPTION: An annual plant, +/- hairy, branching, with stems up to 80 cm. In contrast to ***Sinapis arvensis***, the upper leaves are stalked, deeply-toothed, pinnate or pinnately-lobed. The flowers are yellow, arranged in a raceme. The siliqua is cylindrical in the lower part with a long, wide beak. The section containing the seeds has white hairs. The seeds are small and rounded, with a 20-30 % oil content.

HABITAT: Found in fields, on roadsides, and on rubbish dumps.

PROPERTIES, USES: Cultivated for its seeds which, after grinding, are used in the production of table mustard. They contain a

R. sativa

glycoside, sinalpin, and an enzyme, myrosin, which acts on the glycoside in the presence of water and produces the substance which gives mustard its aroma. Pharmacology uses the seeds to produce mustard plasters, poultices and ointments. On Crete the plant is considered a troublesome weed, but by the same token the tender shoots are used as a vegetable, boiled and made into delicious salads. The plant stimulates the appetite and is indicated as a strong diuretic.

WARNING! Those who suffer from stress or kidney insufficiency must avoid this plant.

A hot drink, made from the fresh white mustard plant (**but not the seeds**), is used for colds and constipation. It is also anti-inflammatory and a digestive aid.

The seeds, after they have been pounded and mixed with olive oil and hot water to make a thick cream, are excellent as a poultice for abcesses, ulcers, respiratory influenza, lumbar and arthritic pain, and ischialgia.

5 g of the seeds with 2-3 litres of water make an excellent foot-bath for scratches, bruises and rheumatism. **WARNING! You must not leave your feet in this mixture for more than 10 minutes!**

An ointment (made by pounding 150 g of roots and adding salt and 2 spoonfuls of kerosene/paraffin), can be smeared on the painful area in cases of asthma, pneumonia, bronchitis, neuralgia and rheumatism.

Folk medicine recommends the placing of powdered mustard seed in our socks, to keep our feet continuously warm. This is especially for those who have cold feet and those who want to go walking in the snow. **Unfortunately however, the rush of blood to the feet that this precipitates can cause heart problems!**

WARNING! The intake of an infusion of the seeds by mouth is completely prohibited. They must also not be used in order to cook tough meat, beans or any type of other pulse or vegetable more quickly; they can prove very dangerous to those who consume them.

NOTES: **Sinapis arvensis L.** differs from **S. alba** in its leaves which are stalked, and the siliqua which is smooth. The plant is edible, but causes the gathering of wind in the stomach and bowels. The oil from the seeds is suitable for lamps.

S. alba

S. alba

S. arvensis

Sisymbrium officinale (L.) Scop. III-V
Hedge mustard

DESCRIPTION: An annual or biennial with the lower leaves pinnately-lobed, the middle lobe larger. Scentless, but has a sharp flavour. The flowers are small, less than 6 mm. The siliqua is also small, 10-20 mm, erect, hairy, fat, sharp-tipped and almost touches the stem.

HABITAT: Olive groves, vineyards, rubbish dumps, up to the mountain zone.

PROPERTIES, USES: As a maceration or infusion, it is used as a disinfectant and expectorant, especially in cases of congestion of the lungs, chronic catarrh, loss of voice and strong cough (inflammations of the pharynx and laryngitis). "A tisane of the leaves, they say, gives the cantor his voice back."

WARNING! The leaves and other parts of the plant, if they are dried, lose their properties. In a poultice, we use the seeds in the same way as mustard (**Sinapis**) for skin conditions such as ulcers, abscesses and inflammation of any kind.

Eaten as a salad, raw or boiled, the plant is said to stimulate the appetite and is diuretic. It is recommended for those who suffer from problems of the urinary tract.

NOTE: Another 3 species of **Sisymbrium** are found on Crete.

- **Sisymbrium irio** L. (**IV-VI**) is almost hairless, with a height of up to 60 cm. It has slender siliquae, 40-65mm, and grows in inhabited areas (on roadsides, amidst ruins, and on rubbish dumps).

- **Sisymbrium orientale** L. (**III-VI**) is an annual, 30-60 cm, hairy, and branching. It has pinnately-lobed leaves with a central,

Sisymbrium irio

dart-like (sagittate) lobe, the upper leaves are entire. Lemon yellow flowers (7 mm) and hairy siliquae, 35-100 mm.

- **Sisymbrium polyceratum L.** The name indicates that this plant produces many siliquae. It is almost unknown.

Sisymbrium orientale

T. creticum?

T. perfoliatum

Thlaspi creticum * (Degen & Jàvporka) Greuter & Burdet V-VII
Cretan penny cress

DESCRIPTION: A perennial, with stems 1-5 cm. Small, basal leaves. Sepals upright, violet, without swellings at their base. The petals are white. Flattened siliquae, with a round or ovoid appearance and a cuneate base.

HABITAT: Found in the alpine and subalpine zone.

PROPERTIES, USES: What we know about its relation **Thlaspi perfoliatum L.** - which Galen refers to as an antidote for poisoning - holds good for **Thlaspi creticum**. The French believe that it neutralises nicotine in smokers. The infusion from its roots is considered sedative, soporific, and aphrodisiac.

NOTE: A third species, recently identified, is **Thlaspi Zaffranii***. This is endemic and found only in the White Mountains.

99

CUCURBITACEAE
(Cucumber family)

Bryonia cretica L.　　　　II-IV
White bryony

DESCRIPTION: A perennial plant with tuberous roots. Stems up to 4 metres, climbing, with simple tendrils. Leaves 5-10 cm with white spots, palmately-lobed, and cordate at the base. Small, greenish flowers, the male ones glandular, with 3 stamens, the female plants on different stems. Calyx with entire or slightly toothed lobes. The fruit (a berry) is cherry red in colour.

HABITAT: On walls, fences, in ditches, in olive roots…

PROPERITES, USES: The root is bitter and sickness-provoking, but it contains a lot of starch and was used in difficult times to make bread.

The plant cleanses the face of freckles and has diuretic and abortive properties. Hippocrates used it to treat tetanus. In a poultice, it was used for abscesses (it makes them open without the need for an invasive surgical procedure), bruises, swellings, epilepsy, snake-bite, ulcers and gangrenous infections. The fruits were once used as a skin depilatory.

WARNING! The plant has toxic properties, and for this reason any use of it in the form of a beverage is strictly prohibited. Dioscurides warns us that the uncontrolled use of this drug can prove dangerous.

Ecbalium elaterium A. Rich.   V-IX
Squirting cucumber

DESCRIPTION: A plant up to 1 metre in height, slightly fleshy, with dense rough hairs and creeping, prostrate stems. Leaves up to 10 cm, stalked, cordate, triangular, and undulate at the margins. Campanulate flowers, lemon yellow, the male flowers up to 20 mm in racemes, the female flowers solitary. The fruit (a capsule) is about 5 cm long, ovoid-elongated, and very hairy. On ripening, it bursts open at the slightest movement, expelling the seeds and, in addition, a thick liquid which is a skin irritant.

HABITAT: Found on the sides of roads, in landslips, and on barren soils, at low and medium altitude.

PROPERTIES, USES: The flavour is bitter, unpleasant and caustic. This is a very strong purgative and diuretic, capable of provoking severe vomiting (a sign of its strength according to Theophrastus).

It was once used in the form of an extract (0.15 g as a dose) for dropsy, intestinal conditions, stomach and intestinal tumours, leucorrhoea, loss of blood during menstruation, intestinal worms, albumen in the blood, acute nephritis and jaundice.

WARNING! A dose of more than 6 g can be fatal!

The inhalation of only one drop of the juice of the fruit can cause terrible nasal catarrh which can last a whole week, and completely decongest the nasal mucous (sinusitis). The same juice, dehydrated in the sun, was once used in eye conditions, toothache, ear tumours, deafness and canker.

Animals, which under normal conditions do not eat this plant, look for it when they are sick, in order to get well again (!).

NOTE: *Cucumis sativus* - the cultivated cucumber - came to us from the East, according to Theophrastus. Its juice soothes pain in the ear (3-5 drops in the evening, before bedtime). Cleansing of the face with cucumber juice helps to tighten the skin. Ladies can use it to maintain a beautiful and fresh complex-

ion. The seeds are an excellent diuretic. We can boil 30-40 seeds with pieces of unpeeled cucumber, strain the mixture through a sieve and give it to the person affected to drink three times per day.

C. sativus

DIPSACACEAE (Teasel family)

***Scabiosa atropurpurea* L. (= *Sixalix atropurpurea* (L.) Greuter & Burdet)**
Mournful widow   **IV-VI**

DESCRIPTION: A biennial, smooth or hairy. Stems 20-100 cm, branching. Opposite leaves, the lower ones elongated-spatulate in shape, the upper ones lobed. The flower-heads are 20-30 mm in diameter, the florets lilac and white.

HABITAT: In uncultivated, open locations, at low altitude.

PROPERTIES, USES: A bitter plant, antiseptic, purgative, sudorific, for the treatment of leucorrhoea and ulcers.

ERICACEAE (Heather family)

Arbutus unedo L.   XI-V
Strawberry tree

DESCRIPTION: A small evergreen tree, 1.5-3 metres in height, with very cracked bark. Alternate, glossy, lanceolate, dentate leaves, 1.5-3 cm. Flowers up to 9 mm, whitish-yellow with green veining, and a jar-shaped corolla. Fruits up to 20 mm in diameter, with a rough surface, originally green, then becoming yellow and finally red - the colour of a strawberry – when fully ripe.
HABITAT: Found in macchia on poor, calcareous soils.
PROPERTIES, USES: The fruits are edible, and suitable for treating stomach upsets. Do not overdo it, however, because *Unedo* means 'only eat one', not more! Unlimited consumption can cause migraine. Dioscurides likened them to the whores of Rome: beautiful, but distend the stomach and cause headaches. Nevertheless, jams and

A. andrachne

A. andrachne

liqueurs are made from the fruit. According to Makryiannis, the fruits were once boiled in wine and the preparation used to wash and treat war wounds.

A tisane made from 30 g of the leaves or bark, dried, and 1 litre of water, has disinfectant (styptic) properties. Distillation of the seeds produces an alcoholic drink which, mixed with honey and cinnamon, is given to those suffering from respiratory or mucous catarrh.

The bark and the leaves are used in tanning. In ancient Greece, torches made from the wood of the strawberry tree were especially prized.

NOTE: *Arbutus andrachne* L. (II-IV) has very beautiful brownish-red bark that is completely smooth, smaller white flowers and orange berries 8-12 mm. According to Theophrastus, the wood was used for the construction of looms.

Erica arborea L.   III-V

Tree heather

DESCRIPTION: An evergreen shrub or small tree, up to 4 metres in height. Linear leaves, like little darts, in bunches of 4, with folded-over tips. Dense inflorescences with numerous flowers. Corolla 2.5-4 mm, white, campanulate with 4 pointed tips. Dark-brown anthers, smaller than the corolla.

HABITAT: Forests and maquis, particularly on acid soils, up to the mountain zone.

PROPERTIES, USES: A nectar-producing plant. One of the best woods for burning.

WARNING! Due to its abundance and its density it ignites very easily and for that reason is considered a hazard where forest fires are concerned.

The branches were once – and in fact still are - used for brooms and to make screens against the wind and sun. They were also used to host silkworm cocoons.

The wood has a very high lustre and is used to make pipes and other small objects.
In folk medicine, the plant is considered to be anti-rheumatic.

E. arborea

Erica manipuliflora Salisb.   VIII-XII
Autumn heather

DESCRIPTION: Resembles ***Erica arborea***, but its height does not exceed 1 metre. It has flowers resembling wonderful, tiny bells, +/- light pink in colour washed with reddish-purple, and anthers larger than the corolla. This is one of the most beautiful decorations of autumn.
HABITAT: In areas of phrygana (garrigue) and maquis, especially on calcareous soils.
PROPERTIES, USES: It was used to disinfect the urinary and reproductive tracts, and in baths to tone the muscles. Dried heather was once much used in fires and ovens.

Chrozophora tinctoria (L.) A. Juss.   IV-X
Turn-sole

DESCRIPTION: An annual, up to 50 cm, ash-green, branching, without a milky juice. Leaves 2-9 cm, stalked, ovate to rhomboid, cuneate at the base, convex, and dentate. Unisexual flowers, hardly visible, the male flowers in bunches, the female flowers almost always solitary. Fruits have fleshy out-growths.

HABITAT: Barren, sterile locations, near to the seashore.

PROPERTIES, USES: Once used to produce a colourant for the hair and for silk. The Dutch used the plant to colour their cheeses. A tisane made from the dried and crushed roots constitutes a febrifuge; the seeds are purgative.

roots with the roots of brambles gives a preparation to treat hypertension and to stimulate the milk glands of nursing mothers.

Euphorbia acanthothamnos Heldr. & Sart. ex Boiss.   III-VII
Greek spiny spurge

DESCRIPTION: A perennial plant, 10-35 cm, forming a hummock, dense and thorny (retains its dried, thorny branches in the following year). Elliptic leaves, bright green in colour. Umbels with 3-4 rays, 2-3 times branched. The bracts surround the golden-yellow cyathia (corolla in a particular vase-shape). Ribbed fruits.

HABITAT: Found up to the sub-alpine zone.

PROPERTIES, USES: **The milky juice causes skin blisters. Internal use is strictly forbidden**. Notwithstanding, a recipe dating from the time of Hippocrates was prescribed for dropsy, 7 drops on a fig, before a meal. The seeds and roots are used in an infusion for catarrh, colds and lithiasis of the gall bladder. In our times, a mixture of the seeds and

Euphorbia chamaesyce L.

DESCRIPTION: An annual, up to 25 cm, with numerous stems, prostrate, thin and branching. Leaves 3-7 mm, thin, opposite, ovate-round, dentate in the upper part, asymmetrical at the base. Flower-cups 1-2 mm, isolated in the axils of the branches. Red glands surrounded by a white membrane, three or five-lobed, which give the impression of a real lobed corolla. Seed capsules small and three-cornered. Tiny seeds, white and wrinkled.

HABITAT: Sandy soils and fields near the sea.

PROPERTIES, USES: The bark is an emetic. The plant was once used for eye conditions, ulcers, scabies, pimples and scorpion bites.

Euphorbia characias L.   XI-V
Large Mediterranean spurge

DESCRIPTION: A perennial, up to 1 metre, woody at the base. Strong stems. Linear-lanceolate leaves, up to 13 cm, numerous and in a dense arrangement. Longish inflorescences with a terminal umbel of 10-20 rays and auxiliary umbels in the axils of the upper leaves. Purplish-black cyathia. The bracts are triangular, convex, and greenish yellow. Hairy capsules.

HABITAT: Found at low and medium altitudes.

PROPERTIES, USES: The milky juice contains a rubbery gum. Dioscurides used it as a purgative, emetic, depilatory, for toothache and for pimples.

WARNING! The 'milk' is caustic.

Euphorbia dendroides L.   III-V
Tree spurge

DESCRIPTION: A small tree up to 3 metres, hairless and producing a milky juice. The branches are in a candelabra-like arrangement. Leaves 25-65 mm, lanceolate, deciduous (easily shed) in the dry season. Umbels of 5-8 rays. The cyathia are yellowish with rhomboid bracts of the same colour. Hairless capsules.

HABITAT: Found on slopes and rocks near the shores, almost exclusively on calcareous soils.

PROPERTIES, USES: The plant was once used for problems of the bile or gall, catarrh, and for its purgative properties. It is said to remove skin pustules and scurf and achieve complete depilation. **WARNING! It is highly toxic. Its use is completely forbidden without a doctor's prescription.**

NOTE: The endemic *Euphorbia sultan-hassei** **Strid** exhibits small botanical differences.

Euphorbia helioscopia L.   II-IV
Sun spurge

DESCRIPTION: A small annual, hairless. Ovate leaves, untoothed. The umbel has 5 rays which form a kind of sun. The cyathia are greenish or yellowish.

HABITAT: Common among cultivated crops, at low altitudes.

PROPERTIES, USES: A strong purgative. **WARNING! The milky juice is poisonous, and the leaves raise pustules when they come into contact with the skin!**

Euphorbia helioscopia

Euphorbia peplis L.   V-X
Purple spurge

DESCRIPTION: An annual plant, prostrate, hairless, fleshy, slightly grey. Stems 5-30 cm, reddish, arranged in the form of a rosette, and branched. The leaves are greenish-blue, fleshy, opposite, elongated and very assymetrical at the base. The cyathia are 12 mm, occurring singly on short flower-stalks, in the leaf axils. Roundish-ovoid glands, brownish-red in colour. The capsules are hairless, with three blunt corners; the seeds are smooth.

HABITAT: Found on sandy beaches.

PROPERTIES, USES: In former times the plant was used to treat gout, dropsy and respiratory conditions. The root is a purgative.

Mercurialis annua L.   I-V
Annual mercury

DESCRIPTION: An annual, up to 50 cm, hairless, and erect, with a quadrangular stem. Leaves petiolate, 1.5-5 cm, ovate to elliptic-lanceolate, dentate. Small yellow flowers, with a three-lobed calyx, the female flowers almost stalkless with two styles, rarely on the same plant with male flowers, which have 15 stamens.

HABITAT: Damp locations around and within inhabited areas.

PROPERTIES, USES: A weed with purgative, sedative and diuretic properties. Once used to treat dropsy.

WARNING! Poisonous! According to Dr. Font Quer "The best thing that we can do is not eat it".

Dioscurides recommended it as a poultice to be placed on the male reproductive organs. If the poultice had been made from male plants, a male child would be conceived. If made from female plants, a female child would be conceived (!).

Ricinus communis L.   III-IX
Castor oil plant

DESCRIPTION: A small tree, up to 4 metres in height, and rapid-growing. The stem is hollow like a syringe, soft and wand-like. Palmately-lobed leaves, alternate, with 5-9 tooth-edged lobes which are acutely pointed at the tip, a glossy green on the upper surface, and fuzzy on the underside. Dense inflorescences, terminal or axillary, which have male flowers with yellow stamens at their base and female flowers with red stigmas at the tips. The fruits are round capsules made up of three compartments, light green in colour and covered by soft thorns. They contain three hairless, ovoid, fleshy seeds, brownish-black in colour and glossy, with light coloured spots which resemble dog ticks.

HABITAT: A tropical plant which has acclimatised itself, growing at low altitudes. In tropical Africa, whence it originates, it can reach a height of 10 metres.

PROPERTIES, USES: According to Jonathan (in the Bible) it was known to the Egyptians, and also in Judaea, where it was cultivated.

Two oils are extracted from ricinus. One of them is obtained under heat, does not freeze at low temperatures and is used for the lubrication of fine mechanisms, especially in aeronautics. The other is the well-known castor oil, which has purgative (laxative) properties due to ricinoline and triglycerine; the only disadvantage is its unpleasant flavour. Today, however, ways have been found to mask it.

Also used in the production of cosmetics, soaps and paints. It is said that the green leaves, placed as a compress on the breasts for a number of days, stimulate the secretion of breast milk. In fact, they cause the secretion of milk not only in nursing mothers who are

deficient in it, but also in women who are not nursing mothers (!) **WARNING! The raw fruits and seeds are extremely toxic to humans! 3-10 of them are fatal!** The fruits are only edible when cooked and **should be consumed only with a doctor's prior approval**. They are rich in starch and fat, but above all in vitamins B and C which, because of the surrounding husk, are not lost when the fruits are cooked. They constitute an excellent food for weak organisms, children, the elderly and all those who have suffered serious illness. The use of the flowers and wood stops diarrhoea, both in humans and animals.

Castanea sativa Mill.   VII
Sweet chestnut

DESCRIPTION: A deciduous tree, up to 30 metres in height, with glossy, lanceolate, dentate leaves, 10-25 cm. Erect male catkins, consisting of a six-part perianth and 10-20 stamens. The female catkins are isolated at the base of the inflorescence. The fruits – chestnuts – are arranged in twos or threes within large, thorny green cupules. The tree begins to produce them at an age of from 25 to 30 years.

HABITAT: Western Crete, on non-calcareous soils. The tree was most probably introduced to the island by the Venetians.

PROPERTIES, USES: Chestnuts are eaten either roasted on the grill or boiled. Various local confectionery products are produced from their flour.

The leaves and bark of the chestnut have an antitussant, febrifuge, disinfectant, expectorant, healing and haemostatic quality (they encourage contraction of the superficial blood-bearing vessels).

NOTE: Unfortunately, many trees are slowly dying near the village of Elos, due to a disease peculiar to the species.

Quercus coccifera L. var. *calliprinos* (Webb.) Homboe   III-IV
Kermes oak

DESCRIPTION: An evergreen, up to 12 metres in height. Leaves 1.5-4 cm, dark green, toothed, thorny. Every cupule is surrounded by short, pointed spines and contains one fruit, the well-known acorn.

HABITAT: Up to an altitude of 1600

metres.

PROPERTIES, USES: The tree is used as the host for an insect, *Cocus ilicis* **Planch**. In

111

bygone days, the female insects were dessicated and produced a red colourant – crimson. Theseus used it to dye the sails of his ship on his expedition to Crete, when he set off to fight the Minotaur. The Spartans dyed their war-clothes with it, in order to conceal spots of blood that might fall on them.

The roots are tonic, sedative and antispasmodic, and stimulate the appetite. A black colourant is extracted from the bark, which Dioscurides recommended for dyeing the hair. Theophrastus tells us that stakes fashioned from its wood were used to surround the hearth, for wheel axles, for lyres and psalteries (ancient musical instruments).

The bark of the tree is rich in tannins, and was once much in demand for the tanning process.

Quercus ilex L.   IV-VI
Holm oak

DESCRIPTION: An evergreen, up to 25 metres in height. Smooth, grey bark. Leaves up to 7 cm, ovate-lanceolate, with entire or slightly toothed edges, which remain on the tree for up to four years. Small male flowers in catkins, tiny female flowers in pairs. Bitter

Q. coccifera

Cocus ilicis

Q. ilex

acorns, inside cupules with soft scales, compressed and downy.

HABITAT: Found in maquis, in gorges and on the banks of streams.

PROPERTIES, USES: The acorns are an excellent food for pigs, whose ham is considered to be of superior quality.

The resistance of the wood to rot is such that it has been used since very ancient times in the construction of ships, houses and underground galleries. The bark contains sought-after tannins. The tree provides one of the best woods for burning.

112

Quercus ithaburensis Decne. *ssp. macrolepis* (Kotschy) Hedge & Yalt.   IV
Valonia oak

DESCRIPTION: A semi-evergreen tree up to 25 metres in height, with leaves 6-12 cm, elongated, serrate, dark green on the upper surface and downy on the underside, falling at the end of winter. Large cupule with long, curved scales.

HABITAT: Found on hills and slopes in the Prefecture of Rethymnon.

PROPERTIES, USES: The oil is used in facial care; it removes freckles and imparts a beautiful, lasting chestnut shade to hair. Gives relief in cases of headache and earache (2-3 drops). Also used in dyeing (black colour) and in tanning.

The acorns were often used, in periods of deprivation and hunger, for human nutrition (Parable of the Prodigal Son). Dioscurides recommended them in cases of dysentery and haemoptysis.

Quercus pubescens Willd.   IV-V
Downy oak

DESCRIPTION: A deciduous tree, up to 25 metres in height. The 'eyes' (nodes), new branches and cupules are hidden by dense grey hairs. Leaves with 4-7 lobes and up to 8 pairs of lateral veins. The fruits are almost stalkless. The cupules have very dense scales.

HABITAT: In the mountain zone. Remnants of ancient forests are to be found.

PROPERTIES, USES: From as early as the time of the Pelasgians (the first Greek tribe) the trees were considered sacred, dedicated to Zeus, and it was believed that his priests could give prophesies when they listened to the rustling of the leaves (oracle of Dodoni). In addition, all of the oaks were believed to

be the homes of the dryads (nymphs of the forests). Flour made from the acorns, rich in proteins and carbohydrates, was used for many years as a food substitute.

The bark and the leaves, in a tisane, constitute an excellent medicine for dysentery and haemorrhages, especially metrorrhagia or uterine haemorrhage (leaves or 5 pinches of pounded bark in 1 litre of water). The same beverage is sufficient to stop incontinence and diarrhoea. Furthermore, in cases of varix, eczema and gingivitis, acorns can be a help either in powder form or as a coffee (the acorns should be roasted and then ground).

Blackstonia perfoliata (L.) Huds.
Yellow-wort   **IV-VIII**

DESCRIPTION: An annual, 10-60 cm, hairless, erect, rarely branching. Leaves blastogenous, opposite, ovate-triangular. In reality, only one leaf is fused (perfoliate). Yellow flowers with a short pistil and 6-12 star-like petals.

HABITAT: Damp locations in forests and areas of maquis.

PROPERTIES, USES: A bitter plant, febrifuge and healing.

Centaurium erythreae Rafn.   **IV-VI**
Common centaury

DESCRIPTION: A biennial, 10-50 cm. Quadrangular stem, with alternating branches in its upper section. Basal leaves 1-5 cm, obovate to elliptic, with and 3-7 veins. The leaves of the stem are smaller, opposite, apiculate, and have three veins. The inflorescence is a dense corymb. The corolla is dark pink with 5 lobes, and the calyx is also divided into five lobes. The flowers open at a temperature of 24° C.

HABITAT: At moderate altitudes and in the mountain zone.

PROPERTIES, USES: A decoction made from the plant is used to dye wool. The addition of alum to it produces a yellow-green or lemon-yellow colour and that of iron sulphide, a brownish-green.

This is one of the best substitutes for quinine. It is also tart, bitter, tonic, stimulatory, healing, antiseptic and a vermifuge, and was once used in cases of dysentery and gangrene.

Centaurium pulchellum (Swartz) Druce IV-VI
Lesser centaury

DESCRIPTION: An annual or biennial, very small, 2-20 cm. The stem is weak, branching from the base, and without a rosette. Leaves ovate-lanceolate, acute. Characteristic of the plant are the 'drowsy' pink flowers, which require a temperature above 28° C for them to open.

HABITAT: Found near the sea, on sandy soils, the edges of swamps and of fields.

PROPERTIES, USES: The name derives from the centaur Chiron who used it as a healing plant. It is considered to be one of the best tonic plants. It is anti-anaemic, anti-scorbutic, a vermifuge and febrifuge. As a poultice, it treats skin ulcers, herpes, shingles, and alopecia.

Centaurium tenuifolium (Hoffl. & Link) Fritsch IV-VI
Slender centaury

DESCRIPTION: An annual, up to 40 cm, without a basal rosette. The stem branches from the middle upwards. Opposite leaves, ovate to elliptic. Numerous flowers, up to 90, which are 12-14 mm long, each on a pedicel at least 2 mm long.

HABITAT: Damp meadows, near the sea.

PROPERTIES, USES: All of the centauria have more or less the same properties. It was once believed that the plant cleansed the blood. It is widely believed to aid the digestion.

Before the appearance of quinine it was used in cases of yellow fever (Greek: 'rigos', hence its popular local name of 'rigohorto').

Geranium molle (L.) ssp. molle   II-IV
Dove's-foot cranesbill

DESCRIPTION: An annual, very hairy, glandular, spreading, greyish-green in colour. Basal leaves, 1.5-4 cm, round, deeply divided into lobes whose tips are divided again into three smaller shallow lobes. Flowers up to 7 cm, pink, with petals two-lobed at the tip, larger than the sepals. Fruits have a large beak. The crushed plant exudes the odour of Chinese ink.

HABITAT: In low and moderate altitude zones.

PROPERTIES, USES: This has the same properties as **G. robertianum**. It is styptic-disinfectant, healing and dilutant (reduces the swelling of the painful area). Also used in gargles for angina and sore throat.

In bygone times it was used to treat haemorrhages, nephritis and contusions.

Geranium robertianum L.   IV-VI
Herb Robert

DESCRIPTION: An annual or biennial up to 50 cm. Hairy, glandular, heavily-scented. Reddish stems. Leaves divided into deeply toothed leaflets. Flowers in pairs on hairy flower-stalks, with sepals that are also hairy and notched, and pinkish-purple petals, 9-13 mm, obovate to cuneate.

HABITAT: Rocky places in the mountain and sub-alpine zone.

PROPERTIES, USES: The plant is diuretic and styptic, used in cases of haemorrhage. Also used in a gargle to treat a sore throat, in a lotion as an eye-wash, and in a poultice in cases of congestion of the breasts in women. It is also said to have been used against sterility (!). The leaves and flowers are the most useful part of the plant. The whole flower emits a nauseating aroma which resembles that of human urine. The stems have a rather bitter, insipid flavour.

NOTE: The sub-species **ssp. purpureum (Vill.) Nyman** is smaller with unnotched sepals, and grows at low altitudes. It probably exhibits the same properties.

GLOBULARIACEAE
(Globularia family)

Globularia alypum L.   II-V
Shrubby globularia

DESCRIPTION: An annual, up to 1 metre, always green. Small, tough, oblanceolate, acute leaves. Heads 1.5 cm in diameter, with tubular blue flowers and numerous pointed bracts. The corolla has two lips, the upper one two-lobed, the lower one three-lobed.
HABITAT: Areas of phrygana (garrigue) at low and medium altitudes.
PROPERTIES, USES: **WARNING! This plant is poisonous!** In antiquity, febrifuge, sedative and purgative qualities were assigned to it, especially where the gall bladder was concerned. On Crete, an infusion used to be prepared from it and given to children who suffered from incontinence. The leaves have a bitter, rather unpleasant taste and drying of them has to take place in the sun and not in the shade, like other plants. They contain globularin, a substance which gives them purgative properties (in a tisane).
The plant is also indicated in cases of remittent fever, headaches caused by digestive difficulties, neuralgia, and for the healing of ulcers of the stomach and duodenum.

Hypericum hircinum L.　　IV-VIII
Stinking tutsan

DESCRIPTION: An evergreen shrub, hairless, much-branching, up to 1.5 metres. Transparent leaves, 1-7.5 cm, opposite, lanceolate and stalkless. When the plants are rubbed, they give off a strong scent, partly resinous and partly that of a goat. Large flowers at the tips of the branching stems, with 5 petals 10-18 mm, gold-yellow, glossy, with numerous stamens considerably larger than the flowers, and ovate-lanceolate sepals.

HABITAT: Damp locations, often alongside water.

PROPERTIES, USES: The flowers, macerated in oil for three days, give us a wonderful medicine for burns and wounds. In Byzantine times the plant was known as 'sword wort', because it was used to treat war wounds.

The juice is considered aphrodisiac (not more than 10 g), as is a tisane (12 g of the root and a few seeds in 300 g of water). It was also used in cases of hysteria and kidney complaints. The plant could be cultivated for decorative purposes.

Photo: Avramakis M.

Hypericum perforatum L.   **V-VII**
Perforate St. John's wort

DESCRIPTION: Up to 80 cm in height, with perennial roots, smooth but with two raised ribs along the length of the stems. Ovate to linear leaves, stalkless, with transparent glands resembling pin-pricks. Yellow flowers, with petals and sepals up to 20 cm, which have black stippling at the edges. Stamens shorter than the petals.

HABITAT: Edges of roads, meadows.

PROPERTIES, USES: The same as those ascribed to **H. hircinum**. It was used in cases of dysentery and jaundice, liver conditions, thrombosis, malaria and lumbago, as a healing agent and febrifuge. It is also diuretic, a menstrual stimulant, and haemostatic. If we rub the leaves with our fingers, they immediately exude an aromatic, resinous scent. The plant is bitter to the taste, insipid and slightly salty. It contains two colouring substances: the yellow substance found in the petals, which is water-soluble, and the red which is resinous and dissolves in alcohol and oil. The two are used to dye wool and silk materials. The substance which has the colour of blood and called 'red water of life' is obtained by distillation. When some parts of the plant are brought to the boil in a corresponding amount of water, a liquid is produced which, if exposed to the sun for 12-15 days in a glass container, transforms itself into a red oil – balsam – to which most of the therapeutic properties of the plant are ascribed.

A liqueur is also produced (by placing 300 g of the flowers and 500 g alcohol and old wine together in a bottle, leaving it in the sun for 15-20 days and then adding sugar, honey, or concentrated grape syrup). It is given for kidney and liver conditions, bronchitis of the lungs and any other condition of the respiratory system.

Both science and folk healers designate this plant as one of the most useful to Man.

It was once believed that the plant averted the evil eye, and this is why a particular beverage is made from it for those who suffer from madness. It has the ability to banish mad moods, revitalise the spirit, soothe the nerves, and banish stress and depression. If we fill our pillow with leaves of this plant, it will put an end to insomnia.

To the English and the Germans this is the plant dedicated to St. John; to the Greeks it is the Baptist's plant.

NOTE: Another 8 species of **Hypericum** are found on Crete, among which 5 are endem-

ic: *H. acyferum*, H. aegypticum, H ambly-* *triquetrifolium.*
calyx*, H. empetrifolium, H. jovis*, H. kel-
leri*, H. perfoliatum, H. trichocaulon*, H.

H. amblycalyx

H. trichocaulon

H. kelleri

H. empetrifolium

121

H. aegypticum

JUGLANDACEAE

Juglans regia L.
Walnut

DESCRIPTION: A large deciduous tree which can reach 20 metres in height. The foliage is pinnate with an unpaired terminal leaflet, with numerous elliptic leaflets, and aromatic. The bark of the trunk is smooth, ashy. The male flowers are in a raceme, the female flowers solitary. The fruit is contained in a fleshy green sheath which opens on ripening to permit the walnut to fall out.

HABITAT: Banks of streams and rivers, damp soils up to 1400 metres. The tree was introduced into Crete.

PROPERTIES, USES: Studies have ascertained its antiseptic and fungicide properties. The bark of the walnut is used, pounded, in a poultice for callouses. An infusion of the leaves is used for the care of the hair, hair loss, sugar diabetes and arthritis. An extract from the leaves and fruit sheath is used for herpes and pimples, and boiled leaves in a poultice for wounds. An infusion made from the freshly picked sheath of the fruit, is used for anaemia. The racemes cause constriction of the capillary vessels, which is very important in cases of haemorrhage, cuts, ecchymosis (contusions), and great blood loss during the period or because of haemorrhoids, diarrhoea or dysentery.

The leaves are also used for eczema, blepharitis in children, the dyeing of woollen materials, and also for the dyeing of our hair.

If we boil four handfuls of leaves in one litre of water we have a strong infusion which will get rid of ants; the solution should be painted on the areas through which the ants pass.

J. regia

LABIATAE (Lamiaceae) (Mint family)

Ballota acetabulosa (L.) Bentham
False dittany   **IV-VI**

DESCRIPTION: A perennial bush up to 80 cm, woody at the base. The stems and leaves are felty, grey-green in colour. The upper leaves are cordate and toothed. 6-12 two-lobed flowers, in whorls. Corolla 15-18 mm, whitish, with a purplish-red blazon and veining. Wide calyx with dense felt in a light green colour, and membranous lips.

HABITAT: Up to the mountain zone.

PROPERTIES, USES: The calyx is used even today, after flowering has finished, as a wick in candles.

In an infusion, it is used in cases of diabetes (it

increases the secretion of insulin and thus reduces the amount of sugar in the blood), arthritis and build-up of uric acid (boil 15 g in half a litre of water until it is reduced by half).

B. acetabulosa

Ballota nigra L. *ssp. uncinata* (Fiori & Béguinot) Patzak (=*Ballota foetida* Lam.)   V-VII
Black horehound

DESCRIPTION: A perennial up to 80 cm, downy, branching, with a heavy scent. Quadrangular stems. Leaves 3-8 cm, ovate, acutely pointed at the tip, toothed and stalked. Whorls with numerous flowers 12-14 mm, pink or violet. Calyx folded along its length, with 5 obtuse-angled teeth.

HABITAT: Abandoned fields, rubbish tips and rubble, at low and medium altitudes.

PROPERTIES, USES: In spite of its bitter flavour and unpleasant smell, bees visit the plant and collect a nectar of superb quality. The plant is diuretic, sudorific, tonic, dilutant, cleansing, calming, and used in cases of hypochondria, spasms and poisonous stings. To destroy intestinal parasites, practical folk medicine advised the introduction into the rectum of a dense paste with the help of fresh stems from garlic or onions which had been smeared with it. After a period of three days, the parasites were said to have disappeared (!).

Lamium purpureum L.   III-V
Red deadnettle

DESCRIPTION: An annual or biennial, often purplish, with a rather unpleasant smell. Cordate to ovate leaves, toothed, petiolate, wrinkled, green or reddish in colour. Pink flowers with a corolla 12-15 mm, the lower lip two-lobed.
HABITAT: Cultivated and fallow fields and meadows up to the mountain zone.
PROPERTIES, USES: A nectar plant, styptic, healing, anticatarrhal and antiscrofulant.

Lavandula stoechas L.   II-IV
French lavender

DESCRIPTION: An evergreen, aromatic shrub, up to 1 metre in height. Linear, greyish leaves, woolly, with folded-over margins. Inflorescence 2-3 cm long, in a dense spike, stalked, with whorls of 6-10 flowers in the axil of hairy, rhomboidal and cordate bracts. The top of the spike is crowned by large ovate-oblong, whitish-violet bracts. Flowers 8 mm, two-lipped, dark violet. Calyx with 5 teeth of which the upper ones are larger.
HABITAT: Areas of phrygana (garrigue) and maquis, on stony soils.
PROPERTIES, USES: It should be mentioned here that all the lavenders exhibit more or less the same properties.
A nectar plant, this lavender was a sought-after antidote to poisoning in bygone years. As an infusion, it is digestive, tonic, antispasmodic and used to disinfect wounds. It produces rapid results in cases of asthma, influenza, liver and spleen complaints, jaundice, congestion, leucorrhoea and weakening of the eyesight. A bath with lavender relieves rheumatism and uric arthritis, and relaxes the nerves and tense muscles. It really is just what is needed (especially where athletes are concerned) in cases of bruising, contusion, sprains, dislocations and wrenches. When inhaled, it speeds up the healing of colds, flu, cardialgia and bronchitis. Used as a gargle, it disinfects wounds in the mouth and helps in a case of paralysis of the tongue, and even in stuttering.

As a compress placed over the liver, it helps the latter to resume its role as the chemical factory of the body.

When rubbed on the chest it strengthens the lungs and accelerates recovery from pneumonia, pleurisy and pulmonary congestion.

When placed in cupboards, it perfumes clothing and repels moths.

NOTE: *Lavandula angustifolia* **Miller** has been imported into Crete and cultivated there.

Lavandula stoechas

Lavandula angustifolia

"This is surely a wonder of nature in blue. Its aroma is a Divine gift…it is one of the most delicate and beautiful. Strew a little lavender between your bedsheets and you will feel as though you are in another world!" says M. Messegué.

Marrubium vulgare L.　　V-VI
White horehound

DESCRIPTION: A perennial plant, aromatic, woody at the base. Stem up to 15 cm with numerous non flower-bearing branches. Thickly-felted leaves, wrinkled, toothed, ovate, rounded at the base. Whorls with numerous flowers. Calyx with 10 teeth. Whitish, two-lipped corolla, the upper lip two-lobed, the lower lip three-lobed.
HABITAT: Barren, degraded locations, rubble, rubbish tips.
PROPERTIES, USES: Once used as a stimulant and febrifuge. An alcohol-based extract of the plant is a substitute for quinine. As an extract, it frees up the respiratory passages and aids the secretion of bile. It also appears to be a diuretic and a urinary antiseptic.

Melissa officinalis L. *ssp. altissima* (Sm.) Arcangeli   V-VII
Balm

DESCRIPTION: A perennial, with stems which exceed 1 metre, erect, branching, downy, glandular, with the aroma (+/-) of rotten lemon. Leaves up to 9 cm, slightly hairy, ovate, deeply toothed, with an obtuse-angled or cordate base. Whorls of yellowish flowers, turning white or pink during the ripening period.

HABITAT: Damp locations, banks of streams.

PROPERTIES, USES: In a tisane – 50 g of balm with the same quantity of artemisia in 200 g of water for cardiac pains, one glass per day for three days. The Arabs were the first to recognise its virtues and gave it the name 'friend of the heart'. It really does assist in its good functioning and stabilises the pulse.

Always in a tisane (one glass every morning), balm is antispasmodic, i.e. it stops painful convulsions and twitches, even those due to stress and agony, acts on the heart (tachycardia and constriction), on the blood circulation (buzzing in the ears and dizziness), on the digestive system (stomach and intestinal cramps), on the nervous system (sleeplessness, swooning, syncope, intellectual exhaustion, migrane and uncontrollable nerves) and on the respiratory system (asthma attacks and coughs). "Lovers who are eaten up with anxiety, fathers full of cares, women tortured by a financial impasse and rivalries, all of you who feel hopelessness and are suffering from life, drink of this 'magic filtre' and you will regain the joy of living", says M. Messegué.

In a tisane, mixed with fern, it is given in cases of amoeba and intestinal parasites (one glass, cold, per day, morning and evening). As a poultice, it is used for neuralgia, rheu-

matic pains, ruptured muscles and wounds. Bee-keepers use the plant to attract and retain bees.

Mentha aquatica L.   VII-IX
Water mint

DESCRIPTION: A perennial, 20-100 cm, branching, aromatic. Leaves 30-90 mm, ovate, toothed and acute. Flowers +/- whitish-pink, in dense whorls which form a terminal, globular head. Calyx with veining, hairy and with 5 long teeth. Four-lobed corolla, the lobes +/- equal.

HABITAT: Wet locations, marshes, the banks of lakes and streams.

PROPERTIES, USES: All of the *Mentha* (mints) have healing properties, especially in the form of a drink. They also play a part in cookery, being used in numerous recipes for sauces etc.

"To be able to list all the properties of menthe, one would have to learn how many fish swim in the Indian Ocean", said **Wilofried de Strabo** in the 12th century.

Mint is tonic, digestive, stimulating, and emollient. It is used in embrocations for headaches and migranes. The oil is considered antiseptic and antimicrobial. As a drink, it treats indigestion, stops stomach pains and soothes burning in the intestinal tract. In a case of obstruction of the intestine (ilium) the infusion of 100 g of dried leaves induces peristaltic movements of the digestive tract, expulsion of gas and a rapid return to normal state. In addition, it strengthens the secretion of the gall-bladder and liver. In cases of burns, a poultice of the leaves produces good results. **Nursing mothers should avoid all species of *Mentha* because they stop lactation.**

NOTES: *Mentha piperita* (peppermint), a cross between *Mentha aquatica* and *Mentha spicata* (garden mint) which is found in gardens and planted in pots, has more or less the same properties. It is the pre-eminent

species of the genus *Mentha* and multiplies through suckers.

The quality of the essential oil depends upon the quantity of menthol it contains.

The various species of *Mentha* hybridise with each other to a great degree.

Mentha longifolia (L.) Huds. *ssp. thyphoides* (Briq.) Harley VII-IX
Horse mint

DESCRIPTION: A perennial, aromatic, up to 130 cm, branching. Greyish leaves, felty on the underside, oblong-lanceolate, toothed, with a small stalk and apiculate. Flowers more or less whitish-pink, small, on extended spikes. Corolla with 4 lobes of which one is torn at the tip.

HABITAT: Damp locations, ditches, streams.

PROPERTIES, USES: Ovid relates that Hades (Pluto), the god of the Underworld, fell in love with the nymph Mynthi. When his wife Persephone heard about it, she changed her into a plant.

This is a stomachic and antispasmodic plant. In Russia, it replaces hops in the aromatisation of beer.

Mentha longifolia

Mentha pulegium L. VI-VIII
Pennyroyal

DESCRIPTION: A perennial plant up to 60 cm, downy, outspreading or upright, very aromatic. Leaves 16-35 mm, ovate, lightly toothed, greyish-green. Lilac-coloured flowers, in loose whorls. Hairy calyx, completely fluted, with the two lower teeth narrower than the three upper ones.

HABITAT: Damp locations, at low altitude, often near the sea.

PROPERTIES, USES: While nursing mothers should avoid all species of *Mentha* because they stop lactation; during pregnancy, on the other hand, it clearly works against nausea, an effect which in general can be obtained by chewing the leaves; it also combats the odour of garlic.

In a poultice, it is used as a softening agent in cases of abscess, boils and bruises. As an infusion, (gargle) it is used for conditions of the pharynx and nose, and for the washing of festering wounds. As a tisane, it soothes stomach pains and – so it is said – combats sugar diabetes.

Villagers drink a glass every evening to avoid colds (it certainly has warming properties) and because they believe that it will keep them young and vigorous.

Mentha pulegium

Mentha spicata L.
Garden mint

DESCRIPTION: A perennial, with erect stems that are square in cross-section. Leaves stemless, lanceolate-elongate, wrinkled, serrate. Thin inflorescences. Individual, characteristic scent.

HABITAT: Marshy locations, streams, springs and generally damp places.

PROPERTIES, USES: The plant was used in antiquity against cholera and as an antiemetic. Dioscurides prescribed it as a poultice for headaches. An infusion was even used as a contraceptive, when a wad soaked in it was placed in the vagina after intercourse. If our knuckles ache because of rheumatism, we only have to rub them with the fresh leaves.

In the Middle Ages, because it was believed that the herb was an aphrodisiac and provoked erotic desires, its consumption was forbidden to soldiers because they would be weakened by it and not fight with the same zeal and force as usual. It is used as a flavouring in cookery, giving an aromatic note to various dishes and sauces.

Ocimum basilicum L.   **IV-X**
Herb basil

DESCRIPTION: Everyone knows this aromatic and decorative plant. It is an annual, with abundant foliage and can reach a height of up to 30 cm. Ovate-elliptic leaves, acute, entire or toothed, mostly uneven on the upper surface, dark green, sometimes becoming violet-coloured, and very variable where size is concerned (small or medium-leaved, black-leaved, crinkly, broad-leaved). Terminal spikes with white or whitish-pink flowers in whorls.

HABITAT: Imported from India by Alexander the Great. Since then, it has been cultivated in all the Mediterranean countries as an aromatic, decorative, and medicinal plant, as well as a flavouring. It is the 'lord of the Cretan courtyard'.

PROPERTIES, USES: The flower stalks and leaves, in a tisane, are used for stomach spasms, nervous stomach, nervous migrane and memory weakness. If we want to spend a peaceful night, all we have to do is drink a cup of boiled basil tisane.

Hippocrates prescribed it for recurrent vomiting, as did Dioscurides, Theophrastus, Galen and Pliny.

The young stems, in salad, act well on stomach upsets and the crushed leaves, in a poultice, draw the poison out of wasp and scorpion stings.

It is particularly used in sauces in Italian cookery (pesto).

WARNING! The plant must not be chewed raw. It causes lethargy, dizziness and liver pain. At the same time however, it stimulates the mammary glands which secrete milk and heals mouth ulcers/thrush (aphtha).

Its flavour and aroma are not pleasing to mosquitos and flies.

*Origanum dictamnus** L.   VI-VIII
Cretan dittany

DESCRIPTION: A perennial, aromatic, with stems up to 20 (-40) cm. Leaves 13-25 mm, discoid to ovate, covered in dense hairs. The spikes are more or less erect, almost hairless. The flowers have a reddish-green to reddish-lilac corolla, surrounded by large reddish bracts. Calyx with 5 teeth.

HABITAT: Found in the clefts of rocks up to an altitude of 1600 metres.

PROPERTIES, USES: A healing plant which was included among the wonder-working plants of the ancients. Its medicinal properties are due to the presence of thymol and carbacrol, and its aromatic properties to puligone. The name originates from two Greek words, - Dikti (the mountain) and thamnos (bush).

Hippocrates prescribed it in a plaster for the gall bladder, lungs and bruises.

According to Theophrastus, the plant stands out because of its virtues and was used on countless occasions, especially at the hour of childbirth. He tells us that "The male flowers of diktamos were placed for protection in the hollow of the stems of giant fennel or reeds, so that they would not lose their properties."

Dioscurides healed battle wounds with the plant.

Aphrodite treated Aeneas with it during the Trojan War. She herself, experiencing the pains of childbirth, retired to Mount Ida on Crete (Psiloritis), gathered leaves of diktamos and used them in the appropriate way (in a poultice, low down on the abdomen – a sure aid in painful childbirth).

Aristotle tells us that "When the wild goats (agrimia) on Psiloritis were wounded by the arrows of hunters, they ate diktamos or chewed it and put it on their wounds, to draw out the poison and the arrow, and thus be healed!"

The plant gives strength and vigour to elderly people and to a weak constitution, and for that is called "erondas" – the plant of youth. There is therefore nothing better than a bath into which we have thrown diktamos leaves! As a tisane or tea, made with 20-30 g of leaves in one litre of water, it constitutes a good tonic and relieves headaches, neuralgia, stomach and liver conditions and period pains. The same amount in an infusion, combats debility and spasms.

A paste, in a poultice, relieves headaches, stomach pains, liver conditions and skin inflammations.

The best vermouths and liqueurs of monastic origin – such as Benedictine or Aquavit, are aromatised with diktamos.

Many people have been killed attempting to gather the plants on sheer cliff faces and rocks. Fortunately, today it is cultivated at Ebaros and included among the products that are exported from the island.

O. dictamnus

Origanum majorana L. (= *Majorana hortensis*) VI-VIII
Marjoram

DESCRIPTION: A perennial, semi-woody plant up to 60 cm. Quadrangular stem, becoming woody, densely branched with small, opposite, obovate to spatulate leaves, glandular, with light greyish down and a sharp, bitter flavour. The leaves, when rubbed, give off a pleasant lavender-like aroma. Small flowers, 2-5 mm, white and in terminal racemes.

HABITAT: A plant native to Cyprus and Turkey which has been cultivated in nearly all the Mediterranean countries since very ancient times.

134

PROPERTIES, USES: The medicinal properties of this plant must be about the same as those of thyme: for headaches, nervous illnesses, hemiplegia (strokes), dizziness, epilepsy, memory disturbances, colds and anorexia. It also helps in the healing of wounds and destroys the tuberculosis bacillus, according to the French doctor Jean Valnet.

We can make a tisane with 5-10 g and drink 1-2 glasses per day. **WARNING! Do not overdo it! Consumption of many such drinks can be dangerous!**

In a poultice, it has good results where liver problems are concerned, and also for wounds (for the latter we add alcohol). 1-2 drops of the extract will stop ear pain. Inhalation of the plant in powdered form relieves nasal congestion.

The leaves and the tips of the tender shoots are used to flavour food.

The ancient Greeks made a perfume that was much in demand among the society ladies of the time; according to Theophrastus, it was so strong that it caused headaches!

Many people grow marjoram in pots and thus perfume and decorate their courtyards, balconies, gardens and the entrances to their houses.

Origanum microphyllum * (Bentham) T. Vogel (=*Majorana maru*)   Vi-VIII

DESCRIPTION: An annual, extremely delicate plant, very aromatic, up to 50 cm, woody at the base, with quadrangular stems. Small leaves, 5 mm, ovate –heart shaped, downy, whitish-green. The flowers have a purple corolla and are arranged in terminal inflorescences. This is the 'sapsycho' of Dioscurides and the 'amarako' of Theophrastus.

HABITAT: Found on Dikti and in the White Mountains, up to an altitude of 1500 metres.

PROPERTIES, USES: Its medicinal properties must be about the same as those of marjoram and thyme.

A drink made from the plant is aromatic and pleasant-tasting. It can be mixed with other plants which do not have its beautiful aroma.

O. microphyllum

135

Origanum onites L. (=*Majorana onites*)
Oregano   **V-VI**

DESCRIPTION: A perennial shrub (phrygano), up to 60 cm. Ovate, entire leaves, slightly toothed, cordate at the base. Flower spikes up to 10 mm, very dense. Corolla 4-5 mm, white, with two lips.

HABITAT: In areas of phrygana (garrigue), up to the mountain zone.

PROPERTIES, USES: A most sought-after constituent of Greek cookery: for salads, roasts, grilled fish, souvlaki etc. Meat which has been sprinkled with oregano clearly keeps longer. All of the species of **Origanum** produce essential oils and can be used for coughs, toothache, blockage of the respiratory paths, minor stomach and intestinal conditions and diarrhoea. In a plaster, the plant helps to heal deep wounds. As an infusion, it is digestive, expectorant, antispasmodic and disinfectant.

Women who wash their breasts with an infusion of oregano (steep a handful of leaves in one litre of water overnight and then filter) keep them beautiful and firm. A pleasant perfume is made from oregano. Placed among the clothes, the plant repels moths.

Origanum vulgare L. *ssp. hirtum* (Link) Letswaart   VI-VIII
Wild oregano

DESCRIPTION: A perennial, downy, woody, aromatic. Stems up to 80 cm. Elongated leaves, stalked, slightly toothed. White, rarely pink flowers, in terminal racemes 5-20 mm which grow longer as they develop. Corolla 4-5mm. Bracts in the form of dense, squared-off prismatic humps.

HABITAT: Up to the mountain zone.

PROPERTIES, USES: A flavouring and aromatic plant with more or less the same properties as those of **Origanum onites**.

Scientific research has revealed its antibiotic properties, in particular of its essential oil, which classify it amongst the antioxidant plants. It has also been shown that Cretan plants contain, by comparison, a larger amount of essential oil.

In an infusion or as a powder, oregano acts as a tonic for those who suffer from iron-deficient anaemia. Added to bath water, it is soothing in cases of neuropsychological disturbance. As a rinse (5-10 drops of essential oil in a glass of water) it is an ideal treatment for toothache. For rheumatism and stiff neck the leaves, heated in a pan, are used as a poultice. In an embrocation, the plant is good for rheumatism. As a tisane, 2-3 small coffee cups stops looseness of the bowels.

NOTE: **Origanum heracleoticum** L. is very slightly different (there are small botanical differences in the formation of the spikelets). **Origanum calcaratum Juss.** (= **O. Tournefortii**) is found to the south-east of Sitia and flowers in **VIII**.

Origanum calcaratum

Prasium majus L.   III-IV
Prasium

DESCRIPTION: A woody shrub up to 1 metre, rather smooth, irregularly branched. Stalked leaves, 2-5 cm, ovate to ovate-lanceolate, with a cordate base and serrated margins. Whorls of 1-2 flowers, 17-23 mm, white or light lilac, the upper lip curved and the lower lip three-lobed. Calyx with 10 veins and two lips.

HABITAT: Stony meadows, phrygana (garrigue), barren areas.

PROPERTIES, USES: The tender shoots are eaten raw or cooked, like spinach, on their own or with other wild greens, and also with pork. The plant has digestive properties, treats ulcers of the stomach and duodenum and regulates the secretion of gastric acid.

In the form of a drink (50 g of leaves and flowers in 1 litre of water) it is a febrifuge, menstrual stimulant and invigorating. Because of its choleric properties, folk healers prescribed it for heart, liver and respiratory conditions.

meadows near to streams.

PROPERTIES, USES: Bees visit the flowers and collect an excellent, sugary nectar.

Prunella vulgaris L.   V-VIII
Self-heal

DESCRIPTION: A perennial, 5-45 cm, creeping, downy, with erect or decumbent stems. Elongated, acute leaves, slightly toothed, sometimes sagittate, with clear veining. The lower leaves are petiolate. Flowers 10-15 mm, dark blue-violet (rarely pink or white) in dense elongated or squarish spikes. Calyx with teeth, ciliate at the edges. Lower lip torn at about the mid-point.

HABITAT: In mountain zones, damp

A styptic and febrifuge plant which was once used to treat diarrhoea. Considered a healing plant throughout Europe. The fresh leaves and the tender stems are used, in a poultice, to stop bleeding in cases of cuts and wounds. When the leaves and stems are placed in water and left to steep, the liquid obtained can be used to rinse the mouth in cases of gingivitis or any other inflammation of the oral cavity, and as a gargle for inflamed throats. The same decoction, when it is filtered, can be used to wash tired eyes. The ointment is used to treat haemorrhoids.

NOTE: *P. cretensis* * **Gand** and *P. laciniata* **L.** are also found on Crete.

P.cretensis

P. laciniata

Rosmarinus officinalis L.   **I-XII**
Rosemary

DESCRIPTION: An evergreen shrub up to 2 metres in height, aromatic with brownish stems. Leaves 1-4 cm, opposite, stalkless, linear, leathery, a dark green glossy colour on the upper surface, with white felt on the underside and rolled over edges. Small inflorescences, covered in star-like hairs, in the axils of the leaves. Corolla 10-12 mm, blue-light lilac, rarely white or pink, with two lips, the upper one torn into two, the lower one trilobate.

HABITAT: Cultivated.

PROPERTIES, USES: A nectar plant. Bees show that they love it.

The essential oil is used in perfumery, for embrocations, washes, to strengthen the circulation, for rheumatism, bruises, wounds and ulcers.

It is a perfect flavouring for sauces, marinades (oil, vinegar and rosemary), grilling on the

spit, soups...

In antiquity it was burned as an offering to please the gods and considered to be the gift of Aphrodite to Mankind. Rosmarinus, the sea rose, was a symbol representing trust at weddings and funerals. Leaves of rosemary were place in the tombs of the Pharaohs, for their scent to accompany them to the kingdom of the dead.

A maceration of rosemary (leaves and flowers) in wine produces an excellent drink in cases of heart weakness, tones up the sight wine, for dysentery.

The powder from the dried leaves is used for cuts and wounds. In cases of rheumatism, we can immerse the painful joint in an infusion or rub it on. A very hot infusion is just what is needed for influenza, colds, rheumatism and dyspepsia. In compresses, it is used for dislocations and stiff neck.

If we mix 3 parts of tincture of rosemary and 1 of lavender we have the famous 'Queen of Hungary water'. For internal use, one coffee spoon per day - but only for adults. Exter-

and improves the memory.

It is also said to stop hair loss and banish sexual insufficiency due to bodily or spiritual exhaustion, and that it was used for abortions. We can use the tender shoots, pounded, for haemorrhoids, and its roots, boiled in nally, it can be used at will, especially as an embrocation in cases of rheumatism, uric arthritis and general body pain. 'If you don't want to have bad dreams again, put a twig of rosemary under your pillow', they say on Crete.

Salvia fruticosa Millet
(= *Salvia triloba* L.)   II-VI
Sage

DESCRIPTION: A large, phrygano plant, an evergreen shrub up to 1.2 metres in height, with a pervading aroma, woody base and grey felt. Leaves up to 9 cm, stalked, undulate, ovate, opposite, greenish-grey, reddish and slightly sculpted on the upper side, greyish on the underside, entire or with two lateral lobes at the base (***var. triloba***). Whorls with 2-6 flowers in the axils of little bracts. Corolla 16-25 mm, blue-violet, pink or white, with the upper lip straight and the lower lip trilobate. Two-lobed calyx with 5 teeth, which often have purple veining. This is a species which takes a variety of forms.

HABITAT: Areas of phrygano and maquis, stony slopes.

PROPERTIES, USES: A nectar plant. The dried leaves are used to make *faskomylo*, 'the Greek tea' which is served in all Greek cafés. If the leaves are fresh, we can add honey to neutralise the bitterness. It gives erotic vigour to those who have lost it due to age, or are physically and mentally tired. It imparts a warmth to the whole body and particularly to the stomach, aiding digestion. It induces abundant urination, accelerates the circulation of the blood and works on the brain cells by soothing the irritation of the nervous system. It reduces the secretion of milk in mothers during the period of weaning and alleviates night sweats during the menopause. It cleanses the blood and combats rheumatic fever, pneumonia and bronchitis, by causing great sweats.

Doctors prescribe it for aerophagia and conditions of the digestive tract. The Arabs asked how a man could ever die if he had sage in his garden!

WARNING! The tea made from it, which is warming, stimulant and tonic, must be avoided by people who suffer from hypertension, and even by those with an irascible temperament.

It revives the facial skin! This can be achieved by holding the face over the steam from a bowl in which we have boiled bunches of sage. Alternatively, cotton wool can be dipped into an infusion and wiped repeatedly over the skin.

Those who suffer from diabetes can dry the leaves and flowers by a fire, powder them and drink one spoonful of the powder in water every morning, for 10-15 days.

An essential oil, produced by distilling, is used in perfumery and soap manufacture.

The plant was once burnt in order to purify and perfume the atmosphere in houses.

Salvia pomifera L.   IV-VI

DESCRIPTION: A perennial up to 1 metre. Single leaves, ovate, velvety, greenish or greyish-green. Whorls with 2-4 flowers, in the axils of the upper leaves. Corolla 30-35 mm, light blue, with a white throat and blue-violet spots, and an upper lip either straight or curved. The lower lip is three-lobed, with a more developed middle lobe. Calyx with two lips, the upper one has three teeth, the lower one two.

HABITAT: In stony locations and maquis, up to 1200 metres, in Western Crete.

PROPERTIES, USES: The name pomifera, meaning apple-bearing, owes itself to a swelling which is caused by an insect and resembles a tiny apple (this is also seen in ***Salvia fruticosa***). The Arabs consider these 'apples' to be very tasty and say that they quench the thirst. In Greece, they are gathered on May 1st and prepared like other sugared fruits.

Salvia pomifera

Salvia verbenaca L.　II-VI and IX-XI
Wild clary

DESCRIPTION: A perennial, 10-80 cm. Stem more or less covered by glandular hairs in the upper part. Leaves oblong, 5-10 cm, +/- lobes and with a wrinkled surface. Flowers 6-10 mm, in spikes, dark blue to dark violet in colour. Bell-shaped calyx, very hairy. A species with many varieties.

HABITAT: Dry, barren areas, roadsides.

PROPERTIES, USES: Once considered a medicine to combat hysteria and sterility. The plant, it is said, cleanses the blood and soothes rheumatic attacks. In cases of pneumonia or bronchitis, consumption of the plant induces great sweats which give the patient relief. It also appears to be stomachic and tonic.

Salvia viridis L.　III-IV
Red-topped sage

DESCRIPTION: An annual, 10-50 cm, hairy. Erect stem, single, rarely branched. Simple leaves, ovate or oblong, downy, slightly toothed. Flowers 14-18 mm, pink or violet-coloured with fine hairs, in a spike which has violet, green or white bracts at its tip.

HABITAT: Barren and stony locations, at moderate altitude.

PROPERTIES, USES: A tonic and stomachic plant. On Crete, it was once believed that the seeds of the plant, boiled in wine, brought male virility!

Satureja calamintha (L.) Scheele (=*Calamintha nepeta* Savi. *ssp. glandulosa*)   VII-X
Calamint

DESCRIPTION: A perennial up to 80 cm, downy, greyish-green, woody at the base, with the aroma of mint. Leaves 10-20 mm, ovate, dentate. Flowers on pedicels, with a little corolla, white or violet, and two-lipped calyx.

HABITAT: In sterile, uncultivated locations, on walls and fences, mostly in the west of the island.

PROPERTIES, USES: Near Georgioupolis it is called 'fliskouni', for the strong smell of mint which it emanates, resembling real mint (***Mentha pulegium***). By extension, it is used like mint.

*Satureja cretica** (.) Briq. (=*Calamintha cretica* (L.) Lam.)   VI-VIII
Cretan calamint

DESCRIPTION: A perennial, densely haired, greyish-green, glandular, woody at the base, with a very strong smell. Stems 10-30 cm. Leaves 6-10 mm, ovate. Waves of 1-3 (-6) flowers. Corolla 10 mm, whitish-pink with a carmine red blazon and two-lipped calyx.

HABITAT: In the White Mountains from the mountain to the alpine zone.

PROPERTIES, USES: It was either once used in the production of incense, or burnt itself as such!

Satureja juliana (=*Micromeria Juliana* (L.) Benth. ex Rechb) IV-VI

Micromeria sp.

DESCRIPTION: A perennial shrub (phrygano), 10-40 cm, hairy, greyish, aromatic. Numerous straight, erect stems. Leaves linear-lanceolate to oblong, 3-8 mm, entire, not pointed at the tip, with folded over edges. Whorls with 4-20 small flowers. Corolla 5 mm, purple.

HABITAT: On rocks at moderate altitude.

PROPERTIES, USES: This plant, with its tonic and aromatic properties, was already known at the time of Dioscurides and Theophrastus. Its properties are of the same value as those of **Satureja thymbra** (Summer savory). Folk healers used it in the form of a beverage to treat stomach acidity and ulcers of the stomach and duodenum, intestinal worms, travel sickness, influenza, bronchitis and colds in general.

As an infusion, it is appetite-stimulating and digestive, used also for diarrhoea, nervous conditions, sleeplessness, disturbances caused by excessive heat, toothache and sore throats. Furthermore, the concentrated infusion is an excellent purgative for constipation.

Crushed, in compresses, it is used for bee stings, bruises and wounds.

Satureja nervosa Desf. (*Micromeria nervosa* (Desf.) Bentham) III-V

DESCRIPTION: A perennial, 10-40 cm. Erect stems with curved hairs. Leaves 4-5 mm, with a very small stalk, opposite, ovate and acute, with conspicuous veining on the underside. Inflorescence in spikes with whorls of 4-20 flowers. Corolla 4-6 mm, purple, two-lipped. Calyx 3-4 mm, covered with hairs.

HABITAT: Rocky locations, areas of phry-

gana (garrigue), on calcareous soils.

PROPERTIES, USES: As an infusion, it is used for gastrointestinal conditions (stomach acidity, ulcers, tendency to vomit).

Satureja spinosa L. VII-VIII

DESCRIPTION: A small shrub, phrygano plant, up to 20 cm. Perennial, aromatic, hummock-shaped. Stems thorny at the tip. Leaves up to 1 cm, oblong-linear. Calyx with 5 teeth covered in white down. Corolla 5-8 mm, pinkish-violet to white, two-lipped with the upper lip straight and smaller than the lower one, which is trilobate.

HABITAT: Grows at high altitudes of around 1500 metres, on Psiloritis and in the White Mountains. Those plants found in the White Mountains have clearly whiter flowers.

PROPERTIES, USES: Probably the same as those of the other species of **Satureja**.

Satureja thymbra L. III-VI
Summer savory

DESCRIPTION: A perennial phrygano plant up to 40 cm, downy, glandular. Leaves 9-14 mm, obovate, and acute. Sparse whorls with numerous mauve, pink or white flowers. Hairy calyx, almost hidden by large bracts of the same size.

HABITAT: Areas of phrygana (garrigue), normally on calcareous soils.

PROPERTIES, USES: Apart from the beverage that is made, the use of this plant in cookery is similar to that of oregano. It was much used by the Romans.

Two drops of the juice in the ears will improve impaired hearing (buzzing). The tisane, as a gargle, heals wounds of the pharynx and mouth. It was once used to combat pediculosis (lousiness) in animals. Wine barrels are washed with an infusion of savory to destroy mildew. The plant was once considered to be an aphrodisiac and for this reason its consumption was forbidden to nuns who cultivated it in their gardens. Indeed, when it is boiled and added to a bath it relaxes and revitalises the function of the reproductive glands. If therefore, you have cunning plans in your head, and want to enjoy love-making, put a handful of savory into a litre of water and drink 2-4 cups of it per day, the last one shortly before you retire to bed!

Syderitis syriaca * ssp. *syriaca*   **V-VI**
Mountain tea, Malotira

DESCRIPTION: A perennial, 10-50 cm, woolly. Leaves 1-6 cm, opposite, the lower ones obovate and slightly toothed, the upper ones 8 cm, linear-lanceolate or oblong, with entire margins. Inflorescences of 5-20 whorls with 6-10 flowers in each. The central bracts are round. Calyx with 5 equally-sized teeth, covered in woolly hairs. Corolla 9-15 mm, hairy, light yellow in colour, two-lipped with the upper lip bilobate and the lower one trilobate.

HABITAT: Found on Psiloritis and in the White Mountains, at altitudes exceeding 1000 metres.

PROPERTIES, USES: The common Greek name *malotira* comes from the Latin 'male' (bad) and 'tirare' (take out), and thus means 'removing what is bad'. Indeed, during the period of the Venetian occupation the plant was considered to be a panacea for colds and conditions of the respiratory system.

This is a plant which is sold and consumed to repletion. It is used to make the famous Cretan mountain tea, being diuretic, tonic, sedative, digestive, antiseptic and beneficial to the blood-carrying vessels of the heart.

It would be a good thing, if it has not already been done, to find a way of rapid cultivation of the plant, otherwise it will become extinct, and that would be a great shame!

Teucrium capitatum L. (= *T. polium* L. *ssp. capitatum* Arcang.) V-VI
Felty germander

DESCRIPTION: A perennial, small shrub, woody, aromatic, covered in white hair. Stems 10-25 cm. Oblong leaves, with shallow teeth and revolute margins. Dense inflorescence, roundish, with a diameter a little more than 10 mm, consisting of numerous small flowers which are white or pink. Calyx with 5 uneven teeth, the upper one large and rounded, those below it acutely pointed at the tip.

HABITAT: Found at low altitude.

PROPERTIES, USES: Hippocrates and Galen prescribed *T. polium ssp. polium* as a tonic, antispasmodic, and to provoke sneezing. In an infusion, it is an anti-inflammatory for the stomach and bowels; because of its bitterness, it is a good idea to add sugar.

"Musaios and Hesiod recommended that those who sought glory and merit be anointed with the plant, and that it should be cultivated and always available in case of snake bites. Physicians gave it in vinegar to those suffering from spleen and in wine to those who suffered from liver problems." Folk medicine recommends it for diabetes.

T. polium

The German popular name 'Marienkraut' and the Greek 'Panayiohorto' reveal much about the therapeutic qualities of this member of the Labiatae family.

NOTES: *T. capitatum* is a plant closely related to *T. polium*, which is not found on Crete. *T. scordium* has more or less the same properties as *T. polium L. ssp. polium*. Eight varieties grow on Crete (*T. alpestre**, *T. brevifolium, T. flavum, T. microphyllum, T. massiliense* and the endemic *T. cuneifolium**, and *T. gracile**), which are probably of great interest from a botanical point of view.

T.cuneifolium

Teucrium divaricatum Sieber ex. Heldr. V-VI

DESCRIPTION: A small bush with a variety of forms, 10-30 cm, hairy. Leaves 10-25 mm, leathery, with small lobes. Flowers up to 10 mm. Corolla spoon-shaped, in a vibrant pink colour with darker veining.

HABITAT: In areas of phrygana (garrigue) or maquis up to the mountain zone.

PROPERTIES, USES: Dioscurides prescribed it as a tisane for poisonous bites, as well as for stomach pains, fevers and colds. For the latter, steam inhalations were recommended.

Thymus capitatus (L.) Hoffmans & Link (= Coridothymus capitatus (L.) Rechenb. fil.) V-VIII
Thyme

DESCRIPTION: A perennial (phrygano) plant, 20-50 cm, much-branching, aromatic, and woody. Leaves up to 10 mm, linear, ciliate at the base, glandular. Deciduous (easily shed) at times of drought. Dense, ovoid flower-spike. Calyx 5 mm, two-lipped, the upper lip with three teeth, shorter than the lower one which has two teeth. Stigma with 20-22 veins, flattened on the side. Corolla up to 10 mm, pinkish-mauve, rarely white, two-lobed. The upper lip has two deep divisions, the lower one is trilobate.

HABITAT: Areas of phrygana (garrigue) on calcareous slopes, from the sea up to the alpine zone.

PROPERTIES, USES: Thyme honey is certainly the best; for this reasons, bees are taken to areas where thyme grows.

Thyme was once used for toothache, coughs, bronchitis, loss of hair and also as a deodorant. Given the large number of biochemical substances it contains, it is used as an anti-

septic and antispasmodic, tonic and febrifuge. Its tonic and invigorating qualities are considered sufficient to combat a number of weaknesses of the constitution, and in particular those of the nervous system (neurasthenia, depression, apathy…), and the circulation (dizziness, migrane, buzzing in the ears…). It regulates the menstrual cycle, eliminates microbes and bacilli by means of its aroma, and destroys infectious viruses which multiply in the body and cause intestinal, nervous and liver conditions.

In an infusion (15-20 g of flowers in one litre of water) it constitutes a strong tonic for the reproductive organs, as well as for children suffering from rachitis. Donkeys suffering from toothache are said to chew thyme in order to get rid of it!

Veterinarians use thyme as a rinse for wounds and ulcers. It is also used as a flavouring and as fuel for burning. The essential oil is used in pharmaceutics and perfumery.

WARNING! Its use is forbidden during

T. capitatus

the period of pregnancy; the plant is a uterine stimulant!

NOTE: ***Thymus leucotrichus Haläcsy***, found in the White Mountains, probably has other properties.

T. leucotrichus

LAURACEAE (Laurel family)

Laurus nobilis L.   III-VI
Sweet bay

DESCRIPTION: An evergreen, aromatic, 2-6 m in height. Leaves 5-10 cm, lanceolate, acute, dark green on the underside, a lighter green on the upper side, with undulate margins. Bisexual flowers, with 4 yellow petals. Black berries, resembling little olives.

HABITAT: Valleys and generally shady, cool places. Sometimes cultivated as a decoration.

PROPERTIES, USES: At ancient Olympia, and later on in Rome, garlands (crowns) were made from the plant for victors, as well as for poets and for battle heroes.

The nymph Dafni, wishing to escape the amorous advances of the god Apollo, fled to her mother Gaia who changed her into a tree. Apollo, in remorse, wove its leaves into a crown and it appears that from then

onwards, the tree was to be dedicated to him. Thus, the priestess of Apollo at the oracle in Delphi acquired divinatory power and uttered the sacred oracle only when she had chewed leaves of sweet bay, or had inhaled smoke from burning bay wood.

The word 'baccalauréat' means a crown of bay with berries (baccae) and was once offered to doctors who had just been adjudged worthy of graduation. Today, it signifies the graduate diploma from a French secondary school.

The plant protects from witchcraft, and for that reason the ancient Greeks hung a branch above their doorways when someone in the house was sick. Theophrastus tells us that the superstitious always had a bay leaf in their mouth, in order to ward off spells and the evil eye.

For indigestion, we can boil dried leaves and drink the tisane. For stomach spasms, we can infuse 4 g of fresh leaves and 8 g. bitter orange in 200 g of water for a quarter of an hour.

Bay is diuretic, invigorating, antispasmodic, expectorant, stimulates menstruation, and has sudorific properties. Its essential oil, because of the spasms which it induces in the bowels, is used in cases of flatulence. An oint-ment relieves pain due to myalgia and rheumatism. Placed in clay jars, bay leaves aromatise and protect sultanas and dried figs from insects and worms.

WARNING! The plant is poisonous! Nevertheless, the leaves are used as a flavouring in many Greek dishes (lentils, stews, sauces etc.).

A. foetida

LEGUMINOSAE (Pea family)

Anagyris foetida L.   XII-III
Bean trefoil

DESCRIPTION: A small tree, 1-4 m in height, with an unpleasant smell and yellow wood. Leaves 3-7 cm, with trifoliate, stalkless leaflets, elliptic to lanceolate, smooth on the upper surface, covered by pliant hairs on the underside. Papilionaceous flowers, large, yellow, in short racemes of a few flowers only, with a standard petal 10-15 mm which bears a black blotch, and wings up to 20 mm. Calyx bell-shaped, hairy, with 5 teeth. Pod (legume) 12-20 mm, asymmetrical with 3-8 large, reniform (kidney-shaped) seeds, violet in colour.

HABITAT: Edges of roads and fields, dry, limestone slopes.

A. foetida

PROPERTIES, USES: **Poisonous! The legumes (seed-pods), which resemble those of beans, have deceived a large number of children, who have been poisoned!** The plant was once used as an emetic and purgative. According to Cretan tradition, Judas was hanged from its branches and for that reason it is worthy of contempt.

Anthyllis vulneraria L. *ssp. rubriflora* (DC) Arcangeli   IV-VI
Kidney vetch

DESCRIPTION: An annual or biennial plant, 10-40 cm, covered in soft hairs. The lower leaves are trefoil or five-part with the top leaflet larger. The leaves of the stems are pinnate, with 7-13 leaflets. Flowers 15-18 mm, purple, concentrated in 1-2 dense heads surrounded by leaf-like bracts, deeply and irregularly divided. Calyx with 4 unequal teeth with purple margins which swell after flowering.
HABITAT: Rocky locations, areas of phrygana (garrigue).

PROPERTIES, USES: A tea made from the plant (steep one spoonful of chopped flowering heads in a litre of water for 10 minutes) is purgative and anti-asthmatic. Washing the hair with the same infusion stops hair loss.
The plant can be used raw in compresses and baths for infected wounds, abscesses, foot ulcers and open sores (syringia).
This is an excellent grazing medium for milk-producing cattle.

Asphaltium bituminosum (L.) Fourr.
(= *Psoralea bituminosa* L.)   IV-VI
Pitch trefoil

DESCRIPTION: A perennial, up to 1 metre, woody at the base, hairy, and smelling of pitch. Leaves 10-60 cm, trefoil, with long stalks, leaflets linear-lanceolate to ovate, with entire margins. Heads on long stalks, 10-30 cm, with 7-10 flowers (15-20 mm). Blue-violet corolla. Pod (legume) with a scythe-like beak.

HABITAT: Roadsides, degraded areas, up to the mountain zone.

PROPERTIES, USES: The leaves, in a tisane, help in the healing of cuts and treatment of wounds. Dioscurides mentions its use in the treatment of yellow fever (malaria), epilepsy, dropsy and snake bites.

Astragalus angustifolius Lam.   V-VII
Milk-vetch sp.

DESCRIPTION: A perennial, low on the ground, hummock-shaped shrub. Numerous stems, woody at the base. Leaves 2.5-4 cm, odd-pinnate with 6-10 pairs of leaflets ending in a terminal leaflet, and a spine as hard as a needle. Flowers 13-23 mm, white, 3-8 in a raceme on a small stalk.

HABITAT: Alpine and sub-alpine zone.

PROPERTIES, USES: It exudes gum tragacanth which is sudorific, sedative and tonic and resembles gum Arabic. Used in confectionery.

Astragalus creticus* Lam. (= Astracantha cretica (Lam.) Podlech   V-VII

DESCRIPTION: A perennial shrub with a low habit, hummock-shaped and with many branches. Leaves 2-5 cm, pinnate with 6-7 pairs of linear-lanceolate hairy leaflets ending in a spine. Flowers 10-12 mm, in pairs, in the axils of the leaves. Whitish-pink standard petal; the wings and keel are light yellow in colour.

HABITAT: Alpine and sub-alpine zone.

PROPERTIES, USES: Dioscurides refers to the plant as sedative, used for respiratory conditions and as a tonic for weakened constitutions.

NOTE: There must be some confusion between the two plants and for that reason they both have the same popular name in Greek – 'kentoukla'. They certainly do resemble one another and are found in the same habitat. They may have the same properties. The juice is collected from a cut made in the stem of the plant during the summer months.

PROPERTIES, USES: The leaves and the pods were once used for their styptic properties. **All of the plant and in particular the seeds are poisonous to ruminants**.

Calicotome villosa Link   III-IV
Spiny broom

DESCRIPTION: A perennial, up to 3 metres, branching, with tough 'steel' spines which cause great pain when they penetrate the skin. The young branches, leaves and calyx +/- hairy. Leaves arranged in threes, stalked, dark green to grey, falling in the summer. Leaflets ovate-lanceolate up to 12 mm. Papilionaceous flowers 12-18 mm, golden yellow, 2-15 in a group (clusters or racemes) which open before the leaves appear. The upper part of the calyx, which is separated from the lower part, stands erect during flowering. Pods (legumes) 2-4 mm, with soft hairs and a thick seam.

HABITAT: Stony areas, rocky slopes and maquis.

Ceratonia siliqua L.   IX-XI
Carob, Locust tree

DESCRIPTION: A bisexual, evergreen tree 4-10 metres in height. Stalked, smooth leaves, with 2-5 pairs of elliptic or ovate, slightly undulate leaflets, 30-50 mm, glossy green in colour. Unisexual flowers, papilionaceous, greenish, almost insignificant. The male flowers, with stamens, are more frequent on wild trees, and the female flowers on cultivated ones. Both lack a corolla; they have a purplish calyx and form raceme-like inflorescences which appear on the trunk or the branches. They bear fruit in the following summer. The pods are 10-30 cm, brownish-violet in colour.

HABITAT: Originates from East Africa. On poor soils, at low altitudes. Often planted as a fruit-producing tree.

PROPERTIES, USES: The fruits – carobs – are sugary and edible. They are used in drinks, water ices and fruit juices (some say even in the production of Coca-cola). An excellent animal feed, especially for horses, and known from very ancient times (Parable of the Prodigal Son). The Moslems make confectionery and liqueurs from them.

The seeds were once used as a measure of weight (carat) for gold and jewellery. Their weight varies between 189 and 205 mg; one carat weighs exactly 200 mg.

The name comes from the Greek word 'kerato' meaning 'horn-like', since the fruit resembles a horn in shape. In Arabic the word became 'kirat' and finally 'carat'.

The tough and shiny wood is used for carving and making walking-sticks.

In medicine, flour made from the carob was used, with good results, for diarrhoea in children as a styptic medicine, because of its high content in pectins. The extract of the bark and leaves is also styptic and the fruit is dilutant and anti-catarrhal in cases of lung and bronchial catarrh, influenza and whooping cough. A tisane can be made with 100 g of carob in 500 g of water and left to boil until only half of the liquid remains.

The carob has a 20-70% sugar content (caramel) from which alcohol of the highest quality is produced. Cellulose, tanning and colouring agents, oils (etc.) are extracted from the caramel.

Cercis siliquastrum L.   **III-IV**
Judas tree

DESCRIPTION: A small tree, up to 10 metres, with many crowns and leaves 7-12 cm, smooth, rounded to discoid, and deciduous. Papilionaceous flowers, dense and a brilliant pink-purple, forming clusters before the appearance of the leaves. Pods 10 cm, brownish-red.

HABITAT: A really Greek tree which is very impressive at the time of flowering. Planted for decoration on Crete, along roadsides and in the cities.

PROPERTIES, USES: According to tradition, it must have been below this tree that Judas betrayed Christ with a kiss.

Once, the floral clusters, which are slightly acid, were eaten in a salad along with other wild greens.

The wood, which is hard and has beautiful veining, is easily smoothed and used in veneering and wood carving. In bygone days, dexterous artisans made wooden containers and flasks for wine and tisipouro, and food plates with covers. Others made saddles for their animals (donkeys, mules and horses).

pharmaceutics, they are considered aphrodisiac and a menstrual stimulant, and help pregnant women to give birth without complications.

Cicer incisum **(Willd) K Maly**   **V-VIII**
Wild chickpea

DESCRIPTION: A perennial, 10-30 cm, creeping, with glandular hairs. The leaves are paired-pinnate, without tendrils, with 1-3 pairs of three or five-lobed leaflets and lateral leaves that are ovate and toothed. Two-lipped calyx. Papilionaceous flowers, violet in colour. Pods with 1-2 edible seeds.

HABITAT: Only in the alpine and sub-alpine zone.

PROPERTIES, USES: The seeds are classified among the most starchy vegetables. In

NOTE: ***Cicer arietinum* L.**, the cultivated chickpea, originates from Asia Minor and was cultivated from ancient times onwards, probably even from the Homeric period.

The plant produces an egg-shaped fruit, bulging and hairy, which encloses one or two spherical seeds with a little projecting tip – the chickpeas. These are roasted to produce 'stragalia', which are somewhat similar in their use to American popcorn.

Coronilla scorpioides (L.) Koch   IV-V
Scorpion senna

DESCRIPTION: An annual plant up to 40 cm, smooth, green-blue. Stalkless leaves, slightly fleshy, the upper ones simple, the others having three leaflets - two lateral ones that are reniform and a larger one at the tip, elliptic to discoid. Heads with 2-5 yellow flowers, 4-5 mm, on a short stalk. Pods 2-6 cm, very bent, with 4-6 corners, in the shape of a scorpion.

HABITAT: At low altitude, on barren, sandy soil and roadsides.

PROPERTIES, USES: **The seeds of this plant are poisonous! They contain a toxic glycoside which is used in very small dosage as an anti-asthmatic and for cardiac complaints.**

C. scorpioides

Coronilla valentina ssp. glauca (L.) Battand   IV-V
Scorpion vetch

DESCRIPTION: A shrub, 50-100 cm, branching, decumbent. Grey-green odd-pinnate leaves, with 2-3 pairs of short leaflets and a larger terminal leaflet. Lateral leaflets 2-6 mm, free, membranous and deciduous. Flowers 7-12 mm, yellow, on a short peduncle and forming a dense spike. Pods 1-5 cm, flattened, with 1-10 biloment compartments inside them.

HABITAT: Stony and rocky soils, forest clearings.

PROPERTIES, USES: **WARNING! Toxic seeds, which are used in medicine as a heart tonic.**

C. valentina

***Glycyrrhiza glabra* L.** **III-V**
Liquorice

DESCRIPTION: A shrub 50-100 cm, with large roots 1-2 m, cylindrical, branching, fleshy. Fluted stems, downy. Paired-pinnate leaves with 9-17 pairs of leaflets which are elliptic-oblong, often sticky. Flowers 8-12 mm, white-violet, papilionaceous, in racemes of many flowers. Pods elongated and flattened.

HABITAT: At low altitude, in barren and uncultivated fields, where it forms large colonies.

PROPERTIES, USES: This nectar plant was imported and cultivated for its sweet roots in bygone days, which were chewed like mastic. Napoleon consumed large quantities of it. Today, it is considered a weed which is difficult to eradicate.

"Sweet root (Glycyrrhiza) has the ability to quench the thirst as soon as it is put in the mouth", asserted Theophrastus. Distillation produces a dark-coloured extract, liquorice (called 'crow's milk' in other countries) which is used for respiratory conditions. Concentrated, it is made into pastilles or long, shiny black tubes.

The drink is made from a decoction in warm water, because the bitter substance contained in the roots dissolves in hot water. If we steep the roots in cold water and add lemon cut

into slices, we have a refreshing drink. Medicinally, because of its anti-inflammatory action (it contains glycorizic acid) it is prescribed for all respiratory conditions which are due to influenza, pneumonia, bronchitis, and asthma.

The root helps in the production of hormones such as hydrocortisone, which explains its anti-inflammatory properties. It can treat stomach ulcers, invigorate kidney glands which have become lethargic after therapy with steroids, and reduce the level of cholesterol in the blood.

WARNING! "The quantity of liquorice which is consumed daily, if at the same time contraception is practiced, must not exceed 10 g, because it encourages water retention, which results in oedema", says Dr. Ursula Selerberg, a member of the German Society of Chemists. It is also used in the production of Chinese ink and beer.

Lotus edulis L.   III-V
Edible lotus

DESCRIPTION: An annual, rather prostrate, and slightly woolly. Leaves with 5 leaflets (a characteristic of **Lotus**), two of which are almost stuck to the stem, the other three standing away from it. Flowers solitary or in pairs. Corolla 10-15 mm, white-yellow. Pod (20-40 x 4-8 mm) fleshy, bendy in the upper part, with a deep channel on the upper ridge.

HABITAT: On sandy clay soils and rocks near the sea.

PROPERTIES, USES: The fresh seeds are eaten like peas.

L. edulis

Lathyrus ochrus (L.) DC.   IV-V

DESCRIPTION: An annual, 20-60 cm, vigorous, climbing, hairless, with winged stems. The lower leaves have a flattened ridge, resembling a leaflet, and tendrils. The upper leaves have 1-2 pairs of ovate leaflets. Flowers 16-18 mm, white-yellow, solitary or in pairs. Calyx with unevenly-sized teeth. Winged pods, up to 6 cm long.
HABITAT: Cultivated in a few places but also self-sowing in fields of grain.
PROPERTIES, USES: The tender tips of the stems, known locally as 'papoulies', are eaten raw with olive oil and lemon dressing. A kind of purée – fava (lentils) - is made from the seeds and very popular in Greece.

Lupinus albus L.   III-V
White lupin

DESCRIPTION: An annual, up to 100 cm, hairy. Digitate leaves, the lower ones 25-35 mm with obovate leaflets, and the upper ones with sphenoid leaflets, smooth on the surface and hairy on the underside. Raceme 5-10 cm, with alternate flowers, white with a standard petal that is blue at the tips. Seed pods 80-100 mm, with large seeds.
HABITAT: An oriental plant, which dislikes lime and is sensitive to the cold. It dies at a temperature of 4° C. Found up to the alpine zone.
PROPERTIES, USES: This is a good animal feed, both in the fresh and dried fodder state. The same goes for its seeds which are given to animals after they have lost their bitterness. Lupins were once systematically cultivated (today much less so) for their seeds which are still eaten, especially during the period of Lenten fasting. We can leave them to soften in salted water until they have lost their bitterness. This was also done in the time of Dioscurides. The lupin is an ideal plant to grow during the period when a field lies fallow – its roots absorb nitrogenous salts from the atmosphere and enrich the earth. It was

once used for rheumatism, arthritis, myalgia, various inflammations, strain, and diabetes (according to one recipe, 2-3 seeds per day).
NOTE: *ssp. graecus* (**Boiss. & Spruner**) **Franco & P. Silva** is also found; it has blue flowers.

161

Lupinus varius L.   II-V
Lupin sp.

DESCRIPTION: An annual, 20-50 (- 70) cm, with dense hairs. Digitate leaves with 9-11 lanceolate, ovate-oblong leaflets, with soft hairs on both surfaces. Linear lateral leaflets. Single raceme-like inflorescences with blue flowers arranged in whorls. The standard petal has a whitish yellow blotch. The seed pod is 4-5 cm, brown-red, covered in soft hairs, flattened, and contains 3-4 round seeds.

HABITAT: In dry, acid, and fallow soils.

PROPERTIES, USES: Once, seeds of this lupin were given to visitors to the Oracle of the Dead at Acheron, to prepare them to communicate with the dead. The alkaloids contained in the seeds brought about a state of ecstasy and loss of the senses, i.e. exactly what the priests wanted for successful communication with the souls of the dead.

Medicago arborea. L.   III-V
Tree medick

DESCRIPTION: A shrub, 1-4 metres in height, with numerous trifoliate leaves and soft hairs. Obovate leaflets, entire or toothed at the margins. Yellow flowers, in a raceme of 4-10, in the leaf axils. Calyx with soft hairs and 5 narrow teeth. Seed pod 12-15 mm in diameter, shaped like a tambourine.

HABITAT: On slopes and roadsides, at low altitude.

PROPERTIES, USES: Often cultivated for decoration. It was introduced to Greece during the period of the Persian Wars. This is a nectar plant. Its leaves are diuretic and healing.

Medicago sativa L.   VI-X
Lucerne

DESCRIPTION: A perennial plant with annual, decumbent branches and a twisted root which is capable of seeking out water up to a depth of 3 metres. Leaves with 3 oblong leaflets, toothed at the tip. Blue and violet, sometimes yellow flowers, in dense axillary racemes. Twisted seed-pod with 2-3 spirals, containing 2-7 kidney-shaped seeds, yellowish-green in colour.

HABITAT: A very useful, high-yield animal feed plant which has been cultivated since antiquity. Known to the ancient Greeks as 'Median grass', it was brought to Greece from Persia during the Persian Wars. The Romans, according to assertions by Virgil, valued it as one of the most worthy plants for a meadow. It is sensitive to cold and damp.

PROPERTIES, USES: There is no better plant for fodder. It is rich in chlorophyll, calcium, phosphorus, iron (double that found in spinach) and contains carotene and a large number of vitamins which are not destroyed by heating. It has antiscorbutic (4 times more that of the orange), haemostatic (due to vitamin K) and fungicide properties. "The plant, shortly before flowering, is eaten raw as a salad. Later on, it can be prepared like spinach or added to soups. The young leaves and the flowering spikes make an appetite-stimulating infusion. The same leaves, when dried, constitute an excellent dietary supplement."

We should avoid giving animals large quantities of the fresh plants, since it can cause fatal bloating.

It does not exhaust the soil, but actually enriches it with nitrogen.

Ononis spinosa L. ssp. diacantha (Reichenb.) Greuter, Matthäs & Risse (= *Ononis antiquorum* L.)   IV-VII
Restharrow

DESCRIPTION: A spiny, perennial plant, with a low habit. The young stems are hairy. Lower leaves trifoliate, with ovate-oblong leaflets, toothed, and entire at the tops of the stems. Flowers with a corolla 6-10 mm, pinkish-red with darker veining.

HABITAT: On barren soils, from the sea up to the sub-alpine zone.

PROPERTIES, USES: The roots, in an infusion, have diuretic and antirheumatic properties, used against gout and the formation of uric lithiasis (30 g of finely chopped roots with a few leaves of mint and fennel in order to neutralise the unpleasant smell of the plant, in half a litre of scalding hot water). The plant also has expectorant and sedative properties and the ability to stimulate the metabolism.

On Crete, they say that the juice of restharrow heals the pain of love (!). Another 10 species are found on the island!

Scorpiurus muricatus L.   III-V
Scorpiurus

DESCRIPTION: An annual, 5-80 cm, +/- hairy, with a variety of forms. The leaves, 3-10 cm, are simple, spatulate to lanceolate, with 3-5 parallel veins. The heads contain 2-5 flowers on large stalks, with a yellow corolla. Seed pod 2-5 cm, spiral in shape, with barbs on the external veins, and half-moon shaped seeds.

HABITAT: Cultivated areas, abandoned fields, roadsides.

PROPERTIES, USES: According to ancient medicine, ideal in cases of scorpion bites. Ancient homeopathy!

Spartium junceum L.　　　IV-VII
Spanish broom

DESCRIPTION: A bush 1-3 (-5) metres in height, with cylindrical stems, erect and hairless, greyish-green in colour. Small leaves, linear-lanceolate, downy on the underside. Inflorescence of loose racemes, with pleasant-smelling flowers up to 2.5 cm, a brilliant yellow colour. Standard petal with soft hairs, membranous calyx with 5 teeth and seed pod 4-8 cm, flattened, with 10-18 seeds.

HABITAT: Up to the mountain zone, preferably on calcareous soils.

PROPERTIES, USES: **WARNING! A poisonous plant, because of an alkaloid substance it contains.**

In an infusion, it was once used as a therapeutic plant for cardiac pains, and as a purgative and emetic (flower stalks in half a litre of scalding hot water, up to three teaspoons per day). It can be used for dropsy, lithiasis (calculi) of the gall bladder and liver disturbances.

As a maceration, 20 g of dried flowers in 500 g of water were once used as a purgative, diuretic, menstrual stimulant, for albumen in the urine, and sugar diabetes. It is said that the content of sugar in the blood is lowered immediately.

Formerly, the stems were used in basket-making and to tie bundles of wood or wild greens, in order to carry them. After the appropriate soaking in water, the shepherds made sandals from the dried-out stems and clothes from their fibres. A yellow colouring agent was obtained from the flowers.

As children, we decked out the house with this plant, pervading it with a sweet scent. A decorative and nectar plant.

Tetragonolobus purpureus **Moench**
Winged pea, Asparagus pea   **II-III**

DESCRIPTION: An annual, 10-40 cm, with soft hairs. Leaves 4 cm, trefoil, with ovate to rhomboid leaflets and ovate-lanceolate lateral leaflets, resembling leaves. Flowers 15-22 mm, solitary or in pairs, with a carmine red standard petal and wings a dark reddish-purple colour, on a stalk smaller than the leaf connected to it. Seed pods 3-9 cm, hairless, with 4 wings at least 2 mm thick, square in cross-section.

HABITAT: Cultivated areas, fallow land, roadsides.

PROPERITES, USES: Once cultivated for its edible fruits (eaten roasted) and as fresh fodder for animals. The plant is healing and styptic.

Trifolium repens **L.**   **IV-VIII**
White clover

DESCRIPTION: A perennial plant with creeping stems 30-40 cm, some of which put out roots at the nodes. Stalked leaves, with 3 leaflets 5-7 mm, broad, inverse cordate or obovate with a white marking. Heads with 8-12 flowers, 10-20 mm, white or white-pink, on a stalk. The flowers are erect or nodding

T. repens

166

according to whether they have been fertilised or not by the swarms of bees which visit them.

HABITAT: Up to the mountain zone.

PROPERTIES, USES: Often cultivated, since it is excellent for animals and grows very rapidly. Treated correctly, it can yield honey, a tea, wine and flour (!).

A leaf with 4 leaflets can sometimes be found amongst the others, the so-called 'four-leafed clover', which is considered to be very lucky for the finder.

The young leaves and the tender shoots are eaten raw or boiled in a salad. When older, they are cooked like spinach. The flavour is very pleasant.

ment for conditions of the liver and the stomach, as well as for respiratory conditions (pneumonia, bronchitis, asthma).

As a plaster, it is used for inflammations, abscesses, boils, arthritis, haematomas, bruises, contusions and ecchymosis.

The seeds are a traditional aphrodisiac, proven to be warming for the kidneys and reproductive organs. This is the reason why it was used by the Chinese for male insufficience.

A flour is made from the seeds which, when mixed with that produced from grain, makes bread sweetly delicious. The plant is an excellent animal fodder.

WARNING to pregnant women! The plant is a uterine stimulant.

Trigonella foenum-graecum L.   III-V
Classical fenugreek

DESCRIPTION: An annual, 10-50 cm, almost hairless. Trifoliate leaves, toothed. 1-2 flowers in the axils of the upper leaves, 8-15 mm, whitish-yellow or white, washed with a purple colour at their base. Seed pods 60-110 mm, linear, slightly bent, with a beak at the tip.

HABITAT: The plant is cultivated. It is also self-sowing in cultivated and abandoned areas at low altitude.

PROPERTIES, USES: "If you rub your body with this plant, your skin will be beautiful, free from any blemish", says a very old Egyptian recipe. The Egyptians used it also as an aid to childbirth and to increase milk secretion.

Today, a tea is made which is much valued in cases of period pain, stomach cramps and travellers' diarrhoea. It is known from very ancient times as a sedative, antiseptic, a treat-

Trigonella graeca (Boiss. & Spruner) Boiss. (= *T. cretica* = *Melilotus graecus*)
Greek trigonella   **IV-V**

DESCRIPTION: An annual, 10-30 cm, erect. Cuneate leaflets, truncated at their base. Raceme of small yellow flowers, 7-10 mm. Disc-like seed pods, 10-20 mm in diameter, flattened, membranous, veiny.
HABITAT: Rocky, limestone areas. An Asiatic plant which is only found on Crete.
PROPERTIES, USES: Probable confusion with *Trigonella foenum-graecum*.

Vicia faba L.   **II-IV**
Broad bean?

DESCRIPTION: An annual, up to 80 cm, smooth and/or downy, with a hollow stem. Grey leaves with 2-3 pairs of leaflets 20-50 mm, without tendrils and with toothed lateral leaflets. Flowers solitary or in threes, in the leaf axils. Corolla with a white standard petal and black wings. Seed pod 80-200 mm, with fat, edible seeds – broad beans.
HABITAT: Cultivated. Only occasionally self-sowing.
PROPERTIES, USES: A nectar plant, known from prehistoric times as a foodstuff. The fresh pods, together with artichokes, are prepared like fresh beans. The tender shoots are eaten raw in a salad, with oil and vinegar added.
The seeds of the broad bean, which are considered –probably erroneously – to be stimulatory and aphrodisiac, are eaten raw, when they are fresh, or carefully boiled and dressed with oil and lemon when they are dried. **Broad beans must not be given to young children, since the plant contains a substance, cyamin, which can be fatal, especially in combination with milk.**

Broad bean flower, mixed with wine and olive oil, can be used as a plaster in cases of congestion of the testicles or tumours of the breast.

The roots have the ability to enrich the soil with nitrogen, something which is very valuable for the fields.

Vicia sativa L.   III-IV
Common vetch

DESCRIPTION: An annual, up to 80 cm, in a variety of forms, climbing, hairy. Leaves with 3-8 pairs of leaflets, tripartite tendrils and lateral leaflets toothed with a dark-coloured, nectar-bearing gland at their base. Flowers 10-30 mm, solitary or in pairs, reddish-purple. Seed pods hairy, black to brown-yellow.
HABITAT: Cultivated, and self-sowing.
PROPERTIES, USES: The quintessential plant for animals. Even the bees visit it compulsively for the rich nectar in the lateral leaflets.
As a tisane, 50 g of the fruit in 300 g of water are diuretic and prescribed in cases of stomach, kidney, gall bladder and liver pain. A poultice with dilutant properties is made from the flour produced from the seeds.

LINACEAE (Flax family)

Linum bienne Miller   IV-VI
Pale flax

DESCRIPTION: An annual, biennial or perennial plant, 6-60 cm, smooth, often branching from the base. Alternate leaves, small, entire, linear to linear-lanceolate with only one vein, without lateral leaflets. Flow-

ers 10-15 mm, light blue in colour, with deciduous petals and sepals acutely pointed at the tip, two or three times smaller than the petals. Fruit: spherical capsules, which open during ripening and contain glistening seeds

Vicia sativa

169

Linum bienne

from which linseed oil is produced.

HABITAT: Pastures and stony soils at low altitude.

PROPERTIES, USES: This is the most common flax in the Mediterranean area. It was cultivated from the prehistoric period onwards and later replaced by ***Linum usitatissimum*** L., the cultivated flax of today. The question could be asked whether this latter species is nothing more than a mutation - an improvement on the former.

Archaeological excavations have ascertained the existence of seeds and linen fabric in Babylon (7000 BC), as well as in the lake-dwellings in the Alps (5000 BC). The wrappings of Egyptian mummies were made from linen, as well as shrouds for the Hebrews and Greeks.

In ancient Greece the plant was known as one for spinning from the Homeric period onwards, by the name of 'linon'. It seems to have been imported from Egypt and from Colchis where, according to Herodotus, it became an exclusive crop and was used in spinning and weaving.

The seeds contain a slimy substance, beneficial for the correct functioning of the bowels (it stops constipation). The oil, rich in acid, has emollient, sedative, purgative and anti-inflammatory properties.

Hippocrates and Theophrastus (5th and 4th centuries BC) used it as a healing plant. Dioscurides (1st century BC) spoke of its emollient properties. In fact, laxative tisanes and softening poultices are made from the powdered linseeds.

It is used everywhere for its thread-like fibres which are extracted from the bark, and for the oil its seeds contain. Linseed oil is used in the production of oil paints and also for a number of manufacturing requirements. It is thus cultivated in a number of countries (Belgium Poland, the Baltic states etc), but no longer on Crete. Linseeds are also one of the best forms of animal feed.

LORANTHACEAE
(Mistletoe family)

Viscum album L. *ssp. abietis* (Wiesb.) Abromeit
XI-IV

Mistletoe

DESCRIPTION: A semi-parasitic plant on pines and other trees, woody with bifurcated branching. Leaves in pairs, leathery, narrow at the base and rounded at the tip, yellowish, with entire edges. The flowers are almost invisible, yellowish with 4 petals, male and female on different plants. White, sticky berries, the prey of birds which transport them here and there.

HABITAT: On Crete, found on Thrypti, appearing only on pines, whereas in the rest of Greece it is met on other trees, such as firs and oaks.

PROPERTIES, USES: Mythology tells us that Persephone used a branch of mistletoe to open the gates of Hades.

The mistletoe on oak trees represented a component in the religious rites of the Celtic tribes and gave protection against witchcraft and the evil eye.

Birds are very fond of it, especially blackbirds, thrushes, and bee-eaters. For many years now, the gum which its berries contain, mixed with honey, has been used to make bird-lime. The birds see a bare branch, perch on it, but cannot leave again, because they are stuck fast to it.

It was once used for epilepsy, spasms and as a means to bring about low blood pressure (hypotension) because of an alkaloid substance it contain (viskin). To lower arterial pressure, 40 g of fresh mistletoe were left for several days in one litre of white wine, filtered and then 100 g drunk per day.

Hippocrates and Pliny considered it a panacea for dizziness, epilepsy and tumours. "Those who suffer repeatedlyfrom migranes, dyspnoea, nervous hiccups, stress, cardiac disturbances, asthma attacks, shortness of breath, increased pulse, inflammations, disturbances of the menopause, let them ask for mistletoe", Maurice Messegué tells us.

The plant is also used for arteriosclerosis, tuberculosis, urine retention, uric arthritis, rheumatism, lithiasis and pain in the kidneys. The plant is nectar-producing.

WARNING! Do not contemplate even the smallest experiment with the fruits. They are too toxic and can prove fatal!

LYTHRACEAE (Loosestrife family)

Lythrum hyssopifolia L.   IV-V
Grass-poli

DESCRIPTION: An annual, 10-60 cm, with reddish, erect stems. Leaves usually alternate. Pink flowers with 4 small petals, 2-3 mm.
HABITAT: In ditches and areas that are periodically damp or flooded.
PROPERTIES, USES: The flowers produce an excellent honey. The plant is healing, styptic and antiscorbutic.

MALVACEAE (Mallow family)

Alcea cretica (Weinm) Greuter   IV-VII
Cretan hollyhock

DESCRIPTION: A perennial up to 2.5 metres. Robust stems, erect, densely haired. Leaves cordate to disc-shaped, +/- lobes. Large flowers, 6-9 cm in diameter, almost stalkless, dark pink to purple. Petals 30-45 mm. Hypocalyx bracts with 6 lobes, joined at the base, +/- the same length as the sepals.
HABITAT: Fences, roadsides, disturbed areas.
PROPERTIES, USES: A beautiful plant which could ideally be used as a decoration. Once, the root was given to children to chew on during the teething period.
NOTES: *Alcea rosea* (cultivated hollyhock) has larger flowers, up to 10 cm, which are white, violet or red. It is a cultivated plant which was introduced into Greece and is met, semi self-sown, along the sides of roads. Division of this family into each respective genus is made on the basis of the hypocalyx bracts or sepals:

Alcea: 6 lobes joined at the base
Althaea: 6-9 lobes narrow at the base
Lavatera: 3 lobes joined at the base
Malva: 2-3 free sepals

172

Malva sylvestris L.
Common mallow

IV-VI

DESCRIPTION: An annual or perennial, up to 150 cm, in a variety of forms, often prostrate, with a twisted root. Mealy leaves, +/- cordate at the base,with 3-7 serrated lobes. Flowers in pairs, light pinkish-mauve in colour with dark veining. Petals 12-20 mm, cuneate, not covering each other, lightly two-lobed. 2-3 free hypocalyx bracts. The fruits, composite capsules, have 2-7 kidney-like yellowish-green seeds, which look like little rounded cheeses or miniature loaves. When we were children, we loved to play with the fruits and often ate them.

HABITAT: Up to the mountain zone, mostly on fertile soils.

PROPERTIES, USES: The plant contains a viscous substance and vitamins A, B, and C. A plaster made from scalded leaves, left on for one night, softens callouses on the feet. As a tea (100 g of dried flowers in one litre of water) it relieves a cough and phlegms and calms inflammation of the digestive and urinary tracts (colitis and intestinal colitis).

It is an ideal antidote for nettle stings. We can rub the irritated area with fresh mallow leaves and the pain will disappear.The fellahin of Egypt boil the roots and then fry them with onions. This is said to be very tasty.

Folk wisdom says "With a vegetable garden and a plot of mallow there will be medicines for the whole family". The flowers are collected when they are still in bud, the leaves during flowering and the roots in autumn.

NOTES: *Malva nicaensis* **All**. differs in its flowers which are smaller, violet-bluish, with petals 10-12 mm on a very short stalk. This is a nectar plant, aromatic and antispasmodic. In an infusion, it is given for conditions of the upper respiratory system and especially for a cantor's hoarseness; in a thick cream, it

is given to avoid difficulties in childbirth. As a poultice, mixed with fat, it is a good analgesic for lumbago and arthritic pains.

Another three types of **Malva** are found on Crete: **M. aegyptia**, **M. cretica** and **M. parviflora** which can have the same or different properties.

Malva nicaensis

Hibiscus esculentus
Okra, Ladies' fingers

DESCRIPTION: A plant up to 2 metres, covered by glandular, rather tough hairs, with palmately-lobed leaves and a long leaf-stalk which resembles that of the vine. It has large, very beautiful flowers of a divine yellow colour with a purple throat. The fruit, a capsule, is large and can exceed 25 cm; it is elongated and has 5 ridges, which narrow slowly as they approach the tip. It contains round seeds.

HABITAT: Our okra came from Africa and is systematically cultivated.

PROPERTIES, USES: The fruit constitutes a vegetable which is easily digestible and pleasing, and can be used without the slightest fear. It causes peristaltic movements along the length of the digestive tract and in this way helps those who suffer from constipation. It is also recommended for conditions of the kidneys, gall-bladder and liver, for obesity and arthritis.

MELIACEAE
(Mahogany family)

Melia azederach L.   IV-V
Indian bead tree, Persian lilac

DESCRIPTION: A large, deciduous tree, rapidly growing, with craggy ash-black bark, and hard, heavy wood, resistant to the dust and air pollution of cities. Rich foliage, with 2-pinnately-divided leaves, long leaf-stalks, and leaflets 2.5-5 cm, ovate-lanceolate, acute and serrated. Blue-violet flowers, aromatic, on long stalks. Fruit almost round, yellow, with a diameter of 6-18 mm.

HABITAT: Originates from the East and is not self-sowing. Takes well to all soils and resists drought and low temperatures.

PROPERTIES, USES: The wood is used in veneering, turning and polishing. Homer mentions that lances were made from it. The roots, in a maceration (6 g in 300 g of water) are used for fever; we can add sugar or honey. In a tincture (3 g. in 300 g of water or wine) in a powder or in olive oil, it is used in embrocations for rheumatic-arthritic conditions. It treats hair loss and destroys lice on the head and in the pubic hair.

MORACEAE (Mulberry family)

Ficus carica L.　　　　　　　VI-IX
Fig

DESCRIPTION: A deciduous tree, 6-8 metres in height, with smooth bark, and thick greyish-silver branches which contain a milky juice.

Alternate leaves, stalked, up to 20 cm, palmately-lobed, cordate at the base, wrinkled on the upper surface, +/- hairy on the underside. Numerous, tiny simple flowers inside a fleshy, pear-shaped receptacle with an open channel at the top. The male flowers are located near the channel, while the female flowers are located towards the bottom and side walls. Remarkable is its pollination by a little insect of the hymenoptera class (**Blastophaga psenes**), which completes its metamorphosis inside the inflorescence and when it exits through the channel as an adult insect, carries on its back a small quantity of pollen which it deposits on the female flow-

ers and then goes to another receptacle to lay its eggs. After this, the pear-shaped receptacle changes into a juicy and sugar-bearing fruit, the fig, 5-7 cm, yellow or brownish violet, with an aromatic, sweet flesh.

HABITAT: Up to the mountain zone, cultivated or self-sowing. Originally grew on rocks – this is still apparent today in the gorges.

PROPERTIES, USES: The name comes from the Titan Sykea, whose mother –the Earth – changed him into a tree, to save him from the wrath of Zeus.

The first fig trees were planted in Athens on the orders of Demeter, goddess of agriculture. Plato had the nickname 'fig-lover'. Xerxes, it is said, wanted to occupy Greece because of its beautiful figs.

For the promulgation of fig trees, cultivars – spring 'male' figs which contain countless male flowers – are used. The cultivars are passed through reeds and bunches are made which are hung on the branches of the 'domesticated' fig. According to Theophrastus, the wood of the fig was used in the making of theatre-seats and the hoop-bases of garlands. During the period of the Peloponnesian War, the black market trade in figs was a normal practice. Pericles wanted to stop it and introduced a law with very stiff penalties. Those who harboured a hatred for others thus took the opportunity to accuse them of illegal fig-trading. These accusers ('fantes' in ancient Greek) were therafter known as sycophants, a name which has lasted until today and in Greek (unlike in English) refers to someone who accuses another without reason.

The fruits are eaten fresh or dried, and are an excellent purgative/laxative. Medicine uses not only the fig, but also the leaves and branches of the tree. The milky juice is used to cauterise boils and wounds. In bygone days, warts and pimples were also treated in

this way. In an infusion, the fig is considered an ideal medicine for sore throats, pharyngitis, colds, gingivitis, chronic diarrhoea, inflammation of the bladder and kidneys, smallpox, measles and scarlet fever.

Meat can be covered with its leaves to tenderise it and roast it more quickly. Very probably, this property of its leaves has led to the belief that it is harmful to sleep beneath a fig tree, because then the muscles relax, the various functions of the body stop, the brain becomes confused and coherence of thought is lost...

Morus alba L. IV-VI
White mulberry

Morus alba

DESCRIPTION: A deciduous tree, 12-15 metres in height, with greyish, ashy bark, and a surface root system. Leaves 6-18 cm, alternate, stalked, ovate, cordate or lobed, with serrate margins, the lower surface slightly downy and the upper surface green and glossy. Small flowers, unisexual, greenish or yellowish, in the form of either male or female catkins, either on the same tree (unisexual) or on different trees (bisexual). After pollination, the female flowers become fleshy and form a false fruit, which is juicy, tart, and has the shape of a blackberry, either white, black or pink, depending on the variety. This fruit is edible when it has ripened.

HABITAT: Originates from China and was brought to Europe and the Mediterranean together with the eggs of silk-worms, by Greek monks during the time of the Emperor Justinian. The trees acclimatised and flourished so much that they are found, semi self-sowing, all over the country. Today they are normally planted, and rarely self-sowing.

177

PROPERTIES, USES: The skin of the root is dilutant and diuretic. The wood is suitable for coach-making and veneering. A number of alcoholic beverages are made from the mulberries.

The leaves of **Morus nigra**, in an infusion (40-80 g in a litre of water) are a good febrifuge; the same infusion, more concentrated, is used in gargles and to soothe toothache. The black mulberries are eaten in cases of diabetes. A syrup is also made to treat mouth ulcers in children, and sore throats. Midwives used an infusion from the leaves for the care of women after childbirth and scorching hot leaves were placed on the pelvis for uterine pain and the loss of amniotic fluid. In France, this action was termed 'culottage', which means 'breeching'.

NOTE: **Morus nigra L**. differs in that its false berries are reddish-black, rich in vitamin C and edible when fully ripe (at an earlier stage they are bitter to the taste). The tree is rather early-blooming. It was also imported from Asia, but at a very early date, long before the Trojan War.

Morus nigra

Morus alba

MYRTACEAE (Myrtle family)

Myrtus communis L.   V-VIII
Myrtle

DESCRIPTION: An evergreen bush up to 5 metres, glandular, aromatic. Leaves up to 3 cm, opposite, stalkless, ovate-lanceolate, acutely pointed at the tip, and leathery with the upper surface shiny and the lower one studded with glands. Flowers up to 3 cm, solitary, five-part, white with a pleasant scent, on a long stalk. Numerous long stamens. Thread-like style. Berry 7-10 mm, blue-black during maturity, with the left-over calyx attached like a hat.

HABITAT: Damp locations, banks of streams. Avoids calcareous soils; also grown as a decorative plant.

PROPERTIES, USES: The ripe berries are eaten together with dried figs. The essential oil, called 'Angel water', is used in perfumery and pharmaceutics for conditions of the upper respiratory tract. In the Middle Ages, embrocations were used containing 'Angel water' in order to acquire a more hale and hearty body.

The leaves and flowers were used to make 'the countess's ointment' for facial care (it smoothed out wrinkles and removed blotches caused by the sun); the women of Illyria and Macedonia certainly used it.

In antiquity, the leaves and fruits were used to make myrtle wine which was drunk in cases of sluggishness of the digestive system. The myrtle was also considered the symbol of happy lovers and was dedicated to Aphrodite.

The heavy wood of the tree, with its beautiful veining, is used in inlay-work.

179

Eucalyptus globulus et amygadalinus Labill.

Eucalyptus

DESCRIPTION: A tree, 30-35 metres in height, with dark green lanceolate leaves, +/- curving. Idiomorphic flowers, with a calyx which opens at the moment of flowering. The whole tree exudes a very individual, aromatic fragrance.

HABITAT: The agronomist and botanist Orphanides introduced the tree from Australia in 1864. It is found preferably on damp and even marshy soil. Through the planting of eucalyptus, the water content of the soil was reduced and completely absorbed, with the result that there were no longer any mosquitos; from that time onwards, it was believed that the eucalyptus drove them away.

PROPERTIES, USES: In pharmaceutics, the leaves are used; they are antiseptic, febrifuge, constrict the peripheral blood-bearing arteries and produce excellent results in conditions of the upper respiratory tract (asthma, bronchitis, colds), remittent fevers, stomach cramps and disturbances of the urinary tract. The infusion is prepared with a handful of leaves pounded in one litre of water; 3-4 cups are drunk per day.

For external use, the leaves stop haemorrhages, relieve the nervous system, soothe migraines, and treat inflammation of the gums (when they are chewed) and mouth conditions. They can also be used in a poultice, as a lotion or in washes for otitis, wounds, inflammation of the nose and vagina, for gonorrhoea and irritation of the anus.

WARNING! In large quantities, eucalyptus is toxic (headache, dizziness, nausea).

OLEACEAE (Olive family)

Olea europaea L. *ssp. europaea*   IV-V
Olive

DESCRIPTION: An evergreen tree up to 10 metres in height, with a long life (millennia), and a robust and gnarled trunk. Leaves 4-10 cm, opposite, lanceolate, acute and entire, the upper surface dark green and the underside silvery. White flowers, very small, in axillary clumps. Corolla with 4 joined lobes. The olive fruit is ovoid to elliptic, fleshy, green to black, and has a very hard stone (pit).

HABITAT: On all soils.

PROPERTIES, USES: Cultivated from very ancient times onwards, the olive is the oldest fruit-bearing tree in the Mediterranean. As a result of her victory over Poseidon for the supremacy of Attica, Athena gave an olive tree as a gift to the city (Athens) which has since then kept her name alive.

Hera anointed herself with olive oil in order to bewitch Zeus. Athletes were anointed with the oil in order to have more strength and suppleness. A piece of bread and a handful of olives still constitute a basic meal. The Christian religion uses olive oil and branches of the tree in its rituals (baptism, Palm Sunday). The olive branch is considered everywhere to be a symbol of peace. In antiquity, branches were used to make the crowns for the victors at the Olympic Games.

Today, olive oil is valued more than ever for its beneficial effects on the human body. It is a gall stimulant, totally effective for those who suffer from gall colics, and used in the production of a large number of plasters. Mixed with red wine, it heals wounds.

In an infusion, the bark of the young branches (30-60 g in one litre of water) is a good febrifuge. The leaves can be used for rheumatism, arthritis and arterial hypertension.

The wood of the olive is an excellent fuel for burning and produces high-quality charcoal. In the Prefecture of Rethymnon, charcoal is still made in the very traditional way in the well-known charcoal burners' chimneys, which require laborious and careful preparation.

Crete is a large producer and exporter of olive oil, and at the same time a great consumer of it, since it is used in almost all of the dishes of Cretan cookery.

NOTE: The sub-species ***ssp. oleaster* (Hoff. & Link) Negodi**, which represents the wild olive, never exceeds the height of a bush. It has branches that are +/- thorny, small leaves and smaller fruit with a fat pit and clearly containing less oil. This is the best subject-material for grafting. Its wood is resistant and dense-textured, easily worked and used for a number of elegant works of art.

O. europaea ssp. oleaster

ONAGRACEAE
(Willowherb family)

Epilobium hirsutum L.　　　　VI-X
Greater willowherb

DESCRIPTION: A perennial, up to 2 metres in height, with subterranean stolons and robust stems, without wings, bearing soft hair. Stalkless leaves, opposite, the upper ones oblong-lanceolate, slightly toothed, semi-periblastic. Flowers 15-35 mm, pinkish-purple with 4 petals, concave at the tip, with 8 stamens and 4 outspread stigmas in the shape of a cross. Long, narrow seed-pod, four-cornered, opening during maturity to allow long, silky hairs to pour out.

HABITAT: Damp locations, banks of streams, ditches, at low and medium altitude.

PROPERTIES, USES: A nectar plant, emollient, dilutant and styptic. Could be cultivated for decoration. The young stems are eaten like asparagus or spinach.

bulbs which penetrate the soil deeply, creating a small, perennial network of tubers. Rosette of tripartite, long-stalked leaves (up to 20 cm), with inverse cordate florets. The flowering stem is hairy, leafless, with 6-12 flowers in an umbel. Corolla with 5 petals, lemon-yellow in colour, 2- 2.5 cm, obovate and with 10 stamens of which 5 are smaller. Propagation is effected via the tuberous rootstock.

HABITAT: Introduced to Malta from South Africa as a decorative plant, it has managed to invade the whole of the Mediterranean area and overwhelm fields and gardens. The limitless expanses covered by its yellow flowers are pleasing to the eye. Western Crete has also been invaded by *Oxalys pes-caprae var. florae pleno* (which has double flowers).

PROPERTIES, USES: As children, we dug for the bitter-sweet subterranean stems of the Bermuda buttercup, in order to eat them.

OXALIDACEAE
(Wood sorrel family)

Oxalys pes-caprae L.   **XII-V**

Bermuda buttercup

DESCRIPTION: A plant growing from

var. florae pleno

PAEONACEAE (Peony family)

Paeonia clusii * F. C. Stern   IV-V
Clusius's peony

DESCRIPTION: A perennial with a rhizome. Stems up to 90 cm, reddish. The lower leaves are double-tripartite, with leaflets deeply divided into acutely pointed lobes. Large flowers, 7-10 cm, white to light pink (rarely completely pink) with 6-8 petals, more or less discoid. The fruits take the shape of an almond and contain black seeds in the centre, with reddish purple seeds around them.

HABITAT: Found in the mountain zone. One of the most beautiful mountain flowers. Walkers descending through the Samaria Gorge can see them around the little chapel of Ayios Nikolaos towards the end of April. This plant is endemic to Crete and Karpathos.

PROPERTIES, USES: The flowers have a nauseating, rather unpleasant odour. Their flavour is insipid, caustic and bitter.

Nuns once used the roots to treat convulsions, epilepsy and even madness. An old botanical treatise states that, if we cover a madman with the plant while he is asleep, he will shortly awake and be completely well. According to Homer, the healing god Paeon, whose name is recorded on a clay tablet from Knossos, treated Pluto with the plant after he had been wounded by Herakles. From then on, it bore his name. Dioscurides strongly recommends 10-12 red seeds in wine for stomach pains, and the black seeds for nightmares. Pliny suggested the red seeds for blood circulation and black seeds to treat gynaecological conditions.

It is used in an infusion (50-60 g of roots in a litre of water) for intestinal pain, jaundice, conditions of the kidneys, bladder and stomach, and as a menstrual stimulant.

The plant was once gathered under a starry sky and hung over the shoulder, in order to ward off malignant illnesses and the evil eye.

P. clusii

PAPAVERACEAE
(Poppy family)

***Fumaria capreolata* L.**   **III-V**
Ramping fumitory

DESCRIPTION: An annual, up to 100 cm, smooth, blue-green, with climbing stems. Alternate leaves, 2-pinnately-lobed, with oblong or ovate margins, often toothed, which usually wrap around the plants alongside them by means of their extended leafstalks or even their leaflets, transformed +/- into tendrils. The inflorescence is a raceme of 10-30 flowers, white or pink. The flowers have a spur, do not exceed 10-14 mm, and consist of 2 sepals and 4 petals, of which the two lateral and the upper one bear dark red shiny spots. The fruits are round.
HABITAT: Cultivated soils, roadsides.
PROPERTIES, USES: In an infusion (30-50 g of the plant in one litre of water or wine), it is used for insomnia, conditions of the digestive tract, and even for skin conditions (shingles, scurvy, scrofula, elephantiasis, herpes and syphilis).

Glaucium flavum Crantz   IV-IX
Yellow horned poppy

DESCRIPTION: A biennial or perennial, up to 90 cm, grey-green, slightly downy, with a milky yellow juice. Leaves wrinkled to the touch, the lower ones pinnately-lobed with undulate margins, the upper ones smaller and periblastic. Flowers 60-90 cm, solitary, with 4 yellow petals and 2 sepals +/- downy. Capsule 15-30 cm, hairless, scythe-shaped, with residual stigmas forming two little horns at the tip.

HABITAT: Shingly, sandy and rocky beaches, abandoned villages.

PROPERTIES, USES: **WARNING! The root is poisonous!** Theophrastus considered the roots to be a very strong purgative and the leaves sufficient to remove ulcers from the eyes of sheep. Dioscurides recommended a tisane of the roots for sciatica, liver complaints and gonorrhoea.

Papaver argemone L.   IV-VI

DESCRIPTION: An annual or biennial, 15-30 cm, with coarse hairs that are very rough to the touch. Flowers 20-60 mm, often with a black blotch at the centre. The petals, which do not overlap, are red and slightly shiny, sometimes whitish. The stamens have violet or blackish threads. The capsule is very elongated, an inverted bell-shape, and normally covered with rows of coarse hairs.

HABITAT: Low and medium altitude.

PROPERTIES, USES: Mixed with the fodder of animals, it predisposes them to flatulence (distended stomach). The petals, in an infusion, seem to be soothing, sudorific, emollient and expectorant. **The fruit is poisonous!**

Papaver rhoeas L. III-V
Corn poppy

DESCRIPTION: An annual, up to 90 cm, covered in coarse hairs. Pinnately-lobed or 2-pinnately-lobed leaves, with toothed lobes, the middle lobe being larger. Flowers 70-100 mm, with 4 disc-shaped petals, a scarlet red in colour and often with a black blotch at the base. The anthers have blackish-blue threads. The capsule is rounded at the base, and smooth.

HABITAT: Fields and ploughed soil. Never absent from cornfields.

PROPERTIES, USES: Mixed in large quantity with animals' grazing material, it can cause poisoning or a propensity to flatulence (distended stomach).

The young plants (rosettes), mixed with other mountain greens, are cooked like spinach. This certainly constituted an excellent delicacy to the ancient Greeks.

The petals were once used mixed with tea (5-10 g to one litre of water) or in a syrup (2 spoonfuls, 3 times per day) as an expectorant. The petals – in an infusion (one pinch in a cup of hot water) – facilitate sleep.

WARNING! The fruits are clearly poisonous. In spring, whole fields are bathed in the red of these poppies. The Assyrians called the plant 'daughter of the fields', while the Greeks considered it the flower of Demeter, goddess of germination. According to Christian tradition, it sprang up from the blood of Christ

and for that reason acquired its red colour. Professor Sp. Marinatos said that it was used as a model for art in the Minoan period.

NOTE: ***Papaver somniferum* L.** (Opium poppy), with its crumpled, white, pink or also red petals, from which opium and heroin are produced elsewhere, is met rarely on Crete.

PHYTOLACCACEAE (Pokeweed family)

P. somniferum

Phytolacca americana L.   VI-IX
American pokeweed

DESCRIPTION: A small tree, 1-3 metres in height. Smooth stems, often reddish. Leaves 10-40 cm, ovate, stalked, with the edges slightly folded over. Inflorescence 10-15 cm, raceme-like, with small flowers (5 mm), white with 10 stamens. Blue-black berries, naked, glossy, round, slightly flattened.

HABITAT: Found at low altitude, in the centre and west of the island.

PROPERTIES, USES: Originally introduced from North America for its berries, which were used to colour wine. This prac-

tice is now prohibited. The leaves of this plant are edible and known as 'sweet spinach of Martinique'.

WARNING! All of the parts of this plant are poisonous to a greater or lesser degree, including the seeds! The roots are used in homeopathy. The fruit constitutes a violent purgative. The dried root is used to cleanse the lymphatic system and especially in glandular fever, tonsilitis, and mastitis

PLANTAGINACEAE
(Plantain family)

Plantago afra L. (= *Plantago psyllium*)
Branched plantain   **IV-VII**

DESCRIPTION: An annual, up to 40 cm, erect, with rich foliage and many glandular hairs. Leaves 3-8 cm, opposite, stalkless, linear to lanceolate with entire or lightly toothed margins. The flowers are distinctive, axillary, surrounded by bracts of the same size, and form dense spherical to ovoid spikes, on long peduncles. The corolla has ovate-lanceolate petals, acutely pointed at the tip, 2mm. The seeds are 2.5-5 mm, dark brownish-red in colour.
HABITAT: Uncultivated fields, areas of phrygana (garrigue).
PROPERTIES, USES: The seeds, because they contain viscous substances, are used as a purgative. Soothing collyria (eyewashes) are also made. The root and the leaves are styptic and healing. The plant is sold in pharmacies.
NOTE: *Plantago arenaria* **Wildest & Kit.** (= *Plantago indica*) differs from *Plantago afra* in that it is not at all glandular and has branches of the same length. Small birds simply cannot get enough of the seeds.

Plantago bellardii All.   **IV-VI**

DESCRIPTION: An annual plant with a low habit, 5-10 cm, with leaves which form a rosette, 1-5 mm in width, erect, linear-lanceolate, with three main veins, covered in soft hairs. 1-7 flowering stems, very woolly. Inflorescence 1-2 cm, dense, leafless.
HABITAT: On sandy and stony soils. Although common, it goes unnoticed.
PROPERTIES, USES: Styptic, healing, suitable for eyewashes.

Plantago lagopus L.   IV-V

DESCRIPTION: A biennial, 30-40 cm, with leaves up to 30 cm forming a basal rosette, lanceolate, sparsely dentate and with 3-7 veins. Rarely, a stem develops with alternate leaves. The flowering stems are fluted, 2-4 times longer than the leaves. Distinctive flowers, in dense, ovoid or round spikes, with 4 smooth, apiculate petals, 4 membranous sepals covered with long smooth hairs, and 4 stamens.

HABITAT: Uncultivated fields, meadows, roadsides.

PROPERTIES, USES: The young rosettes are eaten boiled as a salad.

NOTES: **Plantago lanceolata** L. (ribwort plantain) differs from the above in that it grows to a greater height. This is a plant used for animal feed which has the same properties as **Plantago major**. In an infusion, it is styptic, soothing, anti-inflammatory and an expectorant.

Plantago major L. (Greater plantain) is much larger than the two above-mentioned plants. It has enormous, outspreading basal leaves, ovate-elliptic and long-stalked, with 3-11 veins. Long peduncles rise up out of the centre of the rosette, bearing cylindrical spikes with very small greenish flowers that have a cup-shaped corolla with 4 lobes and 4 stamens. It grows at low altitude, in muddy soil and stagnant water.

According to Dioscurides, the plant was used to heal skin conditions (wounds, boils, anthrax, scrofula). Applied in the form of a compress of pounded, young leaves, it appears to be styptic, anti-diabetic, decongestant, healing and haemostatic. The pounded leaves, mixed up with Vaseline, are also used for haemorrhoids. A tisane (30 g to one litre of water) can assist the breathing, and can

Plantago lanceolata

also be used for eye washes and as a gargle. As a decoction - one spoonful of black seeds to one cup of scalding hot water - it is just what is needed for constipation.

The juice of the young, raw leaves soothes inflammations of the urinary tract and relieves a cough.

Plantago weldenii Rechenb. (= *Plantago coronopus L. ssp. commutata*)   IV-VII
Buck's-horn plantain

Plantago major

DESCRIPTION: An annual or biennial with numerous, arrow-like flowering stems, 4-25 cm. Basal rosette with 'nipped' leaves, somewhat resembling the antlers of a stag. The flower has membranous margins, and is found in the axils of the bracts; the corolla is also membranous.

HABITAT: Sandy and stony locations near the sea.

PROPERTIES, USES: A diuretic, used for lithiasis of the kidneys and gall bladder (100 g in one litre of water, brought to boiling). All of the *Plantago* are haemostatic. Their seeds are used in the preparation of collyria (eye-washes).

PLATANACEAE (Plane family)

Platanus orientalis L.   IV
Oriental plane

DESCRIPTION: A deciduous tree up to 30 metres in height, with a marbled bark and out-spreading branches. The foliage is green in summer. Large leaves, palmate, alternate, with 5-7 deeply divided lobes, entire or toothed, on a long stalk flattened at the base. The female flowers are reddish-purple. Spherical fruits, hanging in groups of 3-4 on the same stalk.

HABITAT: Banks of rivers and streams, damp places. Often planted for its shade.

PROPERTIES, USES: The plane is the tree that offers the best shade, announcing from afar to the thirsty traveller that he will find the cooling spring and hospitable rest he seeks beneath its branches. For this very reason, the people of antiquity considered the tree to be a gift of the gods and revered it.

One of the largest plane trees is located in the square of the village of Krasi. 16 people, holding each other by the hands, cannot encircle its huge trunk. Actually, before the in-filling of

square, 30 people were required. Imagine – its root, which is hollow, was once used as a café consisting of three little tables and their chairs. German scientists reckon that the tree is about 2000 years old. It is certainly common knowledge that some plane trees readily survive for a thousand years. When boiled, the bark and

leaves have antiseptic and haemostatic properties, and are used for frostbite, burns and inflammations of the eyes. The evergreen plane tree, **var. creticus**, is found only on Crete, where 29 such trees have been counted. According to mythology, Zeus, transformed into a bull, abducted the beautiful princess Europa from Phoenicia and slept with her in the shade of a plane tree at Gortys. The divine union was followed by the birth of Minos, the future king who would found the Cretan kingdom. From that time on, this sacred tree no longer shed its leaves. Later, in order to immortalize the event, Gortys minted coins with the sacred plane tree depicted on one side.

var. creticus

PLUMBAGINACEAE
(Sea lavender family)

Acantholimon ulicinum (Willd. Ex Schultes) Boiss. (= *Acantholimon androsaceum*)   V-VIII

DESCRIPTION: A spiny plant, dense, hummock-shaped. Dense foliage, needle-like, 10-20 mm. Short flowering stems with purple or pink flowers and tubular calyx, membranous, remaining on the plant after the petals have fallen.

HABITAT: Found in the alpine and sub-alpine zone.

PROPERTIES, USES: When in full flower, the plants present a pleasing sight on the mountainside. Some people believe that the plant can treat cancer (!).

Limonium sinuatum (L.) Miller

Winged sea lavender   **IV-VIII**

DESCRIPTION: A perennial up to 40 cm, with coarse hairs. Basal rosette with leaves 3-15 cm, pinnately-divided. Erect, fluted stems. Compact inflorescence, umbel-like. Hermaphrodite flowers, blue-violet. Calyx 10-14 mm, funnel-shaped. Small yellowish-white corolla.
HABITAT: Sandy and stony shores, salty soils.
PROPERTIES, USES: A decorative, unassuming plant. The flower-bearing stems are dried and used in the preparation of bouquets. The young stems, and above all the rosettes, are eaten boiled in a salad, either alone or with other greens. The water in which they are boiled is an excellent drink.

POLYGONACEAE (Dock family)

Polygonum aviculare L.   **VI-X**
Knotweed

DESCRIPTION: An annual, prostrate, outspreading, with silver sheathing at the joints. Lanceolate leaves, those of the main stem being larger. Pink or white flowers, in groups of 1-6, in the upper leaf axils. Petals remain after the fruit has been produced.
HABITAT: Seashores, roadsides, up to the sub-alpine zone.
PROPERTIES, USES: For animal feed. The seeds are enticing to small birds; they are emetic and purgative. The whole plant is styptic, healing and haemostatic. In an infusion, it is used for dropsy and bowel pain.

Polygonum equisitiforme Sm.   IV-VI
Hogweed sp.

DESCRIPTION: A perennial, up to 100 cm, with a thick, woody rhizome. The leaves are alternate, stalkless, and elliptic, with wrinkled sheathing at the joints. Small pink or white flowers, in groups of 2-3 in the leaf axils, with 5 elliptic petals (4 mm), 6-8 stamens and 2 styles. The fruit – a nut – is a glossy brown in colour.
HABITAT: Roadsides.
PROPERTIES, USES: A weed. On Crete, a tisane or concoction made from the plant is used as a compress or as a liquid embrocation to stop hair loss.
Every variety of **Polygonum** has pharmaceutical properties, especially useful for mouth ulcers (aphtha) and inflammation of the gums.

Polygonum idaeum* Hayek   V-VI

DESCRIPTION: A perennial with a woody root, ovate-elliptic leaves and few whitish flowers. It is grazed to such a degree that it does not manage to grow to any height but is always prostrate, almost without stems.
HABITAT: Grows on Mt. Psiloritis (at Nida), Mt. Dikti, and in the White Mountains (Volakias).
PROPERTIES, USES: The Greek popular name 'nevrida' derives from the little deer and wild goats which were called 'nevri'.
Folk medicine uses the plant, pounded, in a plaster with healing and analgesic properties. They say that the animals which eat it acquire gilded teeth (!) – at least this was mentioned by the English pilgrim Gerome Dandini (1599).

Polygonum maritimum L.   IV-VIII
Sea knotgrass

DESCRIPTION: A perennial, up to 50 cm. Creeping, with basal woody shoots. Leaves up to 2.5 cm, persistent, greyish, ovate to lanceolate, with revolute margins. Double sheathing on the joints, the second sheath with much fluting. Flowers 3-4 mm, pink or whitish, in groups of 1-4, in the leaf axils. The fruit is a nut, glossy brown in colour.
HABITAT: Found on sand, near to beaches.
PROPERTIES: The word *Polygonum* refers to the many 'knees' (joints or nodes) in the stems.
A tisane of the roots and dried leaves treats diarrhoea and dysentery. The same liquid can be used to clean wounds and make poultices which soothe burns and skin irritations.

Rumex conglomeratus Murray   V-VIII
Clustered dock

DESCRIPTION: A perennial, reproducing through nodes which are produced by the underground stem. The stem is 30-100 cm, erect, branching. Leaves undulate at the margins. Flowers greenish or reddish, in groups, mostly in a leaf axil, on a jointed peduncle.
HABITAT: Found on shaded and wet soils.
PROPERTIES, USES: The young shoots are cooked, like spinach, along with other greens. The leaves are used as a wrapping in dolmades. They are also – since they contain sulphur - used for haemorrhoids and abcesses.
Before the flowers form, the plant constitutes a treat for grazing animals.

Rumex acetosella L.
Dock

DESCRIPTION: A perennial, 10-30 cm. Lanceolate to sagittate leaves, the lower edges of which are outspread or turned upwards. Spike of male flowers on one plant, and of female flowers on the other. Acid, tart flavour.

HABITAT: Roadsides, dry meadows, sandy fields, non-calcareous locations.

PROPERTIES, USES: The acid flavour differentiates it from other plants. **The plant is slightly poisonous!** Even though gourmets enjoy it, **certain others who suffer from arthritis, rheumatism, uric arthritis, kidney problems and problems of the bladder should not even attempt to sample it.**

It is prescribed for those who have stomach problems, haemorrhoids, mouth and pharynx ulcers, suffer from anorexia, or from high fever. In a poultice, it treats skin conditions such as acne and herpes.

PORTULACEAE family

Portulaca oleracea L.   **V-XI**
Purslane

DESCRIPTION: An annual, branching, outspreading. Oblong to obovate leaves, fleshy, smooth, the lower ones opposite, the upper ones alternate. Small flowers, yellow, opening in the morning, with five obovate petals and 2 sepals. Ovoid fruits, filled with thousands of tiny, black, shiny seeds.

HABITAT: Cultivated fields, at low altitude.
PROPERTIES, USES: This is a vegetable which suits everyone - a source of vitamins, without insects or diseases. The leaves are normally eaten raw, in salads, and are refreshing and cooling; when cooked like spinach, they have a delicate flavour.

In antiquity the plant was well-known and certainly used for a number of complaints. Dioscurides recommended it for burns and for stomach ulcers, conditions of the urinary tract and gall bladder, and even for the eyes. Today, it is considered to be a diuretic, useful in lithiasis of the gall bladder, and even an aphrodisiac. A decoction, based on the seeds boiled in milk, helps reduce blood pressure, and soothe the nerves…and helps to bring back that desirable, mental tranquility which allows us to enjoy all the delights of love-making!

PRIMULACEAE
(Primrose family)

Anagallis arvensis L.   VI-IX
Pimpernel

DESCRIPTION: An annual which becomes perennial when it is cultivated at higher altitudes. Dark green leaves, ovate-oblong, +/- acute at the tip. Red, pink or blue flowers, on stalks either shorter than or the same length as, the leaves. Corolla with finely toothed lobes. Ovoid fruits, not at all shiny, with 6-10 flutes.
HABITAT: Cultivated fields, up to the mountain zone.
PROPERTIES, USES: A bitter plant, healing and styptic. It was once used to treat tuberculosis and to remove splinters.
WARNING! The seeds are very poisonous to birds! The name Anagallis derives from the Greek verb meaning 'to laugh with the soul'. In antiquity, the property of causing laughter was attributed to it.

A. arvensis

Cyclamen creticum* Hilderbr.   III-V

Cretan sowbread

DESCRIPTION: A perennial plant up to 20 cm, with an underground tube-like rhizome. The leaves are produced in spring, before the flowers, and resemble those of ivy, being completely cordate with angular margins. The flowers are solitary, white, sometimes slightly pinkish, on hairless stalks, with a corolla 1.5 – 2.5 cm, a funnel-shaped calyx, a globular fruit capsule and coiled, fruit-bearing stem.

HABITAT: In areas of maquis and in the shade of forest trees (shade-loving).

PROPERTIES, USES: **Abandoned by medicine and classified among the poisonous and toxic plants.**

Warriors used to rub it on their arrows to make them deadly. According to Dioscurides its roots, in a decoction made with wine, constituted a strong antidote for deadly poisons. It was used to accelerate delivery at the moment of childbirth, and also to make love philtres.

NOTE: The cultivated cyclamen is a variety of **C. persicum**.

Cyclamen graecum Link   IX-XII
Greek sowbread

DESCRIPTION: A perennial with huge
spherical or slightly flattened tubers up to 25
cm in diameter, and a few self-sowing roots.
Leaves 4-10 cm, cordate, reddish on the
underside and dark green with silver patterns
on the surface, appearing after the flowers.
Curved, whitish-pink corolla with 5 petals
20 x 10 mm, with auricles and purple spots
at the base (neck). Fruit-bearing stem coiled
from the base or from the mid-point.

HABITAT: In stony places in the mountain-
ous and semi-mountainous zone.

PROPERTIES, USES: the ancient Greeks
called it 'tortoise' because of the resemblance
of the tubers to tortoises.

Dangerous to Man! But not, however, to
pigs which seem to enjoy its tubers.

Incredibly beautiful, amongst the grey shades
of autumn! Can be cultivated for decoration.

NOTE: *Cyclamen hederifolium* **Aiton** has
recently been discovered in western Crete.

C. graecum

Lysimachia serpyllifolia Schreiber
V-VI

DESCRIPTION: A plant with numerous perennial roots. Stems up to 40 cm, prostrate and throwing out new roots. Flowers opposite, stalkless, broadly ovate, cordate at the base. Flowers 10 mm, small, star-like, yellow, solitary in the leaf axils, on a long stalk. The fruit is a glistening red berry.

HABITAT: Up to the mountain zone.

PROPERTIES, USES: The almost wondrous properties (primarily haemostatic) which were once ascribed to lysimachia have not been verified by more recent research.

The name *Lysimachia* was given to the plant by Lysimachus, the very powerful lord of Thrace and general of Alexander the Great who was also a physician and probably the first to discover the plant and the healing virtues once assigned to it. In Greek, the verb 'lysimachein' means 'to stop the battle'. Perhaps he was the first to use it to staunch the bleeding from wounds suffered by his soldiers in battle.

NOTE: *Lysimachia serpyllifolia* is only one species of the genus *Lysmachia*!

Primula vulgaris Hudson   III-IV
Primrose

DESCRIPTION: A perennial, low-growing, and hairy. Rosettes with entire leaves, ovate, whitish green, with pronounced veins forming a network. Long flower stems, hairy and bearing only one flower 20-30 mm. Corolla with 5 petals, whitish-yellow, white or pinkish-violet, but with a darker base.

HABITAT: Found in damp locations and deciduous forests in the mountains of western Crete.

PROPERTIES, USES: A nectar plant. The gods used it together with other flowers to make their festive garlands. Today, it is cultivated for decoration. In some countries the flower is used as a political symbol and a means of rapprochement.

The flowers are dried in the shade. The petals are soothing in a case of over-exertion, styptic and sudorific. It can also be used for flu-like colds which are accompanied by headaches and nasal catarrh. The roots, in an infusion, are an expectorant when there is

mucous, phlegm and persistant coughing; in compresses, they relieve painful joints, arthritis and rheumatism.

WARNING! Use of the plant is prohibited to pregnant women and to those sensitive to aspirin.

Samolus valerandi L.   IV-VIII
Brookweed

DESCRIPTION: A perennial, 20-40 cm in height, smooth, very slightly branching, with a hollow stem. Basal rosette of leaves which are whitish-green, ovate, those of the stem being smaller and alternate. Flowers very small, 5 mm, white, with 5 petals joined up to the mid-point, arranged in panicles. Spherical fruits.

HABITAT: Damp locations and water courses.

PROPERTIES, USES: Although they are slightly bitter, the leaves can be eaten in a salad. Animals gorge themselves on them. The plant is healing, appetite-stimulating and antiscorbutic.

PUNICACEAE
(Pomegranate family)

Punica granatum L.   IV-VI
Pomegranate

DESCRIPTION: A small tree, 2-4 metres in height, smooth, usually spiny. The leaves are opposite, often occurring in threes, entire, ovate to lanceolate, and shiny. Flowers funnel-shaped, with petals of a shiny red colour and calyx that is also red, fleshy and five-lobed. The fruit is brownish red, has the shape of an apple with a thick covering, and consists of numerous prismatic, juicy pink grains with a glassy appearance, each one containing a small seed. The grains have a sweet or tart flavour and are divided among small compartments between membrane-like diaphragms which are bitter to the taste. At the opposite end of the fruit stalk there is something resembling a diadem or little crown, which is the remnant of the sepals of the calyx

HABITAT: Of Asiatic origin, the pomegranate has been cultivated in Crete since

very early times. It is sometimes self-sowing along the banks of streams, in ditches and ravines.

PROPERTIES, USES: The best pomegranates grew in Carthage, and for this reason acquired their Latin name 'punica', meaning Punic or Carthaginian.

Hades charmed Persephone with the help of a pomegranate, and managed to kidnap her. Dedicated to Hera, protectoress of marriage, the pomegranate was considered a symbol of love and fertility; it was this fruit, not an apple, that Paris gave to Aphrodite.

Refreshing drinks and syrups are made from its juice. It is used in the preparation of kolyva (seeds and grains offered to the Dead) and wines. In an infusion, the bark was once used as a vermifuge to treat tapeworms and amoeba. The tisane of raw flowers was used as a rinse in cases of gonorrhoea, discharge, haemorrhage, remittent fevers and ulcerative tonsillitis. The flowers and the bark, rich in tannins, are used in leather-tanning and paint manufacture. They also have styptic and tonic properties. The juice is refreshing and helps to maintain lucidity of the mind. An ointment is used against wrinkles and freckles. The seeds of the pomegranate are eaten raw, either alone or with the addition of sugar and rum, which makes them more digestible. In Greece, we prefer to eat them with tsikoudia (raki), especially during the period in which we set up our stills for the distillation of the spirit.

RAFFLESIACEAE (Rafflesia family)

Cytinus hypocistis L.   IV-VI
Cytinus

DESCRIPTION: A perennial, 4-10 cm, growing as a parasite on **Cistus**, where it develops on the root system and produces its own stems which are fleshy and look like little nests. Scale-like bracts for leaves, yellowish-orange or carmine red surrounding 5-10 flowers, yellow and shiny, up to 18 mm. Male flowers at the centre, female flowers on the periphery. The fruit is a berry with a soft texture which bears the residual calyx.

PROPERTIES, USES: The juice of **Cytinus** was recommended by Dioscurides for stomach complaints, and by the pupils of Hippocrates to help mothers-to-be to give birth. Its styptic juice is used in cases of dysentery and haemorrhage.

NOTE: **Cytinus ruber (Fourr.) Kamarov**. has white or whitish-pink flowers and is a parasite on the varieties of Cistus which have pink flowers.

RANUNCULACEAE
(Buttercup family)

Adonis microcarpa DC. ssp. cretica (Huth.) Vierh. (= *Adonis aestivalis*)

Yellow pheasant's eye   III-V

A. ssp. microcarpa

DESCRIPTION: An annual, up to 40 cm, with an erect stem, branching. Stalked leaves, composite (three or four times pinnately-divided), with very narrow, thread-like leaflets. Flowers 1.5 cm, small, solitary, with 5-10 elliptic petals, glossy and normally red, twice as long as the five ovate sepals. The fruit consists of numerous nuts with a short spur.

HABITAT: Found at low and medium altitude.

PROPERTIES, USES: When Adonis, a beautiful youth under the protection of Aphrodite, was mortally wounded by a wild boar, the drops of his blood which fell on the ground gave life to the same number of plants which bear his name. The one-day life of the flower symbolises the short duration of youth. **A poisonous plant! It has heart-stimulating properties and must only be used under the supervision of a doctor.**

NOTE: The sub-species **Adonis microcarpa ssp. microcarpa** mostly has yellow flowers.

A. ssp. cretica

Anemone coronaria L.   XII-IV

Crown or poppy anemone

DESCRIPTION: An anuual, up to 45 cm. Basal leaves tripartite, stalked, with lobed leaflets. Stem with one flower surrounded by three bract-like, whorled leaves, torn into narrow strips. Flowers 3.5-6.5 cm in diameter, with 5-8 elliptic petals which may be red, blue, violet, cream or white in colour, without sepals. The stamens are blue.

HABITAT: Cultivated fields and areas of phrygana (garrigue).

PROPERTIES, USES: The ancient Greeks believed that the wind (anemos) had a great erotic influence on Mankind; they also believed that the wind caused these flowers to open – hence their name. According to mythology, the flowers were born from the blood of Adonis and Aphrodite; still others asserted that they originated from the tears of Persephone or those of her mother, Demeter.

WARNING! All of the anemones, in the raw state as they grow in the meadows, are poisonous and dangerous to animals. Their toxic substance expires on desiccation.

According to Dioscurides, the juice from the

roots, inhaled, cleanses the brain. In desiccated form, it is beneficial for psychoneurotic conditions and neuralgia; it brings light sleep to those suffering from insomnia, relieves

Anemone coronaria

period pains and stops a cough in cases of bronchial pneumonia.

Many people gather anemones to decorate their homes.

Delphinium staphisagria L.　　V-VII
Larkspur sp.

DESCRIPTION: An annual or biennial plant, 30-100 cm in height, erect, without branching, and with protruding hairs. Palmately-lobed leaves with lobes that are elliptic, acutely pointed at the tip, lanceolate or trilobate. Raceme-like inflorescences; dark blue to pink flowers with 5 elliptic petals up to 2 cm, resembling sepals, of which one has a spur. The other four petals are located at the centre and are nectar-bearing. Two of them – the upper ones – also end in a linked spur which inserts into the spur of the so-called sepal. Numerous stamens. Fruit consisting of three sacks with very few seeds.

HABITAT: Found in areas of maquis and cultivated fields, at low and medium altitude, especially in the south of the island.

PROPERTIES, USES: **WARNING! A poisonous plant, and very dangerous! In particular its seeds act as a violent poison on the heart, respiratory and digestive systems**. Dioscurides mentions it and calls it 'flea killer'. Not long ago its seeds were used, pounded in oil, as an insecticide against fleas, canker, and various parasitic insects in general. The flowers are beautiful!

Nigella arvensis L. *ssp. brevifolia Strid* (= *Nigella cretica*)   IV-V
Cretan love-in-a-mist

DESCRIPTION: An annual, up to 40 cm, delicate. Leaves of the stem have extended lobes or are entire. Small flowers, greenish-blue, with ovate, fringed petals at the base, ending in 'nails'. Fruit consisting of 5 little fruits with beak-like tips, joined up to the middle.

HABITAT: Found in areas of phrygana (garrigue) and barren fields, at low altitude.

PROPERTIES, USES: The seeds are used as a flavouring in breadmaking. As an infusion the plant is a menstrual stimulant and stimulates milk secretion.

Nigella damascena L.   IV-V
Love-in-a-mist; Devil-in-a-bush

DESCRIPTION: An elegant, annual plant, up to 50 cm, erect, hairless, very slightly branching. Leaves divided into narrow, acutely tipped threads. Flowers 1.5-3cm in diameter, large, blue-azure, surrounded by a hypanth with hair-like bracts. Corolla with 5 elliptic petals on a short stalk, numerous stamens and an ovary with 5 styles. The fruit is a globular capsule, surrounded by bracts.

HABITAT: Fields under cultivation or set aside.

PROPERTIES, USES: Often cultivated for decoration because of its beautiful flowers. The seeds, crushed, are used to induce sneezing! As an infusion in wine, they are tonic, energizing and diuretic, **but great care must be taken, because this is a dangerous, poisonous drug.**

The ranunculi (*Ranunculus asiaticus* and *creticus*) have large, flamboyant flowers and can be used as decorative plants.

R. asiaticus

R. asiaticus

R. asiaticus

R. creticus

213

Ranunculus ficaria ssp. ficariiformis
(F. Schultz) Rouy & Fouc.   **II-IV**
Lesser celandine
DESCRIPTION: A perennial, low-growing, smooth, vigorous, with slightly fleshy leaves that are dark green, broadly ovate and cordate at the base, +/- toothed. Roots with bulbs in the shape of a fig. Short stems, with large flowers up to 40 mm in diameter, with 8-12 ovate petals of a glossy yellow colour, whitening over the course of time, and 3 greenish-white sepals.

HABITAT: Found in damp places, gardens and fields.

PROPERTIES, USES: The tender young leaves are eaten in a salad or on buttered slices of bread. **With the course of time, the leaves become poisonous and cannot be eaten unless they have been boiled in a large quantity of water.**

The roots, in a tea (50 g to one litre of water) can be used in cases of haemorrhoids. The

bulbs, when they have been boiled in a little water and melted butter drizzled over them, constitute a dish of rare and fine delicacy!

For Galen, the plant dissolved the toughest of callouses and softened very hard nails!

This is one of the first flowers to announce the arrival of spring.

Ranunculus muricatus L.　　　　III-V
Buttercup sp.

DESCRIPTION: An annual, up to 50 cm, branching and smooth. Lower leaves reniform, very toothed, trilobate, with a large stalk; upper leaves oblong with a short stalk. Small flowers, up to 15 mm in diameter, with 5 whitish-yellow petals, slightly larger than the 5 sepals. Fruit glossy, like a nut, with many angular protrusions.

HABITAT: Damp locations, ditches, areas under cultivation.

PROPERTIES, USES: **WARNING! Poisonous to fatal! Poisoning, according to Pausania, announces itself with nervous symptoms, continues with sardonic laughter and ends in a coma and death!**

Reseda lutea L.   III-V
Wild mignonette

DESCRIPTION: An annual or perennial, 20-70 cm. Erect stems, branching, with alternate leaves, unstalked, the lower ones entire, the upper ones pinnate. Long, terminal spikes of numerous small flowers, yellow-green, which have 6 sepals, 7 deeply divided petals, 9 stamens with reddish anthers and a pistil with five styles. The fruit, a bloated capsule, breaks open to expel a large number of small black seeds.

HABITAT: Found on slopes, in areas of scrub, in barren fields, on roadsides, at low and medium altitude.

R. alba

PROPERTIES, USES: Once used as a healing, diuretic and sudorific plant.

If its root is pounded, it emits an odour similar to that of the radish. The young plant, before it begins to flower, is eaten boiled in a salad along with other mountain greens.

A yellow colouring (luteolin) is extracted from the plant and used in the dyeing of silk.

NOTE: Three other species are found on Crete: *R. alba* (White mignonette), *R. luteola* and *R. odorata*. The latter is mostly found on Gavdos.

Crataegus azarolus L.   IV-V
Mediterranean medlar

DESCRIPTION: A small deciduous tree up to 12 metres in height, slightly thorny. The new branches each year are downy-felty on the surface. Leaves have 3-5 lobes, cuneate at the base. The lateral leaves are dentate or ciliate, and sickle-shaped. Flowers white or pink, on a downy stalk. The berries are spherical, edible, orange in colour, with 1-5 pips.

HABITAT: Up to the mountain zone, along fences, roadsides, in agricultural areas.

PROPERTIES, USES: The plant is found in many countries, but its origin is pure Cretan. Its longevity is great, and its lifespan can easily exceed 600 years.

The fruits are eaten raw, in compote or as a jelly. According to Dioscurides, the pounded roots help to withdraw thorns and splinters. They were also ascribed the ability to induce abortion (!)

Generally speaking, crataegus in its many species constitutes the model among shrubs which play a great role in healing the wounds of nature. In this function it is supported by the wild roses, honeysuckles, buckthorns and cypresses (***Rosaceae, Caprifoliaceae, Rhamnaceae, Cupressaceae***) which all together form an ideal biotope, impenetrable to grazing animals and protected from extreme cold, the wind and dampness – i.e. a biotope suitable for the planting and spread of real trees such as the oaks. As it grows, the crataegus tree provides shade unsuited to those spiny plants which dry out, but it will in some other way, for other plants, fulfill the role of a 'wet-nurse'.

In an infusion, the fruits are used to treat diarrhoea; the leaves – also in an infusion, 10 g to every litre of water – are used to treat weakness of the heart and arteriosclerosis. The flowers are also used as a heart tonic; they seem to improve the circulation of the coronary arteries, thus reducing the danger of cardialgia and maintaining arterial pressure at physiological levels.

217

The flowers, dried in the shade, are used in a soothing tea, which is aphrodisiac and diuretic, effective against obesity.

The young leaves are eaten raw in a salad or cooked like spinach.

All those who feel tired, sleep badly, suffer from dizziness, tachycardia, depression, nervousness, buzzing in the ears and strain, all those who want to avoid cholesterol and arteriosclerosis, should drink a cup of crataegus per day, recommends M. Messegué.

NOTE: *Crateagus monogyna* **Jacq**. (Hawthorn) with its small, brownish-red fruits, is also found on Crete in rocky, mountain locations.

C. monogyna

Potentilla reptans L.　　　V-VII
Cinquefoil

DESCRIPTION: A perennial, worthy of note for its creeping stems which throw out roots and can reach to 1 metre in length. Digitate leaves with 5-7 leaflets, obovate to oblong, dentate; entire lateral leaflets. Flowers 17-25 mm, solitary, yellow, with 5 petals, 5 sepals and 5 bracts which form a hypanth.

HABITAT: Found at low altitude, in damp locations, on the banks of streams.

PROPERTIES, USES: The roots have great styptic and healing properties. They are mostly used to treat diarrhoea, dysentery and haemorrhoids.

As a gargle, the dried roots, crushed (20 g in one litre of water) strengthen the gums and treat mouth ulcers. The plant is also a febrifuge.

NOTE: *Potentilla speciosa* **Willd**. has whitish-yellow flowers and grows at high altitude, often on rocks (Gingilos).

P. speciosa

Prunus armeniaca L.   **IV-V**
Apricot

DESCRIPTION: A large deciduous tree, up to 15 metres, with large leaves, ovate, almost round, acute and with toothed edges. 5-part flower, white or pink, stalkless, appearing before the leaves. Fruits +/- round, of different sizes but in yellow shades.

HABITAT: A cultivated tree, originating from central Asia. Brought to the Greek area apparently around the 1st century BC. Imported to Western Europe by the Romans and Arabs.

PROPERTIES: Expectorant, antitussant, purgative, rich in vitamins A and B. Good for children, those suffering from anaemia, and all those who suffer from disorders of the ears and eyes.

A compote of apricots is an excellent treatment for rheumatism. **However, those who suffer from stomach or liver disorders should avoid eating it**.

colic, coughs, diarrhoea and to treat the presence of uric acid in the blood.

The reddish wood of the tree with its fine graining is used in veneering.

Prunus avium L.   **IV-V**
Cherry

DESCRIPTION: A large, conspicuous tree, 10-20 metres in height, with horizontal branches, obovate-oblong to ellipsoid leaves, acutel and dentate, and white flowers forming a stalkless bouquet (umbel). The fruit, sweet cherries, have a variety of shapes and colours.

HABITAT: Cultivated. Imported into Europe by the Roman general Lucullus (117-56 BC).

PROPERTIES, USES: In a beverage, the cherry, and in particular the stalk of the fruit, is a diuretic. It is beneficial to the eyes (contains vitamin A). It can be used for kidney

Prunus dulcis (Miller) D.A.   II-IV
Almond

DESCRIPTION: A deciduous tree. It flowers before the appearance of the leaves, which are lanceolate, toothed, and stalked. The flowers are impressive, white, and fragrant. The exocarp is not fleshy like that of other fruits with stones, but a husk that is grey-green in colour and covered in fine down which contains, enclosed within a woody shell (the almond), 1 or 2 seeds with a white flesh that is sweet or bitter, according to the variety.

HABITAT: Cultivated. A typical Mediterranean tree, most probably a native of Asia Minor, which was taken to the other Mediterranean countries by the Greeks and Romans.

PROPERTIES, USES: The flowers and the green pericarp of the almonds stimulate the function of the stomach and calm asthma and a cough. The bark of the tree is also said to be vermifuge, febrifuge and diuretic. Orgeat, a substance useful to cardiac sufferers, is produced from shelled almonds.
The wood is heavy and hard, suitable for fine woodworking.

Prunus prostrata (Labill.) Ser.   V-VI
Prostrate cherry

DESCRIPTION: A spreading bush, low-growing, up to 1 metre in height. Oblong-linear, elliptic or roundish leaves, stalked with needle-like lateral leaflets. Flowers reddish-pink, small, almost stalkless. Very small, spherical fruit.

HABITAT: Found on dry, limestone rocks or in stony locations in the sub-alpine and alpine zone.

PROPERTIES, USES: Pleasant to eat.

Prunus spinosa L.   III-IV
Sloe, Blackthorn

DESCRIPTION: A small, deciduous tree, thorny, with black branches. Obovate to ellipsoid, dentate leaves. White flowers in dense clusters, appearing before the leaves. The fruits are round berries, blue-black in colour, tart to the taste before ripening and even afterwards quite bitter.
HABITAT: Found on the edges of fields, near streams, and generally in damp places.
PROPERTIES, USES: The flowers, in an infusion, cleanse the system, treat stomach cramps, colics, coughs, respiratory conditions and gonorrhoea in women. The fruits cause contraction of the blood vessels and strengthen the muscular spasms of the bowels and the urinary tract. For this reason they are recommended for diarrhoea and for incontinency. The bark is a febrifuge.

cause poisoning due to the prussic acid they contain.

Prunus webbii (Spach) Vierh.   I-IV
Wild almond

DESCRIPTION: A much-branching thorny bush up to 1.5 metres in height, with linear-oblong leaves. Flowers up to 20 mm, dark pink, single or in pairs. The fruit is a greenish almond, hairy.
HABITAT: At low and medium altitude.
PROPERTIES, USES: In antiquity, wild almonds, served with honey, were considered an excellent treat and a choice confection. They are antispasmodic. In a milky solution, they have beneficial results where respiratory conditions and painful periods are concerned. They are also used for osteomyelitis (tuberculosis of the bones) and for diabetes.
WARNING! Never eat more than 5 wild almonds at any one time, because they can

Pyrus cydonia Miller   IV-V
Quince

DESCRIPTION: A small, deciduous tree with slightly twisted trunk and branches. Leaves large, ovate, alternate, entire, whitish-woolly on the underside and green on the upper surface. Large solitary flowers, white or pink, with 5 petals and a large yellow fruit in a variety of shapes, at first woolly and then smooth, with numerous black seeds. Tough flesh, tart and only moderately sweet, with a pleasing aroma.

HABITAT: Originates from the Caucusus, mainly from regions of eastern Turkey, northern Iran and northern Iraq. It is both cultivated and self-sowing. Solitary trees usually found on the edges of fields where there is dampness, or near to streams. There are no systematically cultivated groves.

PROPERTIES, USES: The quince is eaten cooked or raw. It is used in the preparation of jams, compote, jelly and 'spoon sweets'.

The fruits and the seeds have been designated as healing and styptic for the gastrointestinal tract. The plant is an excellent tonic, recommended after invasive surgery. In a plaster, it is used for haemorrhoids and prolapse of the large intestine. The seeds, roasted, are used for herpes.

In an infusion, it is recommended for dysentery, sluggishness of the digestive system, uterine haemorrhage, inflamed haemorrhoids, kidney and gall-bladder complaints, and also even for inflammations of the respiratory system.

In a decoction (5 g to 100 g of water), the leaves are used for insomnia, neurasthenia, tachycardia, coughing spasms and whooping cough.

The hard wood of the quince, which does

not rot, is used in fine woodworking and in wood-turning. The plant is often used as a parent stock for the grafting of apple or pear.

Pyrus spinosa L. (= *Pyrus amygdali- formis* Villars) III-V
Almond-leaved pear

DESCRIPTION: A small, deciduous tree up to 6 metres in height. The branches are often thorny at the tips. Leaves are linear, lanceolate or obovate, initially hairy. Inflorescence an umbel of 8-12 flowers with 5 sepals and 5 white, elliptic petals. Fruits 2-3 cm, yellowish, almost spherical, and edible in October-November.

HABITAT: Rocky locations, thickets, thin forest, up to the mountain zone.

PROPERTIES, USES: A tree known from very early times. For the inhabitants of Argos it was a substitute for bread. The fresh leaves and its fruit, chewed or in an infusion, are used as a poultice for snake or scorpion bite. Today, it is used as a root-stock for the cultivated pear.

Rosa canina L.   IV-V
Dog rose

DESCRIPTION: A deciduous plant up to 3 metres in height, with a variety of forms. Outspreading stems with curved thorns. Pinnate leaves with 3-7 leaflets, 15-40 mm, obovate or elliptic, dentate, and smooth. Flowers 45-50 mm, pink or white with freely projecting styles, 5 petals and 5 sepals (2 of the latter have acutely pointed, entire tips while the other 3 have narrow lobes), which fall shortly before the ripening of the fruits – smooth red berries 12-20 mm, bottle-shaped. It is said that the leaves, when crushed, give off a sweet fragrance of apple compote.

HABITAT: Along fences, in thickets up to the mountain zone.

PROPERTIES, USES: According to mythology, the rose sprang from the blood of Aphrodite. The plant was called 'dog rose', because in olden times its roots were used to treat mad dogs. According to Pliny, the root acted against hydrophobia, which was transmitted by the rabies virus, and brought healing.

It is an antiscorbutic plant, containing large quantities of vitamin C (3 berries have the same amount as one whole orange), and is a vermifuge and styptic. In a tea (50-60 g to a litre of water) it soothes skin inflammations and relieves chronic eye conditions. The fruits are used for the preparation of tea, syrups, sweet liqueurs and jams. Rose liqueur is recommended as a fortifier for the elderly. There is nothing better for the daily care of our skin, the cleansing of the face and the prevention of the appearance of wrinkles, than rosewater. A handful of petals in our bath water can help to ward off many arthritic and rheumatic problems.

The plant is used as a root-stock for the grafting of a large number of varieties of cultivated roses.

NOTE: The species **R. agrestis, R. dumalis, R. heckeliana, R. pulverulenta** and **R. sempervirens** are also found on Crete.

Rubus sanctus Schreb. (=Rubus ulmifolius)
Blackberry   **V-VI**

DESCRIPTION: A perennial bush, with many bow-like angular stems, smooth or downy, which put out roots in the autumn. They bear large thorns, straight or curved on a wide base. The leaves have 3-5 leaflets, toothed, whitish, and downy on the underside. Branching inflorescences. Corolla with 5 pink petals. The fruits are aggregate, consisting of numerous small berries and little hairs. They ripen in autumn, becoming black and shiny, and are juicy and delicious.
HABITAT: Found at low and medium altitude, in ditches, torrent-beds, on roadsides, and along fences.
PROPERTIES, USES: The leaves are styptic, and used in cases of anaemia and diarrhoea. In an infusion, they bring relief to pregnant women, especially at the time of childbirth, regulate secretions and the function of the glands, help to maintain body weight and good respiratory condition. The leaves and the tips of the stems, in an infusion, are prescribed for heart conditions and for sugar diabetes (90-100 g to 1 litre of water).
The fruits are used to make refreshing cordials or alcoholic drinks, syrups and delicious jams. Their wonderful aroma makes many children's medicines palatable.

Sanguisorba cretica * Hayek   IV-VI

DESCRIPTION: A perennial plant with pinnately-lobed leaves. Flowers arranged in round, pink heads.
HABITAT: Gorges, especially in Samaria.
PROPERTIES, USES: Probably the same as those of the other *Sanguisorba*.

225

Sanguisorba minor Scop.   IV-V
Salad burnet

DESCRIPTION: A perennial, 20-40 cm, greyish. Angular stems, branching. Pinnate leaves, with 4-12 pairs of leaflets smaller than 20 mm. Flowers without petals, in round heads, the upper ones with red styles, the lower ones with yellow styles.
HABITAT: Rocky places on calcareous soils.
PROPERTIES, USES: The leaves are edible and used to flavour salads. The roots and leaves have styptic, anticatarrhal and healing properties. It should be noted that the Latin name means 'it absorbs the blood'.

RUBIACEAE (Madder family)

Galium aparire L.   VI-IX
Goosegrass, Sticky Willie

DESCRIPTION: An annual plant up to 1 metre in height, propped up by other plants around it. The leaves are in whorls of 6-9, reinforced on the upper surface by hook-like spines. The stems and fruits also have these spines, which adhere to clothes and to the hairs of animals. A small, corymb-like inflorescence with white flowers grows from the axils of the leaves, which are larger.
HABITAT: On the edges of fields, in damp places.
PROPERTIES, USES: *Galium* derives from the Greek word 'gala', meaning 'milk'. It is so-named because some species of the genus have the ability to curdle milk.
All parts of the plant have important sudorific, diuretic and soothing properties. According to Theophrastus and Dioscurides, it was used during the period of lactation, to treat

split skin on the breasts of women.

NOTE: These are plants with small flowers; it is difficult to distinguish between them. They are found from the sea shore up to the alpine zone. 23 different species grow on Crete, of which 6 are endemic (*G. extensum*, G. fruticosum*, G. graecum ssp. pseudocanum*, G. incanum ssp. creticum*, G. incrassatum** and *G. incurvum**). Naturally, they may have very interesting properties.

Rubia peregrina L. V-VI
Wild madder

DESCRIPTION: A perennial plant up to 2.5 metres, with creeping stems that are quadrangular and woody at the base. Leaves in whorls of 4-8, tough, stalkless, ovate-oblong, with dentate edges, equipped with small hook-like thorns. Terminal or axillary inflorescences, larger than the leaves, with numerous greenish-yellow flowers. Corolla 4-6 mm, with 5 apiculate lobes. Fleshy black berries.

HABITAT: Areas of maquis, fences, roots of olive trees.

PROPERTIES, USES: The name *Rubia* comes from the Latin 'ruber' and means 'red'. It was probably so-named because its roots are red in colour. The people of antiquity knew it only as a dye plant; the pounded root certainly does produce a red substance, which is produced synthetically today.

Peregrina (wanderer) indicates its ability to be dispersed by clinging to the hairs of animals, or to clothes. The flowers and the root, in an infusion, are used for urinary conditions and for regulating menstruation at a physiological level.

Citrus bergamia
Bergamot

DESCRIPTION: A small tree with oblong-ovate leaves, their stalks winged. Large fruits, shaped like a pear or lemon, yellow or orange in colour, with thick peel and acid, bitter flesh.
HABITAT: Cultivated.
PROPERTIES, USES: Used in the preparation of confectionery.

Citrus decumana
Grapefruit

DESCRIPTION: A robust tree with large elliptic leaves which have a flat, winged stalk. The fruits are large, +/- spherical, slightly flattened at the ends and yellow in colour. The flesh is yellowish.
HABITAT: Cultivated. Originates from the United States.
PROPERTIES, USES: The fruit is used in confectionery; the juice is very refreshing and especially rich in vitamins A, B and C.

Citrus limon Risso
Lemon

DESCRIPTION: A vigorous, evergreen tree up to 8 metres in height, with branches bearing spines. The leaves are glandular, aromatic, leathery and ovate-oblong, slightly serrate, acute, and have a wingless stalk. The flowers are white with 5 petals, occurring singly or in small axillary clusters. The fruit is ovoid and yellow, with a characteristic terminal, nipple-like projection. The pericarp is rich in essential oil and the flesh bitter and aromatic.

HABITAT: Cultivated. Originates from India. Brought to Europe by the Arabs. Very sensitive to cold and ice.

PROPERTIES, USES: The juice of the lemon is acid, refreshing, styptic, good for the stomach and has an antimicrobial action. It is used in the preparation of soft drinks, syrups, perfumes, sweets and for mouthwashes. It is even more useful in the kitchen. Oil of lemon, extracted from the peel, has pectins, resins and bitter substances as its basic constituents.

PROPERTIES, USES: Citrus peel is full of essential oil and vitamins. It is used in pharmaceuticals, confectionery and soap manufacture.

The essential oil, the sodium and potassium salts and vitamins it contains (especially C), make it effective in arthritic-rheumatic conditions, arteriosclerosis, nephritis and all urological conditions.

Citrus medica Risso
Citron, Citrus

DESCRIPTION: A smaller tree than the lemon, with spiny stems and ovate-oblong serrate leaves with wingless stems. The flowers are milky white, with 5 slightly fleshy petals. Bulky fruits, ellipsoidal or breast-shaped with a very thick pericarp, rippled, yellow, greenish or golden yellow in colour, which can weigh from 0.5 to 3 kg. Thin flesh, acid-bitter to the taste.

HABITAT: Cultivated. Brought to Europe in the 6th century BC during the time of the Persian king Cyrus I, either from Persia or India. Theophrastus called it the 'Median apple'.

Citrus nobilis Risso
Mandarin

DESCRIPTION: A small, evergreen tree which does not exceed 2-3 metres in height. Lanceolate leaves, acute, glossy, dark green and much smaller than those of the lemon. Small, fragrant white flowers. Orange-coloured fruits, round, flattened at both ends, with a nipple-like projection where they meet the stalk. One of the smallest of all the citrus fruits. The flesh is sweet and juicy, aromatic, and pleasing to the taste.
HABITAT: Cultivated. Imported from China and Indochina at the beginning of the 19th century.
PROPERTIES, USES: The fruit is eaten raw or used in aromatic drinks and the preparation of liqueurs.
NOTE: The clementine originated from a chance hybridisation of the wild orange (nerantsia) with the mandarin.

Citrus sinensis (L.) Osbeck
Orange

DESCRIPTION: A small, evergreen tree, one of the most beautiful and useful, with leaves that are ovate-lanceolate, elliptic, aromatic, leathery, glandular and have a wingless stalk. The flowers are white, aromatic, with 5 petals. The fruit is round or slightly elongated, with a yellowish-orange peel and sweet or slightly tart juice, never bitter.
HABITAT: Cultivated. Originates from China. There are many varieties: merlin, navel, valencia, blood-orange, tarocco, myridota, sekeria etc.
PROPERTIES, USES: The essential oil is extracted and used in perfumery. The fruits are eaten raw or used in the production of orange juice, marmalades, puddings, a variety of sauces, and confectionery. The orange is the perfect supplier of vitamin C and has antioxidant properties, sufficient to protect smokers and all those who live in a contaminated atmosphere.

***Citrus vulgaris* Risso (=*Citrus auran-tium*)**
Nerantsia

DESCRIPTION: Similar to the orange but smaller in size, and the leaves are tougher and wing-stalked. The fruit resembles the orange but is more flattened at the sides and has an acid-tart flavour.
HABITAT: Cultivated.
PROPERTIES, USES: Used as a root-stock for other citrus varieties and for stands of trees along roads. Delicious 'spoon sweets' are made from the peel of the fruit.

GENERAL INFORMATION RELATING TO THE CITRUS VARIETIES: They undoubtedly originated from Asia. Who brought them here, however? Nobody is certain! Many say that the Arabs brought them, others the Greeks, others the Portuguese, and still others even Herakles! Remember the myth of the 'golden apples of Hesperides'!
One thing is certain; all of the citrus fruits are extremely useful. They contain a great number of essential oils, vitamins A, B and C, iron and glucose, and are not only eaten as they come but also widely used in confectionery, cookery, drinks and perfumery.
In pharmaceutics, the juice of all the species has excellent diuretic properties and is a good medicine for kidney and liver complaints, increases peristaltic movements of the bowels, and is designated digestive, antitoxic, antioxidant and a combatant of infection.

Ruta chalepensis L. II-V
Fringed rue

DESCRIPTION: A perennial plant up to 60 cm in height, heavy-scented, woody at the base, and smooth. Leaves 2-3 times pinnately divided, with sections that are obovate to oblong, and bluish in colour with opaque streaks due to the presence of oil-bearing glands. Flowers arranged in terminal corymbs. Each flower is formed from a glandular, discoid receptacle from which 4 sepals grow, partly joined with each other, to form a calyx, as well as 4-5 free petals which are ovate-oblong, undulate at the lips, fringed, a brilliant yellow colour, and resemble little spoons. The central flower has 5 petals, the rest 4. The fruit is an almost spherical capsule, consisting of 4-5 sections that are apiculate, with angular, kidney-shaped seeds.

HABITAT: Areas of phrygana (garrigue), dry locations, stony slopes.

PROPERTIES, USES: In antiquity, it was used as a general antidote for poisoning and especially for snake-bite. Dioscurides used it as a medicine for breathing difficulties. Pliny informs us that artists ate fringed rue, mixed in with their food, to maintain sharp vision. Leaves of bay mixed with fringed rue and pounded together are used as a plaster in cases of congestion of the male genitals.

According to an old folk saying "Nobody dies in a house where there is fringed rue".

Apart from the essential oil with its pervading odour, it contains a glycoside – rutine. The leaves, steeped in raki, seem to give it tonic qualities. **Nevertheless, it must only be used with great care! The plant has the ability to induce contractions of the uterus and - by extension – to cause bleeding. In other words it has strong abortion-inducing properties (1-10 drops of essential oil).**

NOTE: The sub-species **ssp. *fumariifolia** Boiss. & Heldr**. is a smaller plant, almost prostrate, with light yellow flowers. It is found on Cape Sideros, at the north-eastern tip of Crete.

ssp. fumariifolia

Salix alba L.   III-IV
Willow

DESCRIPTION: A deciduous tree up to 25 metres, with linear-lanceolate, apiculate leaves, 5-10 cm.

HABITAT: Rivers and streams, damp locations.

PROPERTIES, USES: "The leaves and seeds stop impulses and passion in man and woman, and can also banish them completely if they are used systematically and over a long period of time", said Nicholas Culpeper in 1653.

Aspirin owers its efficacy to the willow (salicylic acid) and to the researches carried out by the French chemist Leroux.

Salicylic acid is antiseptic, a febrifuge and analgesic, with a selective efficacy against arthritis and rheumatism.

WARNING! In high doses, of more than 6-10 g, it causes a 'bomb explosion' in the

ears and headaches. At even higher doses it causes blindness and sometimes haemorrhages.

The bark is used for inflammations, rheumatism, arthritis, fever, neuralgia, migrane and pain in general. The rather bitter flavour can function as a light digestive stimulant.

Some use a tisane of the leaves for headaches.

233

SANTALACEAE
(Sandalwood family)

Osyris alba L.   III-V
Osyris

DESCRIPTION: A bisexual, evergreen, parasitic shrub up to 1.2 metres in height (the roots are equipped with suckers), with many twig-like branches. Leaves 1-2 cm, alternate, lanceolate. Small flowers, yellowish, inconspicuous, fragrant; the female flowers are at the ends of short branches, shaped like cups with 3 protrusions and 3 stigmas, the male flowers have 3 broad stamens. Fleshy purple berries, 5-7 mm in diameter.

HABITAT: Stony areas of thicket.

PROPERTIES, USES: Pliny tells us that a type of soap for women used to be made from the purple berries.

SAXIFRAGACEAE
(Saxifrage family)

Saxifraga chryssosplenifolia Boiss.
Saxifrage sp.   IV-VI

DESCRIPTION: A perennial with stems up to 50 cm. Basal rosette with leaves that are discoid, reniform, dentate, and on a long petiole. Leaves of the stems are very small, stalkless, palmately-lobed, and dentate. The flowers, in loose, corymb-like inflorescences, have 5 petals of 6-10 mm, white with red stippling, and 10 stamens.

HABITAT: Rocks and shady places, in the mountain zone. At the beginning of June, the Kamares Cave 'is engulfed' by thousands of these flowers.

PROPERTIES, USES: The saxifrages (there are 4 other species found on Crete) are used for colics of the kidneys and gall-bladder.

SCROFULARIACEAE
(Figwort family)

Antirrhinum majus L. IV-IX
Snapdragon

DESCRIPTION: A perennial plant up to 80 cm, with erect stems. The roots have nodes which produce shoots. Leaves 10-60 x 1.5 mm, opposite or alternate, linear. Flowers in terminal racemes. Corolla 33-38 mm, purple, pink, yellow or white, two-lipped, the upper lip bisected and the lower one trilobate, with a swelling which almost closes the neck. Five-lobed calyx.

HABITAT: A decorative plant, cultivated but also self-sowing in rocky locations, on house walls, ruins, old walls, usually near to villages and up to an altitude of 700 metres. Introduced from Sicily and Spain.

PROPERTIES, USES: We used to play with these flowers as children. By pressing and holding the throat of the flower, we made it open and close its mouth, like a little dog.
Bees visit the plant only when the corolla has been penetrated by a certain type of fat little bug, and collect a rich nectar which produces a good-quality honey.

WARNING! The plant is poisonous!

Cymbalaria muralis P. Gaetner, B. Meyer & Schreb. III-VI
Ivy-leaved toadflax

DESCRIPTION: A perennial, with stems which have the habit of turning downwards towards the ground. Alternate leaves, palmately-lobed, on long stalks. Solitary flowers, 8-10 mm, lilac in colour with a yellow neck, on a long pedicel, in the leaf axils. Short spur.

HABITAT: On walls, rocks, ruins, and in flower- pots, up to the mountain zone.

PROPERTIES, USES: The plant is styptic, healing and antiscorbutic. It was once used against scabies.

Kickxia elatine (L.) Dumortier *ssp. sieberi* (Arcangeli) Hayek   VII-X
Sharp-leaved fluellen

DESCRIPTION: An annual, with prostrate stems, 20-50 cm. Leaves often rounded at the tip, the upper ones triangular or sagittate, with a stem bearing woolly hairs. Solitary flowers, axillary, light yellow, with an upper lip that is brownish-violet in colour.
HABITAT: Sandy locations, fields, near the sea.
PROPERTIES, USES: Healing, purgative, styptic, sedative and dilutant.
NOTE: **Kickxia commutata (Bernh. Ex Reichenb.) Fritsch *ssp. graeca* (Bory a& Chaub.) R. Fernandes**, has whitish-yellow flowers, with a violet upper lip and sagittate, hairy leaves with short stalks. It is an annual but can also be perennial.

K. commutata

Misopates orontium (L.) Rafin   II-V
Lesser snapdragon

DESCRIPTION: An annual, 20-60 cm, with an erect stem, slightly branching, glandular towards the top and hairy towards the bottom. Leaves 2-5 cm, the lower ones opposite, the upper ones alternate, linear and also lanceolate-oblong, acute. Flowers 10-15 mm, purplish-pink on little stalks, in the axils of the upper leaves, with a corolla smaller than the calyx. The fruit is a capsule containing 3 seeds.
HABITAT: Cultivated areas, sandy and stony soils.
PROPERTIES, USES: **WARNING! The plant is poisonous!** Bees visit it if the corolla has first been penetrated by a certain type of small bug.

236

Scrophularia auriculata L.　　**III-IV**

DESCRIPTION: A perennial plant, sturdy, up to 1 metre in height, with a quadrangular, winged and hollow stem. Leaves +/- inverse cordate or rounded at the base, with toothed edges and two lateral leaflets. Brownish-red or brownish-green flowers, whose sepals have white edges. Spherical fruit with an acutely pointed end.

HABITAT: Rivers and streams at low altitude.

PROPERTIES, USES: **WARNING! A poisonous plant!** Its roots contain a toxic alkaloid. The flowers are visited by bees, which collect a good quality nectar. The plant is healing and detergent.

Scrophularia peregrina L.　　**II-IV**
Nettle-leaved figwort

DESCRIPTION: An annual, smooth, up to 90 cm, with a quadrangular stem, often reddish. Leaves up to 10 cm, opposite, alternate at the top of the stem, ovate to cordate, dentate. Flowers 6-9 mm, dark purple, in the axils of the upper leaves, with 5 sepals and a corolla in the form of a swollen column, with a large bilobate upper lip. Stalkless ovary, which develops into a rounded capsule with a narrow beak at the tip.

HABITAT: Set-aside fields, walls, damp locations, gardens.

PROPERTIES, USES: **WARNING! The plant is +/- poisonous!** In an infusion (10-20 g per litre of water) it is tonic, cleansing and invigorating. The leaves are used to make plasters to treat scrofula and toughening of the neck glands. The root, pounded and mixed in equal measure with fat, constitutes an ointment soothing to the pain of herpes, itching and haemorrhoids. Bees collect a sugary substance of good quality from the plant.

Verbascum sinuatum L.   V-IX
Mullein sp.

DESCRIPTION: A biennial plant, 50-100 cm, much-branching, and covered in short-lived felty hairs. The leaves of the rosette are oblong, 15-35 cm, with a short stalk, often lobed, and revolute margins. The leaves of the stem are stalkless. Loose inflorescence, spike-like. The corolla is 5-lobed, 1.5-2 cm in diameter, yellow with a throat bearing red stippling, and has stamens of a vibrant violet colour and slanting anthers. The fruit is round.

HABITAT: Found on roadsides, and in uncultivated fields.

PROPERTIES, USES: The flowers have emollient, antispasmodic and healing properties. In an infusion (10-12 flowers and leaves to 100 g of water) the plant is used as a gargle, not only for coughs, influenza-induced angina, and tonsilitis, but also for insomnia, haemoptysis and conditions of the intestinal and urinary tracts.

NOTE: Some flowers emit a scent strong enough to induce sneezing. This has given rise to a Greek verb, based on the common Greek name 'Phlomos', meaning 'to pour out smoke or a bad odour', or even 'to render render fish and eels senseless with 'phlomos'.

from the magic of Circe.

NOTE: Like the other varieties of **Verbascum** this plant is very hairy and animals do not eat it. In areas that have been over-grazed, it is sometimes only plants of this kind that have been left.

*Verbascum spinosum** L.   V-VIII
Spiny mullein

DESCRIPTION: A perennial phrygano plant up to 50 cm, spiny, forming a hum-mock-shaped bush. Leaves up to 5 cm, oblong-lanceolate, dentate, covered with white down. Corolla 10-18 mm in diameter, yellow.

HABITAT: Stony and dry soils, from the sea right up to the sub-alpine zone in the Sphakia region.

PROPERTIES, USES: Hermes, it is said, gave this plant to Odysseus to protect him

238

Veronica anagallis-aquatica L.   V-VIII
Blue water speedwell

DESCRIPTION: A perennial, 10-80 cm, with smooth stems, fleshy, creeping or erect, which put out roots and vary in the form they take according to whether the plant is in growing in water or not. Quadrangular flower stems. Leaves stalkless, opposite, lanceolate, and toothed. Flowers 5-6 mm, light lilac to white in colour, in a spike on a peduncle in the axils of the upper leaves.
HABITAT: In very damp places, in water.
PROPERTIES, USES: A bitter plant, styptic, stimulant and purgative. Used for conditions of the respiratory tract and stomach. It is eaten by animals, but has the reputation of being harmful to sheep.

SOLANACEAE
(Nightshade family)

Datura innoxia Miller
(= *Datura m. tel* L.)   VII-X

DESCRIPTION An annual, 90-200 cm, hairy, heavily-scented. Large leaves, opposite, long-stalked, acute, slightly angular, hairy. Large flowers, 11-19 cm, white, sometimes with violet shading, resembling a trumpet. Corolla funnel-shaped, wilting with the first rays of the sun. Fruit a hanging capsule, fleshy, ovoid, spiny (with soft, thin spines).
HABITAT: Probably originated from the East Indies. It has become completely acclimatised today. It grows at low altitude among ruins, on rubble and generally in disturbed locations.
PROPERTIES, USES: **WARNING! The plant is extremely poisonous! It contains three alkaloid substances – scopolamine,**

hyoscyamine and atropine. It has a bitter, unpleasant taste and causes nausea. Internal use must be under the complete supervision of a competent medical authority. Poisoning caused by the plant must be dealt with immediately through stomach washing and forced vomiting.

Its medicinal properties are similar to those of belladonna, for neuralgia, rheumatism, spasms and Parkinson's disease. Cigarettes are made from it to treat asthma. It is also used for incontinency, excessive carnal desire, nymphomania and priapism (involuntary erections).

Datura stramonium L.   XII-X
Thorn apple, Jimson weed

DESCRIPTION: An annual, up to 1 metre in height, completely hairless, heavy-scented. Straight, bifurcated stems. Stalked leaves, large, irregularly dentate. Solitary flowers, 6-12 cm in diameter, white or sometimes whitish-violet, trumpet-shaped. Whitish-green calyx, covering two-thirds of the length of the corolla. The ripe fruit is erect, ovate-round, covered in short, sturdy spines which prick only when they have dried out.

HABITAT: Rubbish dumps, on rubble, in disturbed soils, abandoned villages. Some say that it originated from the Black Sea, others from Central America.

PROPERTIES, USES: **WARNING! An extremely poisonous plant! Theophrastus tells us that "3/20 of an ounce (n.b. 1 ounce=30.594 g) is enough for the patient to feel strengthened and well-disposed, that is to say, to be good company. Given twice that dose he will go mad and have hallucinations. Three times the dose, and**

D. stramonium

he will become permanently insane. Four times the dose – and he is dead!"

The witches and soothsayers of the Middle Ages used it for its hallucinogenic properties. The Aztecs also knew the plant.

In some areas, the seeds were used to fatten animals: pigs were given the amount of a thimble-full. Slightly more was given to weak horses.

Hyoscyamus albus L.   III-V
White henbane

DESCRIPTION: An annual, biennial or perennial, 20-80 cm, erect, heavy-scented, covered with glandular hairs which make it sticky. Stalked leaves, ovate with sparse teeth. Flowers 3 cm, on a unilateral spike. Corolla tubular to campanulate, with 5 unequal, rounded lobes, whitish-yellow in colour, with a purple or yellow throat and 5 stamens.
HABITAT: Found on rubbish tips, in house walls, on field walls and in ruins.
PROPERTIES, USES: **WARNING! A very poisonous plant!** Its medicinal use has been attested from Mesopotamia and from the ancient Egyptian Ebers Papyrus (15th century BC). "Due to its hallucinogenic properties, white henbane has occupied an important place among the various magical concoctions, along with belladonna (deadly nightshade) and mandrake. Long before the discovery of chloroform, and probably from the 14th century owards, doctors used the plant in surgery." The essential oil of hyoscyamus is used to combat rheumatic pains. Hyoscyamos in ancient Greek means 'pig's bean'; it is said that pigs can eat the seeds without the slightest fear.

According to Greek mythology, Herakles discovered the hallucinogenic properties of the plant. Dioscurides believed that, with the use of hyoscyamus, the chances of a patient going mad were minimised. As country children, as soon as hyoscyamus flowered, we used to pull off the corolla from the calyx and with great enjoyment, suck the honey which was located on the lower part of the stigma.

H. aureus

Hyoscyamus aureus L.   III-VI
Golden henbane

DESCRIPTION: A plant 20-60 cm in height, sticky, with glandular hairs. Stalked leaves, ovate or round, with sharp teeth. Flowers up to 4.5 cm, in a loose raceme. Funnel-shaped corolla, golden-yellow, with 5 lobes, purple throat, protruding anthers and a woolly calyx.

HABITAT: A plant of Asiatic origin which grows on house and field walls, and in old houses.

PROPERTIES, USES: **WARNING! A poisonous plant!** Hippocrates' pupils gave the seeds of this hallucinogenic plant mixed with wine to sufferers from fever, tetanus and the paralysis which could set in after birth.

The medicinal properties are important: for spasms, brain conditions, neuralgia, nervous cough, whooping cough, incontinence, haemorrhage, haemorrhoids, hernia, ophthalmic congestion, asthma, arthritis, rheumatism, skin and breast inflammation, tumours, dislocations, paralysis of the iris...... Cigarettes were once made from its leaves, to relieve the pain due to breathing difficulties.

WARNING! Do not attempt to use the plant in any way whatsoever without the prior advice of a doctor!

Lycium barbarum L. (=Lycium halimifolium = L. schweinfurthii)   VII-XI
Tea tree sp.

DESCRIPTION: A shrub up to 2.5 metres in height, with arched, supple branches. Narrow, elliptic or lanceolate leaves. Calyx 4 mm, bilobate. Corolla 9 mm, funnel-shaped, violet, turning brown after ripening, terminating in 5 outspread lobes. Protruding stamens. The berry is reddish-orange, and **poisonous**.

HABITAT: Originates from China and has become acclimatised on Crete at low altitude.

PROPERTIES, USES: In certain parts of

the Mediterranean, the tender stems are eaten in a salad.

For the treatment of herpes, fresh leaves are torn up or crushed and applied as a plaster. The infusion of dried leaves is recommended for a cough and can be a substitute for tea. The plant is an ideal nectar source for bees, since it flowers nearly all year round.

Mandragora autumnalis Bertol. (= *Mandragora officinarum*)
IX-XI and III-V

Mandrake

DESCRIPTION: A stemless plant, 10-20 cm, with a perennial, robust, peg-like root often divided into two, clearly resembling the shape of the human body. Leaves in a rosette, large, stalked, ovate-oblong, undulate at the margins. Flowers on stalks which emerge from the centre of the rosette, violet,

M. autumnalis

white or reddish in colour. Bell-shaped calyx, with 5 points, and a corolla of 5 petals, 3-4 x

2-3 cm. Berries up to 3 cm, ovoid, resembling tiny melons, reddish-orange, surrounded by the calyx. **Are they edible? Friends that tried eating them vomited for a period of two days!**

HABITAT: Abandoned and cultivated fields, roadsides.

PROPERTIES, USES: **WARNING! The root is poisonous, being rich in the alkaloids scopolamine, hyoscyamine and atropine. There is no antidote for mandrake! First the affected person falls into a deep coma, then terrible spasms follow, and finally, death.**

The plant was used from very early times as an analgesic and opiate (soporific) and as an anaesthetic during surgical operations. According to Pliny, the patient ate a piece of it and fell into a state of lethargy. The ancient Egyptian Ebers Papyrus, dating from the 15th century BC, refers to it. An extract of mandrake induces complete narcosis. Made from the bark, roots and juice steeped in wine, it was once used in cases of amputation, trepanning, unbearable pain and very deep wounds; the narcosis could last for up to 4 hours. Greek anaesthetists have the mandrake as their emblem.

The similarity between the shape of the mandrake root and that of the human body, and the magical properties ascribed to it, were the reason it was used by witches in their rituals. Superstition prohibited its uprooting under any circumstances by human hand, because it was supposed to bring death. A hole was therefore dug around the root and it was bound by a string to the tail of a dog, which then pulled and uprooted it, while at the same time falling dead, as if struck by lightning (!).

NOTE: The plant which flowers in spring usually has white flowers (***Mandragora var. alba***)

M. autumnalis

Nicotiana glauca R.C. Graham   V-X
Tree tobacco

DESCRIPTION: A small tree, 2-6 metres, greyish, slightly branching, hairless. Leaves 5-25 cm, alternate, long stalked, ovate to acutely pointed, hairless, grey. Large flowers in loose panicles. Calyx campanulate, with 5 acute tips. Corolla 2.5-4.5 cm, yellow, campanulate, narrow, with 5 short lobes. Fruit an elliptic capsule.

HABITAT: Originates from South America and has become completely acclimatised. Found on roadsides, rubbish dumps, in gardens, at low altitude.

PROPERTIES, USES: **WARNING! Poisonous because of the nicotine it contains.** The actual tobacco plant itself is ***Nicotiana tabacum* L.** It is considered that 40-60 g of nicotine constitutes a fatal dose for a human being; this is the amount contained in a large cigar. That it does not cause death is due to the fact that a larger part of the nicotine burns off when the cigar is lit - and also because, with time, the body becomes used to it! Like the normal tobacco plant, ***N. glauca*** is healing and treats wounds. A pinch of tobacco on an open wound immediately stops the bleeding!

N. tabacum

Solanum luteum Miller   VI-IX
Hairy nightshade

DESCRIPTION: An annual, up to 1 metre. Leaves ovate or lanceolate, dentate. White flowers, in loose panicles, with a star-like corolla, five-lobed. Reddish or yellowish berries.

HABITAT: At low altitudes, in cultivated and abandoned fields, on rubbish tips and rubble.

PROPERTIES, USES: **WARNING! The berries are poisonous!** The leaves, however, like the young shoots, well boiled, are eaten along with other wild greens or with courgettes and make an excellent salad. **The plant is dangerous when it is eaten by itself or raw, especially after the fruits have been produced.**

In an embrocation (infusion of 50 g in one litre of water), it relieves itching and haematomas. Its leaves are used in a plaster for treating wounds, certain skin eruptions, ulcers, bruises and burns.

NOTES: *Solanum nigrum*, (Black night shade) which is more common, has the same toxicity. The berries are black. In some places it is cultivated to produce a mauve colouring agent used in the dyeing of silk.

Solanum melongena is the aubergine or eggplant. It originates, as its additional epithet 'Badastan' implies, from India and was unknown to the ancient Greeks. It made its appearance in the Mediterranean during the 16th century.

Solanum tuberosum is the potato. Known from very ancient times to the American Indians, it was brought to Europe in 1524 by the Spanish, but its adoption was a slow process. It was brought to Greece during the time of Capodistrias, but nobody wanted to cultivate it, let alone eat it. Then Capodis-

S. nigrum

trias decided to place guards to protect his potatoes and, as if by magic, the Greeks were persuaded of their worth and began to steal them, while the guards turned a blind eye!

Solanum lycopersicum is the tomato. As its name 'tomatl' suggests, it originates from Peru. The Spanish brought it to Europe and Capucine monks brought it to Greece at the end of the period of Turkish occupation.

Withania somnifera (L.) Dunal VIII-X
Withania

DESCRIPTION: A shrub with entire alternate or opposite leaves. Stems up to 120 cm, branching, downy. The leaves are also downy, 3-10 cm, ovate, obovate or oblong with a cuneate base. Flowers in groups of 4-6 in the leaf axils. Campanulate calyx up to 5mm. Corolla also campanulate, wide open, five-lobed, greenish-yellow, up to 5 mm. Fruit is a red spherical berry 5-8 mm, surrounded by the calyx.
HABITAT: Roadsides, ruins and rocks near the coastal zone.
PROPERTIES, USES: Probably has the same properties as those of the sleep-inducing poppy, and has thus been so named (somnifera).

STYRACACEAE (Storax family)

Styrax officinalis L. IV-V
Storax

DESCRIPTION: A deciduous tree, 2-7 metres in height, with alternate leaves, ovate or oblong, entire, rounded at the tip, and downy on the underside. Flowers in a raceme, white, fragrant, on a stalk 1-2 cm long. Corolla 2 cm, campanulate and terminating in 5-7 lanceolate lobes. Cup-shaped calyx. Fruit covered with white felt.
HABITAT: Areas of maquis, forests, banks of rivers. This is the only representative of its family to be found in the Mediterranean Basin.
PROPERTIES, USES: In antiquity, its gum was used as incense, as it still is by the Roman Catholic Church today. In medicine, Dioscurides prescribed it for coughs and

asthma. A tincture was used for bruises and gonorrhoea. In external use, it has antiseptic properties and combats scabies and lousiness in puberty.
The white wood of storax is hard, heavy and homogeneous, needing special preparation.

THYMELAEACEAE
(Daphne family)

Daphne oleoides Schreber   V-VII
Daphne sp.

DESCRIPTION: An evergreen shrub with many branches, up to 50 cm. Leaves 10-45 mm, alternate, obovate or elliptic, leathery, glandular on the underside. The stems and new leaves are hairy. Flowers white or whitish-yellow, tubular at the base, four-lobed at the top, fragrant, without bracts, in heads of 3-6. Fruit red, toxic.
HABITAT: Found in the mountain and sub-alpine zone, especially on Mount Dikti.
PROPERTIES, USES: **WARNING! The fruits are extremely dangerous, especially to children!**

Daphne sericea Vahl.   III-VI

DESCRIPTION: An evergreen shrub or bush up to 1.5 metres in height, much branching. The leaves are obovate, with revolute margins, hairy on the underside and smooth and glossy on top. Heads consisting of 5-15 flowers, 14 mm, fragrant, pinkish-violet, whitish-yellow or whitish, surrounded by small, soft bracts. Brownish-red berry, **toxic!**
HABITAT: Rocky soils, areas of maquis and phrygana (garrigue).
PROPERTIES, USES: **Although the Daphnes are very beautiful, they are - unfortunately – poisonous**. They were once used internally as an antirheumatic. **Today they are only of historical interest and should be avoided**.

Thymelaea hirsuta   IX-IV
Thymelaea sp.

DESCRIPTION: An evergreen shrub, 40-100 cm, with ovate or lanceolate leaves, 3-8 mm, greenish, fleshy, alternate and in dense formations. Thread-like stems with very dense hairs. Four-part flowers, small, yellow and in axillary bunches of 2-5.
HABITAT: Stony places, at low altitude and in the semi-mountainous zone.
PROPERTIES, USES: This plant was once used to make mooring lines for ships.

ULMACEAE (Elm family)

Ulmus minor Mill. *ssp. canescens* (Melville) Browicz & Ziel   III-V
Mediterranean elm

DESCRIPTION: A deciduous tree, up to 30 metres in height. The young shoots are fragile and delicate. Leaves obovate, ovate or lanceolate, asymmetrical at the base, with 7-12 veins. Small flowers, a vibrant pink colour, appearing before the leaves, with a bell-shaped perianth, which terminates in 4-8 lobes and contains 4-8 stamens. The fruit is a key, whitish green, +/- disc-shaped, membranous, with broad wings and a seed at the centre.
HABITAT: Rare, in the semi-mountainous area, in places which are rather damp.
PROPERTIES, USES: Cultivated since antiquity. The bark in an infusion (50 g in 300 g of water) is sudorific, diuretic, treats dropsy, askitis, herpes, certain skin eruptions, elephantiasis and leprosy. It is drunk cold, before retiring to bed.
Folk medicine uses it for scrofula, rheumatic pains, fevers and cancerous skin abcesses. In a tisane or syrup, many people consider it to be the only treatment for eczema, weak con-

stitution, nervous disorders and insomnia. (100 g of bark in 1 litre of water, left to boil until it has been reduced by half. We can drink a coffee cup full of the liquid 2 or 3 times per day.)

Anethum graveolens L.
Dill

DESCRIPTION: An annual herbaceous plant, aromatic, up to about 60 cm in height, with channelled stems, hollow and greyish-green in colour. Pinnate leaves with thread-like leaflets. Flowers small, yellow, in an umbel. Very fragrant ovoid seeds.

HABITAT: Cultivated.

PROPERTIES, USES: Known from antiquity by the same name. It has an aroma and flavour recalling that of aniseed and is used as an aromatic, principally in cookery. Dill water, which has fragrant and pharmaceutical properties, is distilled from its flowers; dill wine is made from the seeds.

In an infusion (2-3 seeds in 300 g of water) it is diuretic, but it is also used in cases of vomiting, prolonged hiccups, intestinal colic, stomach pain and insomnia.

WARNING! We should avoid consumption of large quantities of an infusion of dill. It can have very destructive results for our sight (cataracts, blindness etc.)

Apium graveolens L.   **IV-V**
Celery

DESCRIPTION: A biennial plant up to 80 cm, with a short, fat, peg-like and branching root. Strong aroma, +/- pleasant. Erect stem, robust, fluted, and hollow. The leaves are pinnate or 2-pinnately-divided, with large toothed florets. The flowers are white, in an umbel.

HABITAT: Self-sowing in damp meadows near the sea, and of course cultivated in gardens and pots.

PROPERTIES, USES: Celery, boiled in milk, is said to dissolve lactic and uric acid, thus destroying the salts which settle in various tissues. The seeds and root, in a tisane, are used for rheumatism, diabetes, colic and lithiasis of the urinary tract. They are also diuretic, helping in the detoxification of the body, and in turn have beneficial effects in cases of gout and the collection of uric acid crystals in the joints.

The water in which they are boiled treats frostbite, stimulates the appetite, facilitiates digestion and improves the function of the urinary tract. Some people even ascribe aphrodisiac qualities to it!

It has been used in homeopathy since 1975. The juice from young leaves is given in cases of fever and the tea (one spoonful of seeds in a cup of water) 2-3 times per day, for wind and dyspepsia. The stems, raw, strengthen the secretions of the mammary glands after birth.

Apium nodiflorum **L.**   **VI-IX**
Fool's water-cress

DESCRIPTION: A perennial up to 1 metre in height, outspreading, with stems that throw out roots. Pinnate leaves, with leaflets that are ovate to lanceolate, and dentate. White flowers in umbels, either on little stalks or stalkless, opposite the leaves. Ovoid, fluted fruit.

HABITAT: In damp places, almost completely in water.

PROPERTIES, USES: **WARNING! This plant is dangerous if consumed in a large quantity!**

NOTE: *Apium* is a Celtic word and means "water with an acrid and burning taste".

Conium maculatum L. IV-VI
Hemlock

DESCRIPTION: A large biennial, up to 2 metres, smooth, heavy-scented, very toxic. Cylindrical stems, hollow, directed outwards, ridged and with purple stipples at the base. Glossy leaves, triangular, 2-4 times-pinnately-divided, the segments very fine. Umbel of small white flowers with 10-20 rays at the top of the stems. Roughly spherical fruit with protruding tips.

HABITAT: Found on fences, rubbish tips, in rubble, on roadsides, and disturbed areas of ground, up to the mountain zone.

PROPERTIES, USES: **WARNING! A very poisonous plant. Two drops of conein, the alkaloid contained in it, on the tongue of a dog or on a dog's wound, are enough to bring death in less than two minutes. 6-8 g constitute a fatal dose for a human. No internal use of any kind is permissible without the advice of a doctor. According to Dioscurides, it has a weakening effect and brings pain and death, while according to Theophrastus it brings death without pain. It is most probable that the juice of the plant brings a painless death, since it reacts upon the nervous system by paralysing it.**

In antiquity, the Athenians used it to execute those who had been condemned to death by the Areopagus (High Court). Socrates was condemned to drink hemlock, which killed him.

Today it is considered a pharmaceutical plant with therapeutic qualities beneficial to oedema, neuralgia, psoriasis and other skin conditions. It has anaesthetic, dilutant, anti-carcinogenic, anti-scrofula, sudorific, and diuretic qualities, used for convulsive coughs, whooping cough, asthma, rheumatism,

arthritis and neuralgia. The leaves and stems are crushed and the paste placed on the affected area as a plaster. An ointment from the plant is used for herpes.

NOTE: *Conium divaricatum* **Boiss. & Orph**. exhibits only the slightest botanical differences.

Crithmum maritimum L.   VII-X
Rock samphire

DESCRIPTION: A perennial, 10-60 cm, woody at the base, hairless. Pinnate or 2-pinnate leaves, triangular, fleshy, greyish, torn into linear sections 1-7 cm long. Umbel with 8-30 rays. Small flowers with yellowish-green petals and tiny sepals. Fruit ovoid-oblong, hairless, deeply fluted, yellowish or red.

HABITAT: Found on beaches, on sandy and rocky soils.

PROPERTIES, USES: The leaves are eaten raw, boiled as a salad, preserved in sugar or steeped in vinegar.

The plant contains essential oils, mineral salts, iodine and vitamins. It is appetite-stimulating, purgative, tonic, gives strength and courage. The essential oil, when rubbed on, is said to act as an unbeatable aphrodisiac for men! Probably the same would apply to women! Sailors once took the fleshy leaves with them on their voyages to protect them against scurvy. In France it was called 'St. Peter's herb'.

HABITAT: Common in green meadows and on roadsides.

Daucus carota L.   VI-IX
Wild carrot

DESCRIPTION: A biennial plant, with a great variety of forms and a tubular root (carrot). Stems up to 1 metre, robust and hairy. Leaves 3-pinnate. Umbel of many white flowers with unequal petals. The central flower of the umbel is often a deep purple in colour, but this is said to have been lost recently because Mankind is rotten! The lower bracts are pinnate and large, the upper ones simple or 3-pinnate. The fruit is elliptic or ovoid. The seeds remain closed for a long time inside the ripe umbel, which folds over during ripening.

PROPERTIES, USES: The root is edible, like the young stems which are eaten boiled with the addition of oil and vinegar. It is also said that good vinegar can be made from the plant. It contains nearly all the mineral salts that we need and appears to have beneficial results against tumours, even those that are cancerous (!), when they are at an early phase. The juice relieves the kidneys and liver in cases of jaundice, as well as arthritic-rheumatic pains. A tea, made from the seeds, rekindles erotic desires in those who have lost them. The carrot is beneficial for the keenness of sight, good for the blood and for children's development.

We should not hesitate to place grated carrot on burns and bruises and to drink a tisane of it when suffering from diarrhoea. Its tannin content produces tangible results.

WARNING! The plant is not recommended for those who suffer from sugar diabetes.

NOTE: The genus **Daucus** is differentiated from the genus **Torilis** by its perpendicular hairs which cover the plant and allow the green colour to show through. By contrast in the latter genus, the short hairs, which are almost contiguous, give the plants an appearance which is more whitish than green.

Eryngium campestre L.   V-VIII
Field eryngio

DESCRIPTION: A perennial, 20-70 cm, with a turnip-like root. The basal leaves are tripartite, spiny, with the central lobe 2-pinnately-lobed. The inflorescence is in the form of a head, whitish-green, ovoid, dense, surrounded by 4-6 narrow bracts, entire or dentate, spiny.

HABITAT: Infertile, uncultivated fields.

PROPERTIES, USES: If we boil a handful of roots in one litre of water for 5 minutes, we have a diuretic beverage, but one that is also useful in cases of liver insufficiencies and wounds.

Known in ancient Greek as 'the plant of love', it constituted the basis for aphrodisiac preparations in ancient Corinth. When the stem has withered, the wind uproots the plant quite easily and rolls it over the ground, hence the French name 'rolling thorn'.

From October to January, an excellent mushroom – **Pleurotus eryngii** – grows on the roots that have remained in the soil.

E. campestre

Eryngium maritimum L.   **VI-VIII**
Sea holly

DESCRIPTION: A perennial plant, 15-60 cm, grey, with erect stems, branching in the upper part. Leathery leaves, the lower ones stalked with 3-4 teeth ending in spines, the upper leaves stalkless. Blue flowers, in heads 1.5-3 cm in diameter, surrounded by 4-7 bracts, elliptic to obovate, 2-4 cm.
HABITAT: Sandy beaches and sand dunes.
PROPERTIES, USES: A most beautiful plant which we should avoid completely when walking barefooted. Can be used for decoration. The root is diuretic and febrifuge. Dioscurides recommended it for bruises.

Ferula communis L.   III-V
Giant fennel

DESCRIPTION: A large perennial shrub, 1-3 metres, robust, with a large inflorescence, much-branching. Thick, cylindrical stem, with fine fluting, hollow inside. Huge leaves, a beautiful green colour, much divided (3-6 times), with linear to thread-like lobes, the lower ones 30-60 cm with a large stalk, the upper ones with an incredibly wide sheath. Terminal umbels with 20-40 rays on a short stem, bearing fertile yellow flowers and surrounded by later umbels on large stalks which bear sterile flowers. Fruit up to 15 mm, flattened, unevenly toothed.

HABITAT: On calcareous soils, often near inhabited areas.

PROPERTIES, USES: The subterranean parts of the plant were once used for remittent fevers. An edible mushroom - ***Pleurotus eryngii var. ferulae*** - often grows on its roots.

The medulla (fleshy part) of the plant, when ignited, burns very slowly, while the bark remains untouched. It was with this that Prometheus deceived Zeus and gave to Man the sacred fire which he had stolen from the forge of Hephaestos.

The plant is dedicated to Dionysos, the god of wine. Canes used to be made from it, with

a pine cone fixed at the end. These canes were strong enough to be used as walking sticks but broke immediately if someone tried to use them to hit the back of another. Dionysos decreed that all those who imbibed wine should only carry a cane of this kind.

A method of fishing for eels involves throwing pounded roots of the plant into still waters. The eels become dizzy, are driven out of hiding, and then easily caught.

Foeniculum vulgare Miller *ssp. piperitum* (Ucria) Coutino   VI-IX
Fennel

DESCRIPTION: Biennial or perennial plant, 0.5-2.5 metres in height, frondy, aromatic, greenish-blue, with linear stems. Leaves have a triangular-oblong perimeter, are stalked at the base, stalkless at the tip, with a wide membranous sheath; 3-4 times pinnate, with thread-like lobes, and are slightly fleshy. Umbels with 4-10 rays, without bracts. Yellow flowers without sepals, only with 5 petals folded over at the edges. Fruits 4-10 mm, ovoid, elliptic with 5 flutes and and aromatic, sharp, slightly sweet taste, like that of dill.

HABITAT: Found on roadsides, banks of streams, in uncultivated fields.

PROPERTIES, USES: Known to the Egyptians and Romans. A plant held in high esteem. The tender stems and leaves are eaten like spinach, by themselves or together with other mountain greens and also with snails. They are also an ingredient of much-coveted little pies.

The plant is diuretic, appetite-stimulating, tonic, regulates the menstrual cycle, increases lactation in women who have given birth and facilitates the elimination of fatty substances. It is also used for flatulence (distended stomach) and in compresses for conditions of the eyes, abcesses, warts and pain associated with blows or knocks. It neutralises even the poison of dangerous mushrooms.

In a tisane (15 g of seeds or 30 g of leaves to one litre of water) it stimulates the nervous system and combats inertia of the digestive tract. The same tisane, drunk by nursing mothers, can relieve colic in babies.

WARNING! A uterine stimulant. Prohibited for pregnant women.

Oenanthe pimpinelloides L.   V-VI
Corky-fruited water dropwort

DESCRIPTION: An erect plant with perennial roots (numerous small tubers). Stems up to 100 cm, single, hollow and fluted. Basal leaves 2-pinnate, with sphenoid or ovate leaflets, divided into 6-7 small lobes. Leaves of the stem 2-pinnate with linear leaflets. Whitish-yellow flowers in umbels of 6-15 rays, without bracts. Hypanth with many bracts which fall after flowering. Fruit 3 mm, cylindrical, angular.

HABITAT: Damp locations, at low and moderate altitude.

PROPERTIES, USES: **WARNING! The root is poisonous. The plant is harmful to animals!**

Petroselinum crispum
Parsley

DESCRIPTION: Resembles celery but is a smaller plant, biennial, with an equally aromatic though quite different flavour. Erect stem, much-branched, with the lower leaves 2- and the upper leaves 3-pinnate. Small, insignificant flowers, greenish-yellow, in umbels. Small, greyish seeds.

HABITAT: Cultivated, but also self-sowing.

PROPERTIES, USES: Contains the essential oil apiol, which gives it its characteristic aroma. Widely used in cookery. In a tisane, it assists digestion. One cup after a large meal is just what our stomach needs, and a little glass every morning for gravel and stones in the kidneys.

Pimpinella tragium Vill. *ssp. depressa** (DC) Tutin   VI-VII

DESCRIPTION: A perennial, aromatic, dwarf, with a thick, woody rhizome, hairy, greyish. Stems 10-15 cm, fragile, and basal leaves pinnate with small leaflets, around 5mm, ovate, deeply toothed. Umbels with 3-5 (-7) rays of small, white flowers.

HABITAT: Alpine zone, in the White Mountains.

PROPERTIES, USES: The plant is diuretic, stomachic, digestive and a tonic for lactation in wet-nurses and women in childbed (one spoonful of pounded seeds morning and evening).

Scandix australis L.   II-IV
Shepherd's needle sp.

DESCRIPTION: An annual, 5-10 cm, with a great variety of forms. Leaves 2-4 pinnate, up to 8 cm long. Umbels with 1-3 rays bearing very small white flowers without sepals and often without a hypanth, the petals on the outside larger than those on the inside. Fruit 1-4 cm, with a beak the same length as the section containing the seed.

S. pecten-veneris

HABITAT: Cultivated and abandoned fields.

PROPERTIES, USES: Diuretic, expectorant and purgative. In folk medicine the tea is considered invigorating, aphrodisiac and a menstrual stimulant.

NOTE: There are three other species of **Scandix** to be found on Crete: **S. australis ssp. brachycarpa, S. macrorhyncha** and **S. pecten-veneris**.

259

Smyrnium olusatrum L.   III-V
Alexanders

DESCRIPTION: A biennial or perennial, 50-150 cm, smooth, with a thick, hollow stem, fluted, branching, and smelling of celery. Leaves up to 30 cm, hairless, stalked at the base, 2-3 pinnate, with large rhomboid-ovate sections, dentate-serrate, sometimes lobed. The upper leaves are pinnate with entire edges. Nodding umbels, with 15-18 rays, no bracts. Fruit 6-8 mm, a shiny black in colour.

HABITAT: On fences, roadsides, demolition sites, mainly in areas where there is some dampness.

PROPERTIES, USES: The young shoots were once cooked as a vegetable and a substitute for celery. The roots and fruits are stomachic, diuretic and anti-asthmatic, while the leaves are antiscorbutic.

Thapsia garganica L.   IV-VI
Thapsia

DESCRIPTION: A perennial, up to 2.5 metres, smooth, greyish-green. The root consists of numerous, tough fibres, the stem is hollow and linear. Stalked leaves, 2-3 pinnate, with linear sections 10-50 mm, entire edges or with 1-2 teeth. Umbel of 5-20 rays, without bracts. Whitish-yellow flowers. Fruit 15-25 mm, oblong-elliptic, with lateral wings 3-6 mm.

HABITAT: Infertile, stony places, up to the mountain zone.

PROPERTIES, USES: The bark of the stem is a strong purgative.

WARNING! The dose should not exceed 70 g! The root causes pustules or vesicles to form on contact with human skin.

Tordylium apulum L.   IV-V
Tordylium

DESCRIPTION: An annual, erect, branching. Leaves pinnate, the lower ones with ovate-rounded leaflets, the upper ones linear, with entire edges. Umbel with 3-8 rays. White flowers, the exterior petals longer, bifurcated, flanked by sepals and bracts. Fruit 5-8 mm, almost spherical, flattened, with swollen edges.

HABITAT: Ploughed and abandoned fields, at low and moderate altitude.

PROPERTIES, USES: According to Dioscurides, physicians recommended the juice of the stem, mixed with wine, for the treatment of kidney conditions.

URTICACEAE (Nettle family)

Parietaria judaica L. (= *Parietaria diffusa, Parietaria officinalis*)   II-V
Pellitory-of-the-wall

DESCRIPTION: A perennial, up to 60 cm, dark green. Erect stems, much-branching, with short hairs. Leaves 2-5 cm, alternate, stalked, ovate-acute, with ciliate edges. Spherical inflorescence, consisting of very few almost inconspicuous flowers, in the leaf axils.

HABITAT: In rock crevices and caves and at the base of damp and shady walls, also in the environs of cities.

PROPERTIES, USES: The Latin name 'paries' means 'wall'. According to Pliny, Pericles used this plant, following the advice of Athena, to heal a workman who had been seriously injured in a fall from the roof of the Parthenon. This gave rise to its common Greek name, 'parthenoudi'.

The flavour is bitter and grassy without the

slightest scent. It is recommended for remittent fevers and for any kind of inflammation, in the form of a hot plaster.

Dioscurides speaks of its refreshing and styptic properties. As a tea (30 g per litre of water), it is used even today to soften the pain of inflammation and to help the elderly who suffer from dysuria (urine retention). A handful of the plant in 300 g of water, of which a glass can be drunk every morning before the meal, helps to eliminate kidney and bladder stones. As a powder, mixed with honey, it relieves asthma and pulmonary tuberculosis. The villages used it as a beverage before going to sleep, to settle any kind of neuropsychic disorder and thus avoid insomnia.

Its pollen is harmful to those who suffer from allergies.

NOTES: *P. cretica* L. is a similar plant, low-growing, with small leaves; it is found on rocks near the sea.

Urtica pilulifera L.　　　　VI-VII
Roman nettle

DESCRIPTION: An annual or biennial plant up to 1 metre, with prickly hairs. Leaves 2-6 cm, long-stalked, opposite, ovate-acute, with deeply toothed edges. Inflorescences in the leaf axils, separated into male and female flowers, the male flowers branching into panicles, the female flowers in the form of a ball, hence the Latin name pilulifera which means 'bearing round balls'.

HABITAT: Uncultivated soils rich in nitrogen, in the vicinity of animals.

PROPERTIES, USES: Once cultivated for its oily, sweetish seeds; goldfinches and canaries adore them. The young stems are eaten raw or boiled in salad, or even cooked like spinach.

The nettle absorbs minerals in the soil, including iron, and for this reason is an excellent tonic against anaemia. Its high vitamin C content ensures the absorption of iron by our bodies.

Due to its styptic properties, it stops bleeding. It is also used in cuts, rheumatism, dropsy, for excess weight and for kidney stones (it dissolves uric acid). As a poultice, it is used for arthritis, pains in the joints, gout, dislocations, neuralgia, tendonitis and ischialgia.

Washing the hair with nettle lotion stops hair loss and eliminates dandruff.

As a tisane, the leaves (boiled until the water is reduced by half) are beneficial in cases of chronic hepatitis, bronchitis and reduced lactation of women in child-bed.

If we are stung by a nettle, rubbing the affected area with leaves of mallow (which often grows nearby) immediately stops the pain. The nettle is the cheapest and most trusted medicine which Nature has given us. The cutting of a branch of nettle and beating of the parts of the body afflicted by arthritis may seem masochistic to us, but it will have a sure result; the pain will recede more quickly. Raw or boiled, nettles are considered an aphrodisiac. They are recommended for women who have not known hedonistic delight, and for men who feel impotent.

NOTE: *Urtica dubia* and *Urtica urens* are also found on Crete.

Urtica dubia

VALERIANACEAE
(Valerian family)

Centranthus ruber (L.) DC   IV-VII
Red valerian

DESCRIPTION: A perennial, up to 80 cm, erect, hairless. Opposite leaves, lanceolate or ovate, grey. Purple flowers, in umbels, with a large, fine, long spur, 5-10 mm, and a single, projecting stamen. The fruit bears a tuft of soft hairs which allow it to fly.

HABITAT: Imported into Crete for cultivation; it has become completely acclimatised. On walls, rocks and at the edges of fields.

PROPERTIES, USES: The flower is insignificant, but the whole plant has a decorative appearance. In Italy the leaves are eaten

in a salad. Steeping the roots in water or alcohol produces an infusion which has antiscorbutic, tranquilising, sedative and antispasmodic properties.

NOTE: *Centranthus sieberi** **Heldr**. is a dwarf plant, up to 20 cm, with elliptic or spatulate leaves, and rounded, pink or purple flowers with a spur 13-17 mm. It grows only in the White Mountains, in the alpine and sub-alpine area, from May to July (**V-VII**).

*Valeriana asarifolia** **Dufresne III-IV**
Cretan valerian

DESCRIPTION: A plant with a perennial rhizome and annual stems up to 50 cm, erect, hairless. Simple basal leaves, discoid or reniform, on a long stalk. Pinnate leaves on the stem. Terminal inflorescence, dense, whitish-pink. Corolla with spur.

HABITAT: Rocks in the semi-mountainous zone. Endemic to Crete and Karpathos.

PROPERTIES, USES: This is a real drug. It has an essential oil with an unpleasant scent, which given in small doses (17-20 drops) causes the slowing down of the heart beat and a slight increase in arterial pressure. In large doses, it reduces it. In an infusion, it has a suppressive effect on the central nervous system and for this reason is used as a light sedative in cases of excitement, hysteria, epileptic fit and neurosis.

The roots have always been considered an effective tranquilliser of plant origin, particularly for children. The plant is used for depression and insomnia, and also for wounds, abcesses and muscle cramps. It is said that cats eat the leaves of valerian in order to cleanse their stomach.

NOTE: The *Valerianella* are herbaceous plants, not easily distinguishable. 10 species are found on Crete. Some are eaten as a salad.

VERBENACEAE (Verbena family)

Lippia citriodora (= *Aloysia tripfylla*) V

DESCRIPTION: A shrub 1-1.5 metres in height. Leaves with a short stalk, lanceolate, glandular, dentate or entire in whorls of 3 or 4. Small white flowers, in axillary or terminal racemes with a whorl-like arrangement. The leaves, when crushed, give off the aroma of lemon, hence the name citriodora, meaning lemon-scented.

HABITAT: Cultivated. Originates from South America.

PROPERTIES, USES: This is a decorative, aromatic and medicinal plant. Folk medicine uses it for stomach complaints. The tisane is believed to stop diarrhoea and is tonic, febrifuge and diuretic. It is recommended for kidney stones.

NOTE: Possible confusion with real lemon balm – *Melissa officinalis*.

Verbena officinalis L.   VI-X
Vervain

DESCRIPTION: A perennial, 30-80 cm, with straight, quadrangular stems. Opposite leaves, pinnate with toothed lobes, the upper leaves stalkless. Tiny flowers, fragrant, pinkish-lilac, in long (10-25 cm) thinly covered spikes. Corolla with 5 petals divided into two lips.

HABITAT: Up to the mountain zone.

PROPERTIES, USES: Considered a sacred plant in antiquity. According to Dioscurides, it was used in an infusion to strengthen the secretions of the mammary glands and for its healing, purgative and tonic properties. It is also beneficial to the womb of women in childbed.

The leaves were once used successfully in a poultice for pleurisy pains and headaches.

The Romans used it in their religious and magic rites. They also made garlands with it for the heralds who were charged with the proclamation of peace or war.

In the Middle Ages it was used in magic spells, for the preparation of liquid medicines, philtres and antidotes. Completely harmless, it tones the nerves, stimulates the liver, cleanses the urinary tract and lowers fever.

WARNING! To be avoided during pregnancy, but can be used at the hour of birth because it strengthens uterine contractions.

Vitex agnus-castus L.   IV-VIII
Chaste tree

DESCRIPTION: A small tree, 1-6 metres in height, aromatic (pepper), decorative, green throughout the summer. The new shoots are quadrangular with a grey felt. Leaves opposite, long-stalked, palmately divided, with 5-7 sections which are linear to lanceolate. Terminal inflorescences, branching, spike-like, with whorls of fragrant flowers. Calyx with 5 teeth and a corolla 6-9 cm, blue-violet, pink or white with 2 lips, the upper one two-lobed, the lower one three-lobed with 4 stamens. The fruit is spherical, reddish with black seeds about the size of a grain of pepper.

HABITAT: Damp places, banks of streams and torrents, at low altitude.

PROPERTIES, USES: The fruit was once used as a flavouring for food (called 'wild pepper').

Odysseus used the strong and supple branches of the plant to bind his comrades to the bellies of sheep to enable them thus to flee from the cave of the Cyclops Polyphemus.

The branches are used everywhere in basket-making and matting.

It is named Castus – pure – because during the period of the Thesmophori, women used its branches for their bedding, believing that thus they would protect their virginity, avoiding any kind of sexual desire or thought. Actually, the ancient Greeks demonstrated its ability to dampen sexual urges and stimulation of the reproductive organs. In other words, it is an anti-aphrodisiac.

Dioscurides observed the emollient properties of its seeds. In the Middle Ages, monks used them to calm desires of the flesh which did not fit in with their calling and monastic life. In an infusion, the plant brings calm and sleep to those who suffer from stress and insomnia.

VITACEAE (Vine family)

Vitis vinifera L. *ssp. sylvestris* (C.C.Gmelin) Hegi   V-VI
Common vine

DESCRIPTION: A sturdy plant, climbing, 10-20 metres, trailing. Palmately lobed leaves, with deep lobes. Branching tendrils, opposite the leaves. Raceme of small yellowish flowers, in the leaf axils, with 4-5 sepals and petals. Grapes consisting of bunches of little berries, black-blue in colour during ripening, slightly acid.

HABITAT: *ssp. Sylvestris*, the wild form of the cultivated wine, climbs up trees and the bushes alongside them and can spread over a wide area. It is found around Lake Kournas and on the banks of streams, mainly in the west of the island. It most likely originates from the shores of the Caspian Sea or Black Sea.

PROPERTIES, USES: The Minoans knew about the vine 6,000 years ago. It was brought to Greece by Dionysos, the god of wine. From the moment that it was discovered that a vine whose stem had been broken off and eaten by a donkey gave more grapes, the value of cultivation was realised! For that reason, in many ancient representations – even on coinage – a donkey appears together with the vine.

Today, Crete is an area of production of table grapes (mostly the variety called *rasaki*), raisins (sultanas), and wine grapes. For red and rosé wines, the varieties *kotsifali, mantilari*, black *romaiko* and *liatiko* are grown, and for white wines *vilana, dafni, thrapsathyri* and *plyto*. White wines are considered to be energising and diuretic, while red wines are tonic and styptic; very dark wines are pleasing, tonic and refreshing.

The vine leaf is full of vitamins and used to make the famous *dolmades* – a truly Greek dish; the tendrils and leaves are also eaten raw. The leaves have been used during peri-

ods of grain scarcity to make flour. Grape juice (verjuice) is a valuable substitute for lemon and oil. It is effective in cases of obesity, since it dissolves fat and facilitates digestion. During the period when the nodes on the vine swell, the sap from the branches (the tears of the vine) is used for eczema, wounds, internal bleeding and eye conditions.

The leaves have styptic properties, stop diarrhoea and tone up the liver functions and the metabolism. A grape cure, over one-two weeks, taking 1-2 kg per day, cleans the liver, kidneys and intestines; it is a full nutrition, comparable to a mother's milk.

Unfortunately, only very little '*petimezi*'- which used to be a substitute for sugar – is made nowadays. There is also *moustalevria*, a type of cream which has flour and grape must as its base ingredients. At one time, both were greatly in demand.

The dried leaves, kept in a glass jar, are used as a plaster for rheumatism, arthritis, pains due to falls, and malignant tumours (a woollen cloth is soaked in a mixture of the leaves pounded in a pestle and mixed up with melted wax, then placed as a plaster on the affected area). We can also use the fresh leaves macerated in wine.

WARNING! Remove the plaster after two hours at the latest, otherwise it will begin to raise pustules. In cases of cancerous ulcers of the skin, only the affected area must be covered, so that no secondary wound is caused around the first one. The grape is forbidden to those who suffer from sugar diabetes and colitis.

ZYGOPHYLACEAE (Caltrop family)

Tribulus terrestris L.   V-IX
Maltese Cross, Small caltrops

DESCRIPTION: An annual, 10-60 cm, creeping, +/- hairy. Opposite leaves, with 5-8 pairs of acute leaflets, accompanied by small, triangular lateral leaflets, Flowers up to 1 cm, solitary, in the leaf axils, with 5 narrow deciduous sepals, 5 rounded petals and 10 stamens. Stalkless ovary. Fruit flanked by very tough spines.

HABITAT: Cultivated areas, roadsides, sandy soils.

PROPERTIES, USES: Extremely painful if we step on the fruits with our bare feet. The Tribulus, to the ancient Greeks, was a weapon of war – a type of mine, we would now say, or caltrop– consisting of four hammer-headed nails which, when they fell on the ground, would always come to rest with one of their points projecting vertically and

thus constituted a source of fear and terror for infantry and horses.

The fruit reduces arterial pressure and is an excellent stimulant for the circulation and the liver. Our neighbours, the Bulgarians, managed to exploit all the properties of the plant and produced a preparation much in demand amongst athletes, which gives fatter muscles and a beautiful body (!)

It is also said to have strong antiviral and antibacterial properties, and to combat herpes. Apparently, its only side-effect (acceptable from the point of view of men) is that it increases erotic urges in the male, as well as the desire to put them into practice.

MONOCOTYLEDONS

AGAVACEAE (Agave family)

Agave Americana L.
Century plant

VI-VIII

DESCRIPTION: A plant with a basal rosette. Leaves fleshy, fatty, 100-200 x 15-25 cm, linear to lanceolate, with spiny edges and teeth, terminationg in a strong, fat, black spine. After 10-15 years, the plant produces a flower-stalk almost 10 metres in height and 12 cm in diameter, woody and taking the shape of a chandelier, which persists after the fruit has been produced. Flowers 7-9 cm, fragrant, yellowish-green, at the ends of horizontal branches. The plant dies after the fruits have matured. It reproduces by means of subterranean stems.

HABITAT: Originates from Mexico and is found on dry and stony soils.

PROPERTIES, USES: Cultivated for decoration.

The juice becomes very sugary during the period that the flower stalk is formed. A rich juice, much sought after in Mexico, is gathered by cutting into it; when distilled, it produces the well-known 'tequila'.

Thanks to their anti-inflammatory and soothing action, the leaves – crushed - produce an ointment that works wonders in cases of acute rheumatism, rheumatoid arthritis, lumbago, pains of the joints, and colds. The same ointment, strengthened with mustard, is used as a poultice in cases of pneumonia; the fever is reduced, there is profuse expectoration, and the symptoms of pneumonia disappear.

Alisma plantago-aquatica L. VI-XI
Common water plantain

DESCRIPTION: A perennial, aquatic, up to 1 metre, with broad, lanceolate leaves, rounded at the base. The plant takes a variety of forms, on or beneath the surface of water, hairless, with very large stalks. Leafless stem, in a raceme-like arrangement. Numerous flowers in whorls, with 3 white or light lilac-coloured petals.

HABITAT: In water (non-stagnant) up to an altitude of 1000 metres.

PROPERTIES, USES: The submerged stem is styptic, antibacterial, soothing and diuretic. Dried and pulverised, it was once used for rabies, scurvy, haematuria, kidney colics, to reduce arterial pressure and to cleanse the liver.

An ideal plant for the decoration of ornamental ponds and streams.

AMARYLLIDACEAE
(Daffodil family)

Narcissus tazetta L. XII-III
Bunch-flowered narcissus

DESCRIPTION: A perennial plant with a bulb. Leaves flat or channelled, up to 75 cm in length. Sturdy stem, up to 65 cm in height, with 3-15 aromatic flowers, 2.5-3.5 cm, in the axil of a membranous spathe which reaches a length of 6.5 cm. Tubular corolla, delicate, with 6 parts, 8-22 mm, flattened-out, acute, white or cream. Secondary corolla in the form of a cup, yellow or orange.

HABITAT: Cultivated and abandoned

areas, maquis, damp meadows, gardens. Often cultivated.

PROPERTIES, USES: These beautiful flowers with their intoxicating scent are pleasing to the eye and their scent a delight to the nose during the winter months.

Narcissus was the son of the god Kifisos and a nymph. Because of his great beauty, all the nymphs were in love with him. Nevertheless, he did not reciprocate their feelings, because he loved only himself. Then the gods decided to punish him and one day, while he was admiring his reflection in the waters of a spring on Mount Helikon, in his ecstasy he fell into the water and drowned. A flower with a golden crown was left, which today nods its head over the waters of lakes, springs and streams.

The emetic properties of the plant were known in antiquity. It was used for epilepsy, spasms and remittent fevers. The flowers, when distilled, yield a superb essential oil which is used in perfumery and in the manufacture of drinks.

NOTE: ***Narcissus serotinus*** L., which flowers in autumn in low-lying and barren locations, has very thin stems bearing 1-2 white flowers, with a secondary, very small corolla, orange-coloured, and 1-2 cylindrical leaves which appear after flowering.

N. serotinus

Pancratium maritimum L. **VIII-IX**
Sea daffodil

DESCRIPTION: A perennial plant with thick bulbs and a sturdy, flattened stem. Grey leaves 1-2 x 15 cm, linear, appearing after flowering. Vigorous, dense inflorescence. Spathe with 2 openings, 5-7 cm. Umbel with 3-15 white, fragrant flowers, with a stigma 6-8 cm long. Linear sections of the perianth 3-5 cm in length. Secondary funnel-shaped corolla, 20-45 mm, with 12 teeth and stamens on all sides. Capsules full of black seeds.

HABITAT: Sand and sand-dunes, near the sea.

PROPERTIES, USES: The beauty of this flower did not escape the notice of Minoan artists. It can be seen in various representations, such as in the wall paintings of Santorini and on the Palaiokastro sarcophagus (Heraklion Museum).

Unfortunately this plant is in great danger of extinction, because of the large complexes of hotels which have sprung up near the sea and above all on the sand-dunes, which constitute its biotope. In view of such a threat, it certainly merits our affection and protection. **WARNING! The high alkaloid content of the plant makes its usage dangerous without medical advice.**

Sternbergia lutea (L.) Ker-Gawler ex Sprengel IX-XI
Common sternbergia

DESCRIPTION: A perennial, with bulbs, similar to the crocus. Leaves in groups of 4-6, very long, appearing together with the flowers, lanceolate, slightly channelled, with finely toothed margins. Flower stalk up to 20 cm, the flower appearing in the axil of a tubular spathe. Corolla 5-20 mm, funnel-shaped, with sections of perianth about 4 cm long, rounded, a brilliant yellow colour; ovary in an inferior position. Fruit a fleshy capsule. The flowers take three years to appear.
HABITAT: Areas of phrygana (garrigue) and rocky slopes up to an altitude of 600 metres.

PROPERTIES, USES: **WARNING! The bulb is a violent purgative!** The plant is cultivated for decoration.

NOTES: ***Sternbergia greuteriana*** * **Kamari & R. Artelari** is endemic, clearly resembles **S. lutea** but has narrower leaves, smaller flowers and is found up to 1200 metres, particularly in eastern Crete and on Karpathos.

***Sternbergia sicula* Tineo ex Guss.**, a characteristic species on Sicily, has sections of perianth which are acutely pointed at the tip and the plant is slightly smaller than **S. lutea.** The photograph was taken on Parnassos.

Sternbergia sicula

Sternbergia greuteriana

ARACEAE (Arum family)

Arisarum vulgare **Targ-Toz**   **II-V**
Friar's cowl

DESCRIPTION: A plant 20-40 cm in height, perennial due to its tuberous root. Basal leaves, long-stalked, ovate-sagittate. The spathe, which is green with purple ridges, 3-5 cm long, is joined at the base to form a tube 2-3.5 cm. The upper part of it is bent over in the form of a hood and covers the spadix. This in turn bends forwards and bears 20 male flowers which dominate the 4-6 female ones. The upper part of the spadix is greenish in colour. The berries are fleshy, and also greenish.

HABITAT: Olive groves, forests, walls.

PROPERTIES, USES: **WARNING! The plant is toxic! The leaves and tubers are emetic.**

Used externally, it is healing. Hippocrates gave it the name 'snake', because the stems of the leaves reminded him of snakeskin.

NOTE: The **ARACEAE** family is characterised by a spike (the spadix) surrounded by a torn bract (the spathe), which affords it protection.

Arum concinnatum Schott. (= *Arum italicum* = *Arum nickelii*)   IV-V
Large cuckoo pint

DESCRIPTION: A perennial with tuberous roots. The leaves appear in autumn, green with white veining on the upper surface, on a stalk 18-40 cm, with a sagittate blade with two triangular auricles at the base, and very drooping. Spathe 15-40 cm, with a base wrapped in a tube 3-8.5 cm long, yellow-greenish, and a spadix with male flowers in the upper part, female flowers in the lower, and a terminal section that is robust, yellow and without flowers. Red berries.

HABITAT: Fields and olive groves.

PROPERTIES, USES: The underground tuber and the leaves are styptic. The leaves were once used for rheumatism and ulcers.

NOTE: Five other species of arum are found on Crete: ***A.alpinum, A. creticum, A. cyrenaicum, A. idaeum*, A. purpureospathum*.***

A. creticum

A. idaeum

Biarum davisii* Turill and _Biarum tenuifolium* ssp. idomenaeum_ (Schott.) P.C. Boyce IX-XI

Cretan and narrow-leaved biarums

DESCRIPTION: Flowers in the autumn immediately after the first rains. Its roots grow from the bulbs, which range in size between that of a hazelnut and a potato. The flowering stem issues from one single bulb and bears a whitish-pink (**B. davisii**) or brownish-red flower (**B.tenuifolium**).

HABITAT: In meadows and pastures up to an altitude of 1000 metres.

278

B. davisii

B. tenuifolium

PROPERTIES, USES: **The fresh bulbs are toxic! When they are boiled, they lose their toxicity. WARNING! The plants can induce abortion, and people who eat them suffer sexual impotence (!)**

Even today it is said that the plant is widely used by women who want to savour total erotic delight and lasciviousness, free from the consequences of an undesired pregnancy(!).

Dracunculus vulgaris Schott. IV-VI
Dragon arum, Great dragon

DESCRIPTION: A perennial which exceeds 1 metre in height, with a thick, fleshy and tuberous root. Leaves with a long stalk, pinnate with 9-15 pairs of elliptic, oblong or lanceolate leaflets, with purplish-black spots. Spathe 20-50 cm, nude, greenish on the outside, brownish-red inside, the lower part wrapped and the upper part flat, with an undulate margin. Spadix of the same length as the spathe. Occasionally, a few infertile flowers form the dividing line between the male and the female flowers. The upper part of the spadix has no flowers and is a dark purple in colour. The berries are reddish-orange.
HABITAT: Barren and uncultivated areas, clumps of trees, coppices, ruins.
PROPERTIES, USES: **WARNING! A poisonous plant! Even animals refuse to go near it!**
If the plant – which is really impressive - is to be cultivated in a garden, it is a good idea to cut off the flower spike before it blooms, otherwise the plant will give off a strong stench of rotting matter.

The plant was used as a decorative motif on a sarcophagus from eastern Crete (Heraklion Museum).

In antiquity, these strange plants were connected with the snakes which represented the secrets of the Underworld, or Hades.

NOTE: The variety *var. alba* (with white flowers) is found only on Crete, on the southern slopes of Psiloritis, up to 1500 metres. Some botanists also distinguish another *var. creticus*, which has larger spots on its stems and flower-stalks.

Tamus communis L.   I-V

Black bryony

DESCRIPTION: A perennial vine-like plant, hairless, climbing, up to 4 metres, with a thick underground stem. The stems above ground are fluted, without tendrils, and wind in a clockwise direction. Cordate leaves, sometimes three-lobed, alternate, glossy, with a large stalk. Flowers very small, yellowish-green, with six petals, the male ones bell-like with 6 stamens and the female ones shaped like water-jars, with a stalkless ovary. Male inflorescences oblong, up to 16 cm, female up to 1 cm. Berries 10-15 mm, a vibrant red colour.

HABITAT: Forests, thickets, olive groves, banks of streams.

PROPERTIES, USES: **WARNING! A poisonous plant which contains a substance that is a skin irritant**. Notwithstanding this fact, the tender shoots are eaten boiled as a salad or cooked in a casserole with onions, or in an omelette. Dioscurides recommended the berries for those who had facial freckles. In modern homeopathy, a substance is extracted from the root which treats sunburn. The plant also seems to be purgative, diuretic and healing.

GRAMINEAE (Poaceae) (Grass family)

Arundo donax L.   VII-X
Giant reed

DESCRIPTION: The largest grass in Europe. Perennial, sturdy, up to 6 metres in height, with a creeping rhizome which tends to become woody. The woody stem, single or with short lateral branches, flowers every two years. Leaf blades up to 60 cm, greyish-green with wrinkled edges. Inflorescence 30-60 cm, in the shape of a panicle which becomes white during maturity. The spikes have 2-4 flowers with external membranous bracts, smooth and with soft hairs on the inside of the throat, ending in a short beard.

HABITAT: In damp to waterlogged soils, on roadsides and the banks of streams.

PROPERTIES, USES: Probably originates from central Asia. Pan made his pipes from it, using the tubular stems of the reed.

It is used in the making of baskets and mats, for fishing, as plant supports, for wind-breaks and to cover the terraces of houses and huts. It is noteworthy that the large grasses do not lose their leaves in winter.

Avena sativa L. IV-V
Wild oat sp.

DESCRIPTION: An annual, erect, hollow and knotty, 1-1.5 metres in height. The leaves have a sheath and an awn that is linear and apiculate with rough lips. Terminal inflorescence, a panicle with short spikelets which bear two flowers and do not fall during ripening.

HABITAT: Cultivated and semi self-sowing, very common.

PROPERTIES, USES: The fruits have excellent nutritional value, being rich in vitamins B and C, starch, proteins and fatty substances. Not cultivated by the ancient Greeks and Romans.

In an extract or tisane, it tones the nerves, and appears to be ideal for the treatment of depression and loss of strength.

In a poultice, the flour is used for skin complaints: eczema, skin irritations and herpes zoster (!). (**Varicella zoster, shingles**).

NOTE: *A. barbata* **Pott ex Link** (Bearded wild oat) and *sterilis* L. (Winter wild oat) are self-sowing on Crete.

Cynodon dactylon Rich. IV-VII
Bermuda grass

DESCRIPTION: A perennial with small roots and yellowish shoots, on long, creeping stems. Leaves small, delicate, greyish-green. Tiny violet flowers, on spikes that resemble fingers.

HABITAT: This plant constitutes a headache for gardeners; it grows everywhere and it is almost impossible to uproot and eradicate it.

PROPERTIES, USES: The whole plant is diuretic, sudorific, cleanses the body and rejuvenates it. It can be used for all conditions of the urinary tract (kidney and gall bladder inflammation, uric arthritis and kidney colic), for cellulitis, liver and gall-bladder colics.

IRIDACEAE (Iris family)

Crocus boryi Gay   IV-XII
Crocus sp.
DESCRIPTION: A perennial plant without a stem. Leaves (3-7) and flowers grow from one underground bulb (corm). The flowers are white without veins and have reddish or orange stigmas and white anthers. The coverings of the bulbs are shiny and tough.
HABITAT: Found at low and medium altitudes, in the central and eastern part of the island.
NOTES: **Crocus boryi ssp. tournefortii Greuter, Mathäs & Risse** has blue or bluish-violet flowers and the bulb sheaths are thick and membranous.
Crocus cartwrightianus Herbert (Greek saffron crocus) has smaller flowers, a variety of colours and a netted bulb sheath. It is found only in western Crete.
The crocuses have only three anthers, not six like the varieties of colchicum and sternbergia.

C. boryi

C. cartwrightianus

Crocus laevigatus Bory & Chaub.
X-XII

DESCRIPTION: Differs from **C. boryi** in its flowers, which are white with 1-3 dark, vertical, distinctive veins on the outside of the three external petals. The throat is yellow, the anthers white, and the stigmas are divided into numerous linear arms. Maximum of 4 leaves, 1-2.5 mm wide. The sheath of the bulb is tough and smooth.
HABITAT: Up to the mountain zone.

*Crocus oreocreticus** B.L. Butt   X-XII

DESCRIPTION: Differs from **C. laeviga-tus** in its leaves which number 7-15, the violet or purple flowers with their dark veining and the silver or yellowish shading on the external surface of the petals. Generally, all of the parts of this plant are narrower.

HABITAT: In the mountain and sub-alpine zone.

Crocus sieberi Gay. *ssp. sieberi**
IV-V (-VIII)

DESCRIPTION: One of the most beautiful, and clearly the largest, of the Cretan crocuses. White flowers with external striping and a yellow throat. Yellow anthers, stigmas yellow or yellowish-orange, divided into three cuneate arms. 4-8 leaves, 1.5-6 mm in width, and a netted bulb sheath.

HABITAT: Mountain, sub-alpine and alpine regions, where the snow melts.

PROPERTIES, USES: The stigmas of the crocus – saffron – are used in medicine, cookery and dyeing. Many cheeses and types of pasta owe their colour to saffron. In a solution of one part of saffron to 100.000 parts of water, the yellow colour still remains. 140,000 crocus flowers are required to obtain one kilogram of saffron.

As a flavouring, saffron is aphrodisiac, a menstrual stimulant, an abortive, diuretic, appetite-stimulating, tonic, digestive and emollient. In the form of a syrup it brings relief when rubbed onto the gums. Dioscurides mentions that it was used for many different types of inflammation.

The cultivated crocus (**Crocus sativus**) is grown in the area of Kozani (northern Greece), in the villages of Krokos, Karyditsa and Ano Komi, which have provided the whole of Europe with precious saffron for three hundred years.

The retail price is set at 3 Euros/gr, i.e. 3,000 Euros per kilo (!).

Evidence for the cultivation of the crocus dates from 2300 BC. On the voyage of the Argonauts, Medea, daughter of the king of Colchis, gave Jason the juice of the Caucasian crocus - which had grown from the blood of Prometheus - to protect him from the fiery breath of the bulls which guarded the golden fleece.

Gladiolus italicus L., *Gynandriris monophylla* Boiss. & Heldr. and *sisyrinchium* (L.) Parl. (Barbary nut) (= *Moraea mediterranea* and *sisyrinchium)* and *Hermodactylus tuberosus* (L.) Mill. (Snake's head, Widow iris) *(= Iris tyberosa*) are purely decorative plants.

G. italicus

G. sisyrinchium

H. tuberosus

Iris germanica L.   IV-V

Tall bearded iris, German iris

DESCRIPTION: A plant with a fat rhizome. Stems up to 90 cm, hollow. Broad leaves, sword-like. On every stem there are 2-3 fragrant flowers, about 10 cm, with 4 external violet petals and 2 internal ones which are dark lilac.

HABITIAT: Probably originates from the eastern Mediterranean and has almost acclimatised. Found both cultivated and self-sowing, always in the neighbourhood of settlements.

PROPERTIES, USES: The raw rhizome is emetic and purgative. Dried, it is diuretic, vermifuge, tonic and expectorant. It is often used to impart the scent of violets to washing. In antiquity, it was used to aromatise wine; the oil was used as a body deodorant!

NOTE: The self-sowing varieties *Iris planifolia* (Mill.) **Fiori,** *pseudacorus* **L.** (Yellow flag) and *unguicularis** **Poir**. are found on Crete.

I. germanica

290

Iris planifolia

LILIACEAE (Lily family)

Allium cepa L.
Onion

DESCRIPTION: A biennial or perennial vegetable. Green leaves, oblong, cylindrical, cannular. The underground bulb consists of consecutive layers. A leafless cylindrical stalk, thick, hollow, grows from the centre and terminates in a bulky, ball-shaped umbel with white or greenish flowers which tend to take on a purple colour, with 6 petals, a long stalk and 2-4 bracts. The dried bulbs – onions – may have white, bronze, red or reddish skins according to their variety, which are always delicate. The pungent and aromatic flavour is due to the presence of sulphurous volatile oils which cause reddening of the eyes and bring tears to them.

HABITAT: Cultivated.

PROPERTIES, USES: As raw onions and onion soup are considered to be tonic and to lower arterial pressure, an onion a day can do nothing but good.

Onions, crushed to a pulp and mixed with salt, make an excellent ointment for burns.

Herodotus and Homer tell us that the heroes enjoyed onions because they believed that they would make them braver on the battlefield. The philosophers also taught the same, because they believed that the onion strengthened the body and nourished the spirit. In antiquity, they were used as a disinfectant for the plague.

When onions are eaten raw, they activate the digestive secretions of the stomach, give us appetite and tone up our bodies.

WARNING! Forbidden to those who have stomach ulcers (they cause indigestion) and to those suffering from haemophthysia (they cause hyperaemia).

Folk medicine prescribes boiled onions for the woman who has just given birth so that she will produce abundant milk, and onion juice (half a coffee cup per day) for diabetics, in order to bring their sugar back to physiological levels.

Onions contain vitamins C, H, PP and various inorganic salts. They give women a wonderful complexion and a skin which resembles that of the rose and lily. People who are afraid of the strong smell only have to use a mint spray for the mouth, to eat a peeled apple, or a spoonful of honey, chew two celery leaves, or a coffee bean.

The onion is aphrodisiac to the degree that it tones up the body. It is also anti-anaemic, purgative (it removes undigested food from the body) and diuretic (rubbing it over the kidneys or lower part of the stomach noticeably increases the production of urine). 3-4 drops of the juice are recommended for pain in the ears.

An onion diet produces wonderful results in those suffering from kidney colics, kidney and bladder stones, oedema, urine retention, albumen in the urine, uric arthritis and rheumatism. The onion has the ability, through perspiration, to neutralise toxins in the system.

In a poultice, it is used for migraines, insect stings and dog bites. The hot onion is just what is needed for sore throats and haemorrhoids, and onions roasted on glowing embers for chilblains, split skin, abcesses, boils and ulcers. The fresh juice is the only thing to use for bee and wasp stings.

It is said that the Bulgarians, who eat large

A. porum

quantities of onions, enjoy the greatest longevity and that in Transylvania, where they are widely consumed, cancer is unknown.

The skins of the bulbs have colouring properties and give fabric a soft golden brown colour which is fixed with alum. They are also used to dye eggs at Easter, giving them a marble-like appearance when they are wrapped in onion skins before boiling.

NOTES: *Allium porum* L. (the cultivated leek) has diuretic and purgative properties.

Allium sativum L.
Garlic

DESCRIPTION: A perennial plant which can reach 60 cm and whose bulb consists of a number of little bulbs – the so-called 'cloves' – wrapped in a membrane. Umbel of white or pink flowers, at first wrapped in a membrane. The scent is strong and unpleasant.

HABITAT: Cultivated. It originates from central Asia.

PROPERTIES, USES: For arthritis and wounds, we can crush 3-4 cloves of garlic in a mortar and put the paste on the affected part.

A clove of garlic per day lowers blood pressure through diastolic action on the peripheral blood vessels, and combats obesity.

In antiquity, the Greek infantry and Roman legionaries consumed large quantities of garlic before battles, because they were convinced that it would give them the necessary strength to defeat their opponents. Athletes did the same.

As a treatment for alopecia (temporary significant loss of hair) nothing is better than an ointment made from pounded garlic, olive oil and gunpowder. The area to be treated is shaved and then the ointment put directly on the skin. The pain is unbearable! It is impossible to keep still! It burns! The result, however, is incontrovertible.

Women who suffer from mastitis after giving birth can use garlic as a poultice. As a liniment, it is recommended for styes of the eye. It certainly reduces the amount of cholesterol in the blood and also the danger of stroke and cardiac thrombosis. It stimulates the immune system and acts as an antibiotic. An embrocation can destroy warts, boils, and condylomas.

A. scordoprassum

If it is added to food, it safeguards against infections, improves the condition of the coronary arteries and reduces the sugar content of the blood – here, vitamin C is consumed without being stored in the body. Garlic is also a vermifuge, diuretic, anti-asthmatic and relieves toothache.

NOTE: Fresh celery can reduce the strong odour of garlic emitted by our lungs and the pores of the skin.

A further 20 species of **Allium** are found on Crete in the wild state: *A. amethystinum, A.*

ampeloprasum, A. chamaespathum, A. cal-limischon ssp. haemostictum, A. commuta-tum, A. neapolitanum, (Naples garlic), *A. roseum,* (Rosy garlic), *A. subhirsutum, A. trifoliatum.*

Many of these, known as wild leeks, are gathered before flowering and used in casseroles, cooked like spinach.

A. amethystinum?

A. ampeloprasum?

A. haemostictum

295

A. nigrum

A. trifoliatum

A. neapolitanum

A. roseum

296

A. sibhirsutum

Aloe vera (L.) Burn fil.   V-VI
Aloe sp.

DESCRIPTION: A perennial plant with leaves 30-60 cm in a dense basal rosette, lanceolate, thick, greyish with white stippling, dentate. Flower stalk 30-50 cm, leafless. Flowers 2.5-3 cm, tubular, yellow, drooping. Fruit a three-cornered capsule.

HABITAT: Stony and sandy places near the sea. Of African origin, known in Greece from Classical times.

PROPERTIES, USES: The resin of this plant energises the stomach functions when they have become inactive, stimulates the appetite and aids digestion. It is also a bile stimulant, menstrual stimulant, and purgative.

The Arabs assigned it a mysterious power, capable of driving out evil spirits. The thick juice is a unique help to wounds and burns of all kinds. It is also used for dry skin and especially for eczema around the eyes, and for fungal infections such as scurf.

WARNING! Its use is prohibited during pregnancy, and in cases of uterine haemorrhage, haematuria and haemorrhoids.

Asparagus aphyllus L. *ssp. orientalis* (Baker) P.H. Davis

Asparagus sp.

DESCRIPTION: A plant up to 1 metre in height, with a finely fluted stem. Branches 1-5 cm, sturdy, solitary or in groups of 2-3, with a very tough thorn. At the base of the branches, there are 1-2 leaves so small that they resemble membranous scales. 2-8 yellowish flowers, on a stalkl 1-3 mm, with 0-2 bracts at the base. Blackish-blue berries, 5-8 mm.

HABITAT: Roadsides and the edges of fields, particularly in barren fields, up to the mountain zone.

PROPERTIES, USES: The tender shoots (asparagus) are much sought after. They are consumed in the same way as cultivated asparagus. It is believed that they regulate the heart beat and have an effect in cases of bronchitis and pulmonary tuberculosis. In homeopathy, asparagus is recommended f or rheumatism and dropsy.

According to Theophrastus, asparagus was the favourite food of the gods.

Asphodelus aestivus **Brot.**
(= *A. ramosus*)   **III-VI**
Common asphodel

DESCRIPTION: A perennial plant with thick, spindle-like roots. Leaves 25-45 cm long x 2-4 cm, basal, slightly keeled. Flower spike on a sturdy stem, up to 1.5 metres, branching. Flowers with 6 white petals, 10-16 mm, with a central red vein. Bracts 10-15 mm, membranous. Capsules +/- rounded, fluted. The whole plant emits a sweet, unpleasant scent which often causes nausea.

HABITAT: Areas of phrygana (garrigue), meadows, often in large colonies, up to the mountain zone.

PROPERTIES, USES: For the ancient Greeks, the asphodel was a symbol of mourning. They planted it in cemeteries, so that the starchy roots could be used as nourishment for the souls of the dead. Homer, describing the return of the soul of Achilles from the kingdom of the Dead, tells us "How, with giant steps, he crosses the meadow of asphodels".

The bulbs contain so much starch that, if they are boiled in a large quantity of water, they can be used for food in periods of famine. Shoemakers used to pound them in a mortar and make a very strong glue, idea for leather. Even alcohol can be produced from the bulbs.

The plant has heart-tonic, expectorant, emetic, diuretic and healing properties. In an infusion it was once used in cases of sudorific pleurisy, oedema due to cardiac disturbances, dropsy, cirrhosis of the liver (20 g of the bulb, 20 g of alcohol, 400 g of water and honey). For the cure and healing of gangrene and common ulcers, for inflammation of the breasts (mastitis), of the testicles (orchitis) and for boils, an ointment was made from the grated bulb, boiled in wine until it formed a cream. Another ointment, based on the bulbs and olive oil in the proportion 5 – 2, was used for alopecia, burns, chilblains and ear pains. For eczema, sulphur is mixed with the crushed bulb and a little olive oil added.

Ancient authors, first among them Dioscurides, considered the asphodel a panacea for all ills. Perhaps it has antimicrobial, and antibiotic properties and enzymes which are not as yet fully known to us.

Colchicum cretense

Colchicum cretense* Greuter   **IX-XI**
Cretan autumn crocus
DESCRIPTION: Differs from **Colchicum pusillum** in its leaves which are 5-8 in number and appear after flowering.
HABITAT: Mountain zone.
NOTE: **C. cupanii** has small leaves and two narrow, fluted leaves, which grow together with the flower in the autumn. **C. cousturieri*** greatly resembles it, but has darker petals, and two bow-like outspreading leaves which are acutely pointed at the tip. It grows only on the Koufonisi islands and Chrysi, in the south of Crete.

Colchicum macrophyllum B.L. Burtt.
IX-XI

DESCRIPTION: 3-4 very large leaves (35x14 cm), which appear in spring and are elliptic with parallel pleats. Large autumnal flowers which produce (downwards) an elongated stigma, growing directly from the corm, while upwards they open into 6 lobes with 6 stamens and 3 fine styles, curved at the tips. The lobes (the petals, up to 80 mm), are pink with purple stippling at the edges. The anthers (8-10 mm) are purple, with yellow pollen. The fruit, which is the size of a walnut and of an inky colour, ripens around 9 months after flowering.

HABITAT: Found at low and medium altitude.

Colchicum pusillum Sieber   X-XI

DESCRIPTION: A dwarf plant up to 2 cm, with an egg-like bulb. 3-6 leaves up to 140 x 1-2(-5) mm, appearing at the time of flowering. Pink, lilac or white flowers with petals 10-20 mm, purplish-black or brown anthers bearing yellow pollen, and styles of the same length.

HABITAT: Rocky locations at low altitude.

PROPERTIES, USES: **WARNING! Despite their important therapeutic properties, colchicum bulbs must on no account be consumed raw, and certainly not at all without the approval of a physician.**

This is actually a very poisonous plant, even fatal, without a known antidote to date. Clearly, everything depends on the strength of the dose.

The name derives from its homeland, far-off Colchis, where it was used to annihilate undesirable persons and dangerous animals. The Argonauts were the ones who brought it to Greek territory, and Dioscurides and Theophrastus studied it.

It has anti-arthritic properties and relieves the pain of gout and rheumatism (bulbs and seeds). It is also used for neuralgia and phlebitis.

Being cytostatic, (it stops cell division, and stops nucleus division), it acts on chromosomes, attacks new cells, such as the cancerous, the cerebral and reproductive, with the result that it is responsible to a certain extent for teratogenesis. Its cytostatic property allows it to be used against cancer and leukaemia as an ancillary in cases of radiotherapy and x-rays using

cobalt. It is also used in cases of uraemia, measles, influenza, smallpox, chicken-pox, hepatitis, various polymorphic inflammations, and other conditions which are caused by viruses.

NOTE: There are many species of colchicum to be found in Greece and Crete. Nobody knows with certainty, however, which one the Argonauts brought from Colchis. Probably all the colchicums have more or less the same properties.

Drimia maritima (L.) Stearn
(= *Urginea maritima*) (= *Charybdis*
maritima)   VIII-X
Sea squill

DESCRIPTION: A perennial, 50-150 cm, with a very large bulb, up to 18 cm in diameter. Basal leaves 30-100 x 3-10 cm, lanceolate, appearing after flowering. Terminal, raceme-like inflorescences, long and dense, with more than 50 flowers which have 6 white, star-like petals with green or purple veining and greenish anthers.

HABITAT: Meadows, rocky soils, phrygana (garrigue), up to the mountain zone.

PROPERTIES, USES: The very strong diuretic properties of the bulb and its irritant and pustule-raising effect on the skin were known to Hippocrates and Galen. Its fleshy covering was used to treat cardiac disturbances.

According to whether the flowering is late or early, villagers can predict whether the winter will be severe or mild.

At one exhibition of Cretan and other Greek products there was a soap and a cream on display, produced in Rethymnon from olive oil and sea squill, to be used for cosmetic and therapeutic purposes. It seems from this that the plant significantly strengthens hair growth and combats the problems of acne, skin oiliness, and pimples.

Lilium candidum L.
Madonna lily

V

DESCRIPTION: A perennial plant with a bulb, up to 120 cm. The basal leaves are lanceolate, up to 30 cm long, with 3-5 parallel veins; the leaves of the stem are similar, but considerably smaller. Flowers up to 8 cm, dead-white, with petals slightly turned over, and yellow anthers.

HABITAT: Occurs rarely self-sown on Crete. We found a number of plants in a field in the locality of Doxa, in the Prefecture of Heraklion, but these may, however, have been planted for decorative purposes.

PROPERTIES, USES: This is the white lily which we can see in wall-paintings from Amnisos, dated to 1600 BC (Heraklion Museum).

A symbol of purity, wisdom, beauty, virtue and hope, it is believed to be the flower that the Archangel Gabriel offered to the Virgin on the day of the Annunciation.

It grew for the first time, or so mythology tells us, from a drop of milk which fell from the breast of the goddess Hera when she was suckling Herakles.

The essential oil treats wounds and burns. Once, the distilled water from the flower of the lily was used for eye illnesses. The fleshy part of the bulb, when it has been cooked in a mixture of water and milk and placed on boils, whitlows, inflammations, chilblains, wounds, split skin, haemorrhoids, burns and cracked skin of the breast, brings good results. The oil, extracted by boiling the bulbs, is excellent for first and second degree burns. The stamens stop all pains of the stomach, kidneys and teeth; they are also antispasmodic and a menstrual stimulant (!).

Muscari comosum (L.) Miller   III-V
Tassel hyacinth

DESCRIPTION: A perennial plant growing from a bulb, with a strong stem 15-50 cm, leafless. Basal leaves 3-7 with a width of up to 20 mm, linear, shorter than the stem. Longish, loose flower spike. In the lower part the flowers are fertile, bell-shaped, brownish-white with 6 yellowish-beige teeth, and at the top the flowers are sterile, blue-violet and form a tuft.

HABITAT: Cultivated and abandoned fields, up to an altitude of 800 metres.

PROPERTIES, USES: Edible. The bucolic poet Theokritos tells us that a village repast consisted, above all else, of 'volvi' (bulbs of this plant), snails and wine. Large quantities of them are eaten on Crete.

NOTE: 'Volvi' normally refers to varieties of **Muscari**. According to one specialist, the best are those which have white flowers (!). However, only **Ornithogalum**, has white flowers. The plants which that specialist showed me were actually **Ornithogalum narbonense**!

Muscari commutatum Guss.   IV-V
Dark grape hyacinth

DESCRIPTION: A perennial, growing from a bulb, up to 30 cm. Basal leaves lanceolate, gutter-like. Short, dense raceme-like inflorescences with ovoid flowers, a dark violet colour, almost black, the lower ones fertile and with 6 teeth, the upper ones (up to 4), of a lighter colour, and infertile.

HABITAT: Barren soils and hills up to an altitude of 400 metres.

PROPERTIES, USES: The bulbs of all the *Muscari* are eaten, although they exhibit a certain bitterness. They are larger or smaller, sweeter or more bitter, according to the species. They are boiled two or three times, changing the water each time.

They are a tonic for the weakened organism, give those suffering from tuberculosis and rachitis an appetite, and cure inflammations of the liver. As a compress, they are used for external pains (bruises, rheumatism, abcesses, sprains…).

NOTES: Another 6 species of *Muscari* are found on Crete. Of these, the most common are: *Muscari neglectum* **Guss ex Ten** (= *Muscari racemosum*), (Common grape hyacinth) which differs from the species described above in that the teeth of the flower are white and the leaves are shorter than the inflorescence. This is a small plant, up to 10 cm.

Muscari parviflorum **Desf.**, which flowers in the autumn.

Muscari spreitzenhoferi* **(Heild. Ex Osterm.),** which has yellowish flowers and is found up to 2100 metres.

Muscari dionysicum **Rech.**, found in the region of Sitia.

M. neglectum

M. spreitzenhoferi

M. dionysicum

Ornithogalum narbonense L.   IV-VII
Star of Bethlehem sp.

DESCRIPTION: A perennial plant growing from a bulb, up to 60 cm. The leaves, which lack a white vein in the middle, appear together with the flowers. Long, cylindrical flower-spike, with white flowers on a flat flower-stalk.

HABITAT: Meadows, roadsides, barren fields at moderate and low altitude.

PROPERTIES, USES: The bulbs are eaten like those of **Muscari**, but said to be more tasty.

O. narbonense

NOTE: Another 6-7 species of *Ornithogalum* are found on Crete, of which most are of great beauty, such as *O. arabicum, O. nutans* (Drooping Star of Bethlehem), *O. creticum, O. divergens*, and *O excapum*.

O. arabicum

O. nutans

O. creticum

O. divergens

309

R. aculeatus

tion. The tender stems are eaten like asparagus. The subterranean parts of the plant were included in the preparation of the 'syrup of the five roots'; the identities of the other four roots are, unfortunately, unknown. The seeds, char-grilled and ground, can be a substitute for coffee.

During ripening, the branches are used for decoration.

Smilax aspera L.　　　　VIII-XI
Common smilax

DESCRIPTION: A bisexual, woody, evergreen climber, with long stems bearing thorns. Leaves up to 10 cm, alternate, cordate or sagittate. Lateral leaflets with 2 tendrils. Umbel consisting of 5-3- small flowers with a pleasant scent. Petals 2-4 mm, yellowish-green. The berries are a dark red, and

Ruscus aculeatus L.　　　　II-IV
Butcher's broom

DESCRIPTION: An evergreen shrub up to 80 cm. The stems (branchlets), have a length of hardly 2.5 cm; they are green, flattened out, inflexible, ovate-lanceolate with a truncated tip, and resemble leaves. They grow in the axils of scale-like, membranous leaves which fall quickly, and they carry out all the functions of the leaves. The flowers are small, greenish, often solitary, in the axil of a small, lance-like bract, on the surface of the stems/leaves (branchlets). Male and female flowers are found on different plants. Relatively large, round berries, 1.5 cm in diameter, a lively, glossy red colour.
HABITAT: In maquis, on roadsides and in fields, on rocks.
PROPERTIES, USES: The underground roots are used for disturbances of the circula-

310

S. aspera

attractive to birds.

HABITAT: Maquis, roadsides and the edges of fields.

PROPERTIES, USES: According to mythology, the nymph Smilax was changed into a plant, when she realized that her love for Krokos was without hope.

The roots of the plant are purgative and sudorific.

The tulips (*Tulipa*) are purely decorative plants. Four species are found on Crete: *T. cretica**, (Cretan tulip), *T. doerfleri**, *T. goulimyi*, and *T. saxatilis* (Rock tulip).

T. doerfleri

T. saxatilis

T. cretica

T. goulimyi?

ORCHIDACEAE (Orchid family)

These are the wild orchids, a number of which are known by the following common names: bee orchid, man orchid, wasp orchid, monkey orchid.

For details of these plants, the reader is directed to the book "The Orchids of Crete and Karpathos". There are more than 70 self-sowing species on Crete.

The orchids are much better known for their beautiful flowers than for their properties and uses. Nevertheless, we know that their bulbs are nutritious, tonic, excellent for those who are recuperating, and effective against dysentery. Today in Greece, and particularly in Turkey, a kind of sweet drink – salepi – is

O. episcopalis

made from their bulbs. On Crete this is almost non-existent, but in northern Greece the tradition continues, especially using the bulbs of **Dactylorrhiza sambucina.** Fortunately, this species of orchid, which is found at an altitude of over 100 metres, is not threatened with extinction.

O. boryi

O. ariadnae

O. simia

Dactylorrhiza sambucina

TYPHACEAE family

Thypha domingensis (Pers.) Stendel
IV-VII

Reed-mace or bulrush or roadman's hammer
DESCRIPTION: A perennial up to 3 metres in height. Flat leaves, very long, with a width of 5-12 mm. The male and female flower-spikes are completely distinctive; the female flowers are a light brown in colour with simple scales, while the male flowers have toothed scales.

HABITAT: Large colonies in marshes and water-filled trenches.

PROPERTIES, USES: The leaves, after steeping, can be used for a short period of time to make baskets and chairs. The root is styptic. As a plaster, it relieves varices.

316

GLOSSARY OF TERMS
(not in alphabetical order)

Labiate

Tubular

Glandular: Description usually applied to leaves or flowers bearing glands which emit a scent and secrete various sticky or resinous substances.

Florets: There are two types, the labiate which resemble normal petals, and the tubular.

Corolla

Pedicel (flower stalk)

leaf

Leaf stalk (petiole)

Roots

Pedicel, Peduncle: Flower stalk, i.e. the stalk which bears the flower (pedicel) or flowers which make up the inflorescence (peduncle)

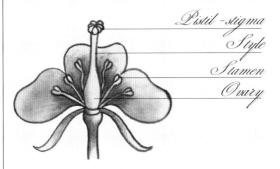

Pistil -stigma

Style

Stamen

Ovary

Flower: Consists of the pistil or stigma, style, ovary, stamens, petals sepals and flower stalk.

Male   *Hermaphrodite*   *Female*

Flowers:
✓ According to the genus, these may be male, female or hermaphrodite – i.e. they may have only male reproductive organs (stamens and anthers), only female ones (pistil and stigma), or both together.

317

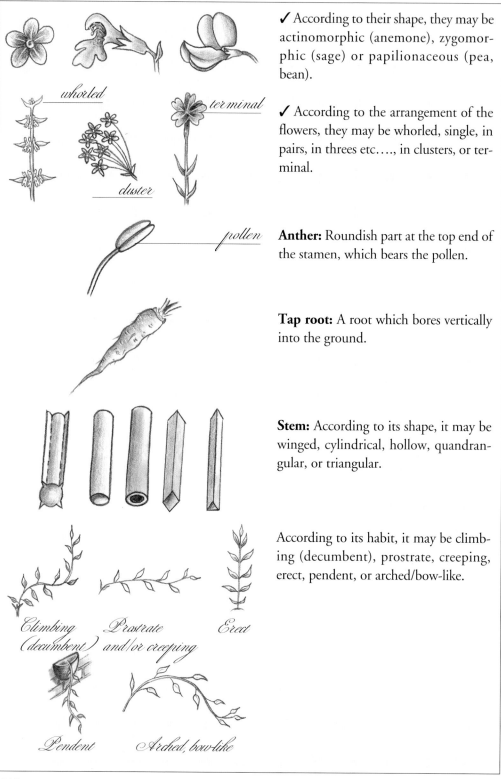

✓ According to their shape, they may be actinomorphic (anemone), zygomorphic (sage) or papilionaceous (pea, bean).

✓ According to the arrangement of the flowers, they may be whorled, single, in pairs, in threes etc…., in clusters, or terminal.

whorled

terminal

cluster

pollen

Anther: Roundish part at the top end of the stamen, which bears the pollen.

Tap root: A root which bores vertically into the ground.

Stem: According to its shape, it may be winged, cylindrical, hollow, quandrangular, or triangular.

According to its habit, it may be climbing (decumbent), prostrate, creeping, erect, pendent, or arched/bow-like.

Climbing (decumbent)   *Prostrate and/or creeping*   *Erect*

Pendent   *Arched, bow-like*

Bract: Usually a small leaf which accompanies the flower or inflorescence.

Knee: Organ which curves downwards at a steep angle, such as the lip in various species of orchids (*Ophrys* and *Serapias*).
Tree: A woody plant exceeding 3 metres in height, the trunk of which is exposed from the roots up to the branches and leaves.
Sapling: A small tree which branches at the base.
Cluster: A number of leaves or flowers which grow from the same point.
Bisexual: A plant which has only male or only female flowers and for this reason cannot be pollinated without the help of a second plant bearing flowers of the opposite gender.

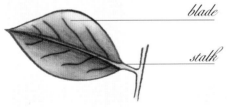

Blade: The level, flat part of the leaf.
Stalked: Parts which bear a stalk (peduncle, pedicel) or stem (petiole, i.e. petiolate).

Terminal: Found at the end, either applied to a leaf or a flower.

Epicalyx: A small, second calyx outside the main calyx of some flowers (e.g. pinks).
Stalkless: Parts which lack a stalk (pedicel or peduncle) or stem (petiole).

Deciduous: Parts of the plant which are shed relatively early and easily, which do not remain on the plant.
Scrub: Thicket of small, wild saplings.
Papillary: Part bearing papilla.

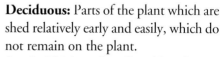

Catkin: A spike-like, elongated inflorescence consisting of small, inconspicuous flowers, such as in the chestnut.

rotary   *tubular*   *cup-shaped*

Calyx: A leaf-like sheath, rather like bracts joined at the base, which protects the flower. It can be funnel-shaped, two-lipped, cup-shaped, tubular, rotary, or campanulate.

funnel-shaped, campanulate   *calyx*

capsule siliqua   *berry*   *samara*

Fruit: According to the type, we can speak of an achene (chicory), a drupe (cherry, plum), a nutlet (cynoglossum), a nut (walnut, hazelnut), a capsule (pinks, silenes), siliqua (mustard, brassica), capsule (poppy), berry (grape), samara (sycamore) and pod, legume (beans, peas)

capsule   *drupe*   *nut*

achene   *nutlet*   *pod, legume*

tubular

labiate

leaf-sheath

Capitulum: The head bears numerous flowers, relatively small in size, which are only tubular or only labiate, or both together.

Leaf-sheath: A membranous, flattened, seimi-periblastic stem which terminates in a leaf.

Tuber, condyle: An underground, fleshy bulb, full of nutrient substances for the plant, which will reproduce in the following year.

Cupule: a component which resembles a cup and surrounds the fruits of various trees such as the oaks (acorns). May also be spiny.

Scale: A very small, membranous leaf.
Lobe: A deep, rounded division at the perimeter of a leaf or petal.
Macchia: The name given in the Mediterranean region to the dense group of various plants, small trees and shrubs (such as Kermes oak, myrtle, lentisc, tree heather, autumn heather, spiny broom, gorse and oleander) which form an almost impenetrable expanse of thicket.
Axil: Name given to the angle formed between the leaf and the stem or branch.

paracorolla

stipules

sheath, ochrea

Leaf-stalk, petiole: Narrow section of a leaf which connects it to the stem or branch, in some way the extension of the central nerve of the leaf-blade.

Solitary: Bearing only one flower or leaf.

Unisexual: A plant bearing male and female flowers at the same time.

Veining: The pattern formed by the network of veins, normally on the leaves.

Filament: The very thin thread-like part connectiong the anther to the corolla.

Nail: Part of a leaf or flower which narrows gradually until it terminates in an elongated, pointed tip.

Paracorolla: Secondary corolla of the flower which is usually found in the narcissi.

Stipules: Small leaflets at the base of a leaf, rather like the bracts at the base of a flower.

Perianth: All of the parts of the flower located around the reproductive organs, i.e. the calyx, sepals, and petals.

Sheath, ochrea: Found around the joints of the stems of certain plants such as the reeds and equisetum.

Felt: hairy covering

Spur: A type of protrusion at the back of the flower, +/- large, which is formed either by some mutation of a sepal or petal, or even of a number of them together. Often bears nectar.

Hummock-shaped: Phrygano scrub forming a hummock or pillow-shape

Beak: Terminal section of a part of a leaf, petal, sepal or fruit, in the shape of a nose.

Rhizome: An underground, perennial stem, often horizontal and long, which plays a role in the reproduction of certain plants.

Rosette: Outspread leaves, in a circular arrangement around the base of a stem.

Spathe: A membranous casing or large coloured bract at the end of a stem which surrounds the flower or the whole inflorescence in some plants such as the narcissi (*Amaryllidaceae*), onions (*Allium*), *arum* and *dragon arum*.

Spadix: Inflorescence in the form of a spike which is found inside the spathe of *arum* and *dragon arum*.

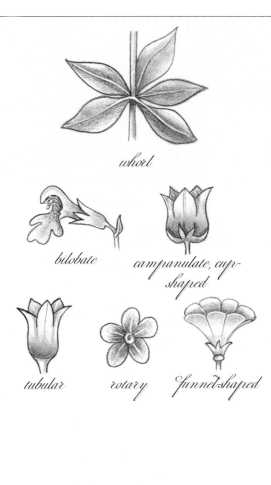

whorl

bilobate

campanulate, cup-shaped

tubular

rotary

funnel-shaped

Whorl: An arrangement of flowers or leaves which all originate at the same level around the axis (stem or branch) which bears them.

Corolla: The sum total of the petals of a flower. It can be labiate or bilobate, campanulate, cup-shaped, tubular, rotary or funnel-shaped, in exactly the same way as the calyx.

Stamen: Consists of a hair-like, thread-like stem which has a swollen section at its tip - the anther – which bears the pollen.

Stolon: An external, creeping root which ends in a node and periodically creates self-sown roots from which new plants form, as for example in the strawberry.

Inflorescence: This take many forms and is designated a bostryx, raceme, dichasium, catkin, capitulum, corymb, cyme, cone, umbel, spike or panicle.

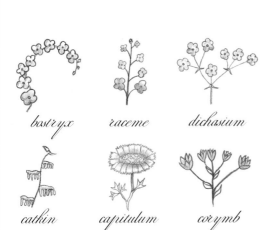

bostryx

raceme

dichasium

catkin

capitulum

corymb

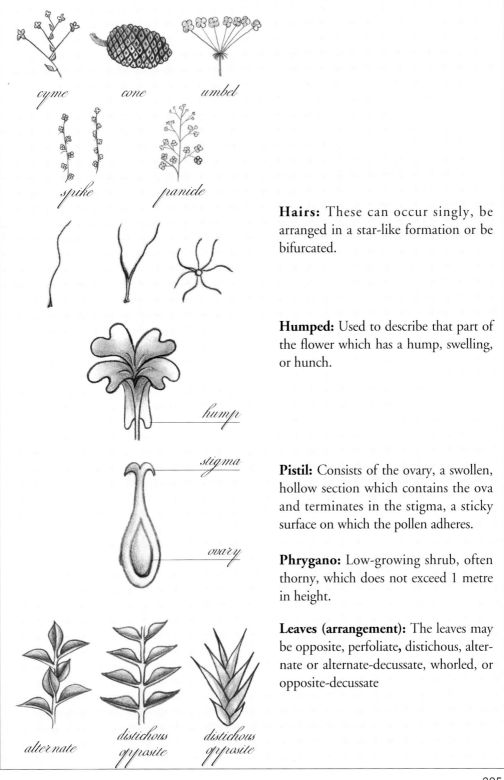

cyme   *cone*   *umbel*

spike   *panicle*

hump

stigma

ovary

alternate   *distichous opposite*   *distichous opposite*

Hairs: These can occur singly, be arranged in a star-like formation or be bifurcated.

Humped: Used to describe that part of the flower which has a hump, swelling, or hunch.

Pistil: Consists of the ovary, a swollen, hollow section which contains the ova and terminates in the stigma, a sticky surface on which the pollen adheres.

Phrygano: Low-growing shrub, often thorny, which does not exceed 1 metre in height.

Leaves (arrangement): The leaves may be opposite, perfoliate, distichous, alternate or alternate-decussate, whorled, or opposite-decussate

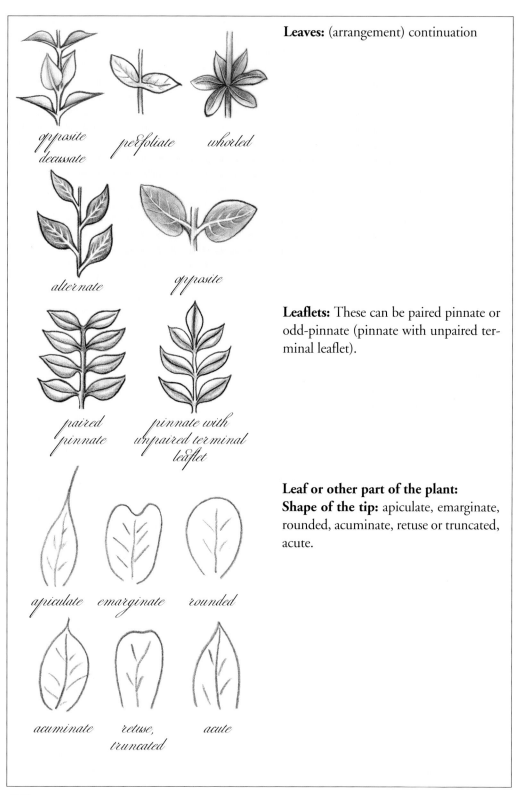

Leaves: (arrangement) continuation

opposite
decussate

perfoliate

whorled

alternate

opposite

Leaflets: These can be paired pinnate or odd-pinnate (pinnate with unpaired terminal leaflet).

paired
pinnate

pinnate with
unpaired terminal
leaflet

Leaf or other part of the plant:
Shape of the tip: apiculate, emarginate, rounded, acuminate, retuse or truncated, acute.

apiculate   emarginate   rounded

acuminate   retuse,   acute
             truncated

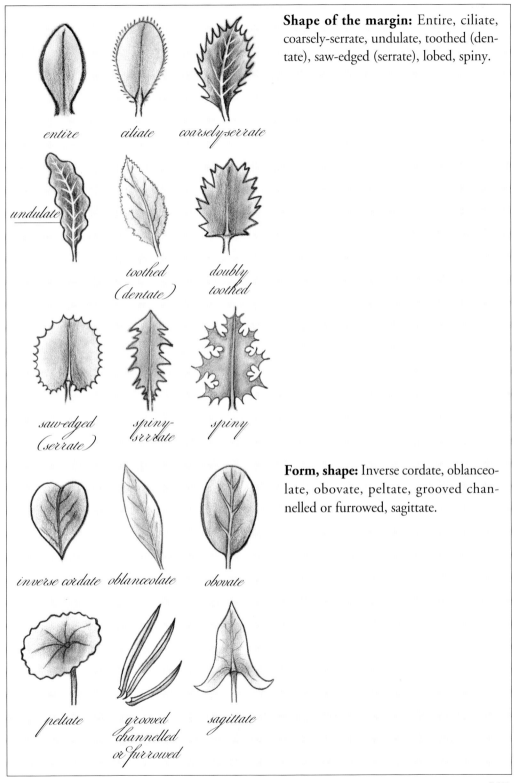

Shape of the margin: Entire, ciliate, coarsely-serrate, undulate, toothed (dentate), saw-edged (serrate), lobed, spiny.

entire

ciliate

coarsely serrate

undulate

toothed (dentate)

doubly toothed

saw-edged (serrate)

spiny-serrate

spiny

Form, shape: Inverse cordate, oblanceolate, obovate, peltate, grooved channelled or furrowed, sagittate.

inverse cordate

oblanceolate

obovate

peltate

grooved channelled or furrowed

sagittate

Form, shape: continuation
acerose or awl-like, cauline, bractose, labiate, linear, deltoid, bilobate, orbicular, pinnately-lobed, 2-pinnately-lobed, deeply divided, two or three times deeply divided (2-3 pinnate), bisegmented, bifurcated, elliptic or elliptoid, pinnate with terminal tendril,

acerose

sessile

labiate

linear

deltoid

bilobate

discoid

pinnately lobed

2-pinnately lobed

2-3 pinnate

bisegmented

bifurcated

elliptic or elliptoied

Pinnate with terminal tendril

Form, shape: continuation
semi-tubular, cordate, lanceolate, deeply toothed, reniform, filiform or thead-shaped, palmately lobed, digitate, pedate, periblastic or sheathed, oblong or elongated, rhomboid, sword-like or sword-shaped, spatulate, sphenoid (cuneate), tubular, ribbon-like, trefoil or trifoliate, ovate.

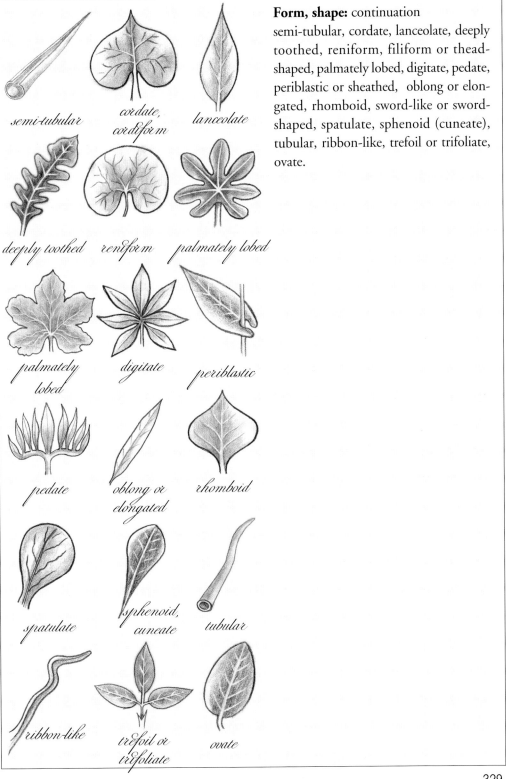

semi-tubular

cordate, cordiform

lanceolate

deeply toothed

reniform

palmately lobed

palmately lobed

digitate

periblastic

pedate

oblong or elongated

rhomboid

spatulate

sphenoid, cuneate

tubular

ribbon-like

trefoil or trifoliate

ovate

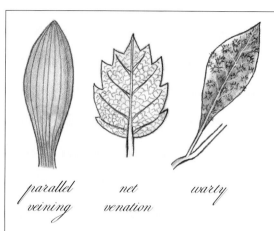

parallel
veining   *net*   *warty*
             venation

Leaves can bear hairy, wart-like patches, and a whole network of veins (in the orchids the veining is always parallel), and they can also be hairy, velvety, downy, smooth, wrinkled, leathery, and fleshy.

A plant:
(in terms of its lifespan) can be a biennial, an annual, or a perennial
(in terms of its form) can be a tree, a bush, phrygano, hummock-shaped, herbaceous (low-growing like moss, grass, herbs).

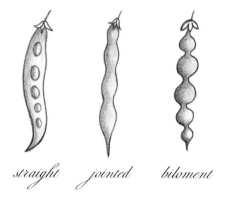

straight   *jointed*   *biloment*

Shell, pod or husk: This type of fruit can be straight, jointed, or biloment.

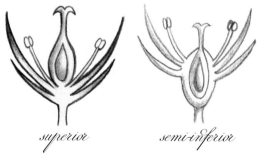

superior   *semi-inferior*

Ovary: This can be in a superior, semi-inferior, or inferior position

inferior

auride

Auricle: An ear-like swelling

INDEX OF COMMON ENGLISH NAMES

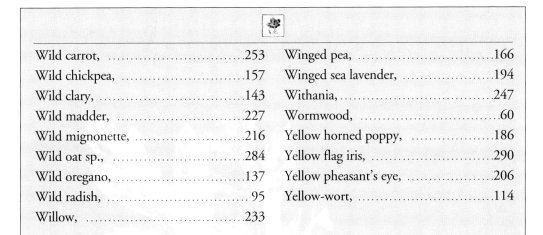

INDEX OF PLANTS BASED ON THEIR SCIENTIFIC LATIN NAMES

Synonyms are given in brackets * Indicates a plant endemic to Crete

MONOCOTYLEDONAE

1. Αλιμπέρτης Αντώνης, *Οι ορχιδέες της Κρήτης και της Καρπάθου*, Ηράκλειο 1998
2. Αραμπατζής Ι. Θεόδωρος, Θάμνοι και Δέντρα στην Ελλάδα, Δράμα 1998
3. Αραμπατζής Θεόδωρος, Αγριολούλουδα του Παρθένου Δάσους της Δράμας, Δράμα 1997
4. Berclay Colville, *Crete. Checklist of the vascular plants*, Berlin-Dahlem 1986
5. Bonnier G. De Layens G., **Flore complète portative de la France, de la Suisse et de la Belgique**
6. Bayer E., Finkenzeller X., Buttler K.P., Grau J., *Guide de la flore méditerranéenne*, Paris 1990
7. Boisvert Clotilde, *La cuisine des plantes sauvages,* Paris 1984
8. Γεωργίου Κυριάκος & Δεληπέτρου Πηνελόπη, *Απειλούμενα Ενδημικά Είδη Χλωρίδας στη Νότια Ελλάδα,* Ηράκλειο 2001
9. Delforge Pierre, *Guide des orchidées d'Europe, d'Afrique et du Proche-Orient*, Lausanne-Paris 1994
10. Διοσκουρίδης, **Περί ύλης ιατρικής,** Αθήνα
11. Fielding John and Turland Nicholas *Flowers of Crete*, Kew 2005
12. Huxley A. and Taylor W., *Flowers of Greece and the Aegean*, London 1977
13. Heldreich Χελντραϊχ Θεόδωρος, *Λεξικό των δημωδών ονομάτων των φυτών της Ελλάδος*, Αθήνα 1980
14. Kit Tan with G. Iatrou, *Endemic Plants of Greece. The Peloponnese,* Köbenhavn 2001
15. Κυριακίδης Ευάγγελος, Γαλανίδου Νένα, Ισαακίδου Βαλασία, Σαρπάκη Ανάγια, Καπετάνιος Ανδρέας, Ψιλάκης Νίκος, Κυπριωτάκης Ζαχαρίας, *Η πολιτισμική αξία των φυτών και των ζώων στην Κρήτη από τη Νεολιθική εποχή μέχρι σήμερα,* Ηράκλειο 2001
16. Kretzschmar H & G. Eccarius W., *Orchideen auf Rhodos*, 2001
17. Kretzschmar H & G. Eccarius W., *Ορχιδέες Κρήτη και Δωδεκάνησα,* Ηράκλειο 2004
18. Kreutz C.A.J., *Die Orchideen der Türkei,* Landgaaf/ Raalte 1998
19. Kreutz C.A.J., **Die Orchideen von Rhodos und Karpathos** Raalte & Landgraaf 2002
20. Lipper / Podlech, *Pflanzen der Mittelmeer Küsten*, München 1989

21. Lambraki Myrsini, *Plantes, herbes, légumes verts, fruits,* Héraklion 2001

22. Μεσεγκέ Μωρίς, *Τα βότανα και η υγεία μας* Αθήνα

23. Μπάουμαν Έλμουτ, *Η ελληνική χλωρίδα στο μύθο, στην τέχνη και στη λογοτεχνία*, Αθήνα 1984

24. Ντάγκλας Σλίνγκερ, *Σεξουαλικά μυστικά,* Αθήνα

25. Pelt Jean-Marie, *Le tour du monde d' un écologiste,*

26. Pignati S., *Flora d`Italia,* Bologna 1982

27. Polunin Oleg, *Flowers of Greece and the Balkans*, Oxford 1987

28. Polunin O. and Huxley A., *Flowers of the Mediterranean*, London 1974

29. Rechinger K.H.fil., *Flora Aegea,* Wien 1943

30. Schönfelder Ing. et Pet., *Guide de la Flore Mediterranéenne*, Fribourg 1988

31. Σφήκας Γεώργιος, *Αγριολούλουδα της Κρήτης*, Αθήνα 1987

32. Σφήκας Γεώργιος, *Τα Ενδημικά Φυτά της Ελλάδας,* Αθήνα 1996

33. Sfikas Georges, *Plantes médicinales de la Grèce,* Athènes

34. Σπύρου Λάμπρος, *Τα βότανα*, Αθήνα 1984

35. Strid Arne, *Φυτά του Ολύμπου,* Αθήνα 1980

36. Strid Arne, *Mountain Flora of Greece,* Cambridge 1986

37. Strid Arne, *Flora Hellenica,* Königstein Germany 1997

38. The Herb Society`s, *Πλήρης Οδηγός Φαρμακευτικών Βοτάνων,* Αθήνα

39. Tutin G.& Others, *Flora Europea,* Cambridge 1980

40. Turland N.J.L. Chitton & J.R. Press, *Flora of the Cretan area,* London 1993

41. Ψιλάκης Νίκος και Μαρία, *Τα βότανα στην κουζίνα* Ηράκλειο

42. Ζαχαρόπουλος Ιγνάτιος, *Σύγχρονη πλήρης θεραπευτική με τα βότανα,* Αθήνα

43. Χαβάκης Ιωάννης, *Φυτά και βότανα της Κρήτης*, Αθήνα

CONTENTS

By the same author:

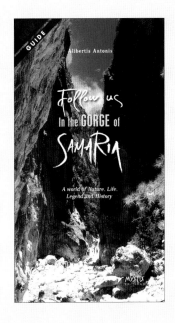

By the same publisher:

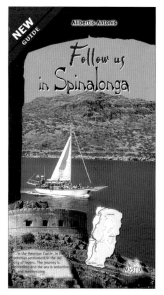

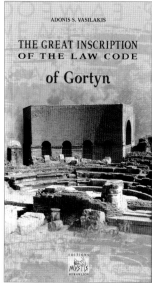

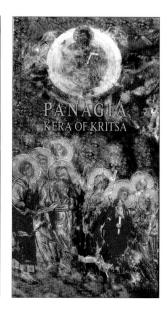

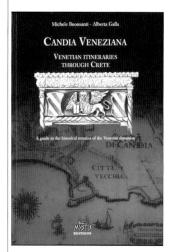

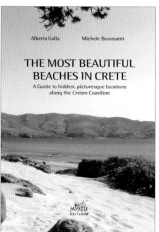

BIOGRAPHICAL NOTE

 10th August 1943, in Perastra, a village swathed in greenery on the island of Tenos. I spent my childhood years there; they were carefree, easy-going years, in the midst of a society that was humane and warm, where Nature defined all the pursuits of men.

After my studies in Athens and France, I worked for 36 years as a teacher of French in Heraklion on Crete, and in Athens. Certainly, all through this time, Nature continued to fascinate me and exhort me to become involved with her.

Now a pensioner, I devote my time to the discovery and photography of plants from all over Greece, in search of all those idyllic places that our country offers in such plenty, and to the writing of books on a number of subjects. Six books have already been published: *The orchids of Crete and Karpathos* (3rd edition), *The Samaria Gorge and its plants*, the guide books *Come with us to the Samaria Gorge* and *Come with us to Spinalonga*, the novel *Hallo, King Minos*, and the present reference book *The healing, aromatic and edible plants of Crete*.

I have always believed that unlimited powers lie hidden within us and that we can do wonderful things as long as the will, daring and perseverance are there.